Envisioning the Congregation, Practicing the Gospel

Envisioning the Congregation, Practicing the Gospel

A Guide for Pastors and Lay Leaders

John W. Stewart

William B. Eerdmans Publishing Company
Grand Rapids, Michigan / Cambridge, U.K.

Published 2015 by
Wm. B. Eerdmans Publishing Co.
2140 Oak Industrial Drive N.E., Grand Rapids, Michigan 49505 /
P.O. Box 163, Cambridge CB3 9PU U.K.
www.eerdmans.com

Printed in the United States of America

21 20 19 18 17 16 15   7 6 5 4 3 2 1

Library of Congress Cataloging-in-Publication Data

Stewart, John W. (John William), 1934-
   Envisioning the congregation, practicing the gospel:
   a guide for pastors and lay leaders / John W. Stewart.
     pages   cm
   Includes bibliographical references.
   ISBN 978-0-8028-7164-0 (pbk.: alk. paper)
   1. Church. 2. Mission of the church. 3. Protestant churches.
   I. Title.

BV600.3.S744   2015
253 — dc23

               2014047112

To Members and Friends
at the Westminster Presbyterian Church
in Grand Rapids, Michigan
where many of the ideas in this book
were first planted and a few blossomed.

Contents

Preface

The gestation period for this book has been unusually long. Some of its proposals were first conceived in a center-city Presbyterian congregation in Grand Rapids, Michigan, where a few matured. Later, seminary students whittled away at and honed most every idea I put forward. Further, I field-tested many of the initiatives proposed for this book in numerous mainline congregations across the country. Some flourished; others evaporated.

As will become apparent, I approach the life and witness of contemporary mainline Protestant congregations as a practical theologian. By that I mean as one of those pastors and scholars who seeks to integrate (a) the biblical and theological norms of the Christian faith, (b) the time-honored practices of Christian worship and lifestyles, and (c) the findings of sociologists who interpret the sociocultural contexts within which every congregation must minister and witness.

I was trained initially as a pastor and, later, as a historian of American culture and society. Over the past two decades, I have explored the emerging academic field of "congregational studies." Entering this newer department of practical theology has required some academic retooling and encounters with new, and sometimes unfamiliar, sociological literature and research methodologies. Hence, the good-natured teasing of friends and colleagues about the delayed birth of this book has not been totally unfair.

As will become obvious, I have sought to bring to the attention of lay leaders of congregations a wide variety of resources to help equip them in their calling to lead. I am well aware that most of the books and articles I mention will not be available to most lay leaders, though they may find and borrow some from pastors' and churches' libraries. To compensate for the inaccessibility of significant resources, I have summarized or quoted writers' salient points and perspectives. Further, where possible, I have entered websites and Internet articles, including those produced in Wikipedia. In all, my intent has been to introduce lay leaders to insightful and encouraging resources.

In a book such as this, my Reformed theological and ecclesiological inclinations will soon become evident. Experiences from my pastorates in the Midwest and from my seminary teaching in the East will inevitably surface. In fact, they provide many of the illustrations used. Equally obvious, I trust, will be my deep respect for the women and men who are called to lead contemporary congregations. Theirs is a noble calling in the kingdom of God.

Acknowledgments

This book would have been inconceivable without the encouragement and contributions of friends and colleagues. I owe them an
enormous debt of gratitude. Even the following list is incomplete:
Eileen Best, Linda Bieze, Laurence Bratschie, Robert and Betty
Coughenour, Clinton and Cathy Cozier, Jerry and Janet Diggins, Wes
Granberg-Michaelson, P. Douglas and Barbara Kindschi, Daniel L.
and Margaret Migliore, Donald and Bethany Gordon, the late Mar-
ian Randlett Glover, Olivia Stewart Robertson, Richard R. and Sally
Osmer, E. Stanley Ott, Brian Phillips, Jon Pott, Phillip J. Reed, Jack
Roeda, Allen D. Timm, Carolyn Timmer, John Witvliet.

As will become apparent, I have relied on a select group of schol-
ars from whom I have learned — and lifted! — much. Notable among
these are Nancy Ammerman, Mark Chaves, Kenda Creasy Dean,
Daniel L. Migliore, Jürgen Moltmann, Richard R. Osmer, Marjorie J.
Thompson, Geoffrey Wainwright, Nicholas Wolterstorff, and Robert
Wuthnow. Just beneath the surface here are my former mentors at the
University of Michigan, including the late Timothy L. Smith, James C.
Turner, and especially the late John Higham, who urged his students
to "join historical scholarship with contemporary social concern."
These historians of American culture shaped my understanding of
the ways Protestant churches intersect with American society.

My wife, Maureen Stewart, is not only my best friend but she is
also my most trusted consultant and editor. Her steady encouragement has never waned. She deserves far more of my gratitude than
I am able to express.

CHAPTER 1

Reimagining the Future of Protestant Congregations

Then the Lord ... said: "Write the vision; make it plain ... so that a runner may read it."

— HABAKKUK 2:2

Why This Book?

Nearly two decades ago, while serving as a pastor in a western Michigan city, I searched for a book — or any resource! — that would provide thoughtful lay colleagues a clear, theologically concise, and biblically informed explanation of the distinctive vocation and mission practices of ordinary American Protestant congregations.

Later, while helping to prepare seminarians for their vocations as pastors, I searched in vain for one volume that would integrate three pivotal perspectives on contemporary Protestant congregations: an explanation of why the Christian gospel serves as a congregation's normative conviction; a description of how biblically-generated practices of discipleship can be nurtured through Christian communities; and analyses of values in American culture that infiltrate and often disorient Christian communities.

In both settings I knew that I was after what theologians call *ecclesiology* — that is, an exposition of the biblical origins, distinctive marks, essential practices, and Kingdom-inspired mission of Christian churches. During this same period, however, I came across the writings of the late Peter Drucker, renowned authority on contemporary American organizations and their management. Drucker once insisted that most nonprofit organizations in America could not answer three questions: *What business are you in? How is business?* and *What business ought you to be in?* We now know that Drucker meant to include American congregations when he put forward those barbed, metaphor-laced questions. I remain haunted by them.

This book's classification rests somewhere between a *textbook* and a *testimony*. As a *textbook* about ecclesiology, it focuses only on traditional, ecumenical Protestant congregations in contemporary American society — what we usually call *mainline* churches. They are the kinds of Christian communities I study and with whom I consult.[1] As a *testimony*, this book is an affirmation (*apologia!*) of the mission and ministries of congregations seeking to be faithful in a culture that competes for Christians' loyalties.

The line between description and prescription is very thin here. Both textbook-like research and testimonial affirmations point to urgent leadership tasks if these congregations are to thrive in the twenty-first century. Obviously, no congregation, past or present, can live outside its socio-cultural context. But any congregation can learn to name and critique the intrusions of the secular values that jeopardize its divine calling.

That is no easy assignment when congregations in rural North Dakota or Mississippi are so obviously different from those in Manhattan or central Los Angeles. Yet every congregation is called to be the "salt of the earth" and a "light of the world" in its own social setting. At the same time, leaders in every Christian community ought to be able to explain why and how their identity and mission is grounded in the affirmation that, "here is one body and one Spirit, [we] were called to the one hope … one Lord, one faith, one baptism, one God and Father of all, who is above all and through all and in all" (Eph. 4:4-5).

In short, this book addresses a continual challenge: how can Christian communities remain faithful to our risen Lord and his mission while being in the world but not captive to it?

1. There is a growing uneasiness among scholars with the word "mainline" to categorize this genre of congregations. The term "mainline" carries overtones of social significance rather than ecclesial or theological orientation. Currently, the term "ecumenical" is suggested as a better adjective. Throughout this book, however, I will continue to use "mainline," for it still has popularity among sociologists, survey takers, and journalists of American religious trends.

For Whom Is It Written?

The following pages address lay leaders and pastors of established Protestant congregations, especially those who belong to the Baby Boomer generation and their immediate successors, Generation X or Gen Xers. Currently, these are the folks who usually lead and shape the futures of today's North American mainline congregations.[2] Boomers, born between 1946 and 1965, came of age during the Vietnam era. The Gen Xers, born between 1965 and 1983, came of age in the last third of the twentieth century. Thus the ages of current mainline leaders are, in rounded figures, between fifty and seventy-five. Both groups have lived and worked in eras of significant social and cultural changes: shifts in patterns of work and family, high enrollment in higher education, assassinations of prominent leaders, two controversial wars, a growing gap between the economically endowed and the economically deprived, and a "new morality," often called "expressive individualism."

Sociologists such as Robert Wuthnow and Wade Clark Roof have probed deeply into the religious attitudes and faith practices of these cohorts of Americans and charted the "restructuring of American religion" as the twentieth century wound down. In my encounters across this nation, most of these Boomer and Gen-Xer leaders are able, faithful, and well-intentioned. Yet many oversee their congregations' ministries within a frame of reference that seems out of sync with basic Christian convictions and the practices of Christian discipleship.

Furthermore, most of these leaders, who are well educated, typically appear unaware of the current research and abundant resources that can better illumine a congregation's purpose, practices, and contexts. *One primary intent of this book, therefore, is to broker the findings of some of these studies for these congregational leaders.* I have tried to ensure that the studies — biblical, theological, sociological, and organizational — referenced herein are readily comprehensible for any inquisitive and patient lay leader.

2. In 2008 my denomination, the Presbyterian Church (USA), created a profile of its key lay leaders, called elders. Their median age at the time was 60; 52 percent were women; 66 percent had earned college or graduate degrees; and 46 percent of these elders had annual incomes of $90,000 or higher, while 8 percent earned $30,000 or less. Further, the median age of Presbyterian pastors was 56. Source: Research Services, Presbyterian Church (USA), www.pcusa.org/research/panel.

At the same time, I am fully aware that most scholarly publications about congregations are probably inaccessible to lay leaders. To help compensate for that dilemma, I have incorporated summaries and lengthier quotations. As will become apparent, the publications in the newer academic field of "congregational studies" are especially insightful and relevant. In a real sense, scholarly publications, along with specialized websites, are gifts for the stewards of local congregational ministries. As Stanley Hauerwas once wrote, "The theologian's task is not to present something new but to help the church to know what it has been given" (Hauerwas, 134).

Agendas Close to the Surface

Drucker's barbed questions deserve *theological* answers, not simply programmatic ones. Theologians use the term "ecclesiology" when trying to describe the origins, nature, liturgies, practices, and mission of Christian communities. Because it is a foundational topic in Christian theology, writers on ecclesiology seek to make clear the essential affirmations and distinctive characteristics of a faithful Christian community. This book, then, is an ecclesiology for Protestant congregations. Or, in the words of the theologian Jürgen Moltmann, it seeks to "bring out what is *specific, strange and special*" about Christian congregations.

At the same time, however, the venerable adage "The church reformed is always in need of being reformed according to the Word of God" still holds. Two important assumptions are explicit in this wise saying. One is that the Word of God is the normative criterion by which Christians and their congregations determine their commitments and mission. "The Scriptures principally teach," the respected Westminster Shorter Catechism (1647) affirms, "what man [sic] is to believe concerning God and what duty God requires of man."

The second assumption is that leaders of the people of God in every era and cultural context are continually called, through the empowering presence of the Holy Spirit, to discern and appraise their congregation's practices and call to missional responsibilities. That calling is no trivial assignment. It is a weighty responsibility for leaders to manage different styles of communal worship, identify faithful practices, ensure financial stability, hone governance protocols, endorse missional priorities, measure accomplishments, name cultural inhibitors, and reframe established programs. Efforts to transform congregation-based ministries are especially challenging when a consensus among independence-asserting leaders and consumer-oriented members is not automatically forthcoming.

"Where there is no vision," the Scriptures say, "the people perish" (Prov. 29:18, KJV). I contend that without a faithful, shared, informed *theological* vision, congregations rarely flourish. But Christian communities can also perish with a *myopic* or *distorted* vision. I fear that many mainline congregations have neglected their "first love" (Rev. 2:4) as stewards of the gospel. As we shall find, once-lively Protestant congregations scattered across the American landscape now seem weary, confused, and self-contained. Many are no longer restorers of hope in their surrounding communities. In this book, I hope to provide for lay leaders a constructive alternative to any dour trajectory that would consign mainline congregations to an "also ran" status in American Protestantism.

This book will affirm that the congregation is called to be the localized, particular expression of the Body of Christ. I stand with those Protestant theologians who understand the word "church" to mean, primarily, a congregation of Christian disciples in a specific time and place. I take with utmost seriousness the biblical promise of Jesus that "where two or three are gathered in my name, I am there among them" (Matt. 18:20). When a congregation, empowered by the Holy Spirit, remains faithful to the gospel and creatively enacts the gospel-driven practices that Jesus expects of his followers, then that congregation can be reassured it is truly a localized community of the people of God.

The community of Jesus' followers does not better or more fully exist in institutional structures above or apart from local congregations. Such affirmations do not exclude or devalue one congregation covenanting with others. In fact, it is of special benefit when congregations join with others across a worldwide network to learn how to (a) bear witness to the gospel; (b) equip leaders for the "work of ministry;" and (c) speak for social justice and righteousness. When referring to such a worldwide, ecumenical network of churches, I will capitalize the term "Church."

Finally, two seasoned authorities on American congregations,

Nancy Ammerman and Carl Dudley, state passionately why congregations matter:

> Congregations have never been more important. In a mobile and fragmented world they are a spiritual home, a gathering place where caring, trusting relationships are built and nurtured. In a world where outsiders' voices are often kept silent, congregations invite those voices to speak. In a world of great need, congregations provide support and comfort, food and shelter, training and advocacy. In a world that seeks moral and spiritual guidance but has no clear tradition to guide it, congregations preserve and renew traditions, calling their members and communities to accountability and vision. Although doomsayers of a generation ago may have thought congregations were islands of complacency or dinosaurs on their way to extinction, it is clear that the obituaries were premature. (Ammerman and Dudley 2003, 1)

How This Book Is Organized

The introductory essay in chapter 2 offers a brief appraisal of the American cultural influences now embedded in Protestant congregations. Drawing on the insights of historians and sociologists of American religion, I contend that many contemporary American secular values, often unacknowledged, regulate and remain unchecked in many mainline Protestant congregations.

Because the gospel of Jesus Christ both generates and critiques the people of God, the third chapter seeks to clarify what Protestant Christians mean by the term "gospel." Successive chapters describe how the Christian gospel is to be embodied in five foundational practices required of all Christian communities. These five practices, I will contend, find their primal model in the second chapter of the Acts of the Apostles.

Since the ordinary terms for these practices — fellowship, witness, service, education, and worship — have lost their edge and energy, I have dared to revert to the classical names for them: *koinonia*, or hospitable belonging; *mathētēs*, or informed discipling; *martyria*, or grace-filled witnessing; *diakonia*, or compassionate serving; and *leitourgia*, or passionate worship. Having tested these Greek-language terms in congregations across America, as well as in South Korea, South Africa, and Egypt, I am increasingly confident these classical, New Testament terms have transcultural recognition and practical utility in congregations in the United States.

Variations on these "Fab 5" practices (as a colleague once dubbed them) can usually be found in any textbook on Christian ecclesiology. I contend that these gospel-infused *faithful practices* are normative, indispensable, and doable for congregations who seek to remain faithful to their risen Lord. As with any organization, practices rather than public announcements reveal its true identity. These five faithful practices, I believe, distinguish a Christian community from any mere voluntary organization or neighborhood center where folks convene for religious entertainment.

Confessions Worth Mentioning

I readily acknowledge that other vital and faithful Christian congregations in America fall outside this mainline or ecumenical category. Further, Protestant congregations with different institutional heritages and structures, or those with a preponderance of members from one racial or ethnic background, or those independent congregations that are unaffiliated with a larger denomination also remain unexamined here. And a survey of other congregations, such as Roman Catholic parishes and Orthodox churches, would bulge out the boundaries of this book, even if I knew very much about them, which I do not.

We academic types are addicted to footnotes for good reasons. An attribution in a footnote usually acknowledges an author's sources and honors the works of others. In this book, however, I have reserved footnotes for supplementary comments and for pointing the reader to helpful resources. To identify fully the sources from which I quote or to which I refer, please consult "Works Cited" in the final pages of the book.

One last stylistic note: I have tried to organize sequential topics and subtopics by using different typefaces and bulleted sentences. Italicized words and phrases are reserved for organizational purposes, particular emphases, and book titles. I hope these stylistic techniques will help the reader better *visualize* how ideas flow and connect.

CHAPTER 2

Cultural Impulses in American Congregations

We have this treasure in clay jars....

— 2 CORINTHIANS 4:7

Christian congregations — now numbering more than 350,000 — are among America's most enduring institutions. Many pre-date the nation's public school system, most governmental bureaucracies, and the concept of the American business corporation. New York City's Marble Collegiate Church, organized in 1628 by the Dutch West India Company, remains as one of the oldest continuing congregations in the "New World." King George III of England issued the deed to the property of First Presbyterian Church in Pittsburgh, Pennsylvania, before the American Revolution; and many currently active New England congregations, as well as Anglican or Southern Episcopalian ones, existed long before the Pittsburgh Presbyterians.

Current non-mainline congregations are equally long-lasting. For example, the Bethel African Methodist Episcopal congregation in Baltimore, Maryland, traces its origins to the 1780s, and priests in a Roman Catholic parish in Mobile, Alabama, have been saying Mass continuously since 1704. Today, the total number of Protestant congregations of all persuasions is actually growing. Few will deny what sociologist R. Stephen Warner concluded: "The congregation remains the bedrock of the American religious system. It is in congregations that religious commitment is nurtured and through them most voluntary religious activity is channeled" (Warner 1994, 54).

Nevertheless, in America's mainline, ecumenically oriented Protestant congregations, seismic changes are currently underway. Baffling transformations are no longer merely on the horizon.

The Quandary of Membership Decline

The decline in membership in mainline congregations is well known and widely publicized. According to the *Yearbook of American and Canadian Churches*, membership in these kinds of congregations peaked in the late-1960s. Between 1960 and 2000 their membership declined between 20 and 40 percent.[1] The much-publicized "American Religious Identification Survey" of 2008 revealed that the number of people identified with mainline denominations had fallen to 13 percent by 2001; whereas a decade *earlier* that number was 18 percent.

During the same decade, "nondenominational" evangelicals increased their share of the population from 5 percent to nearly 12 percent. If Baptists and Pentecostal churches were added to the "independents," the survey predicts that these evangelicals would outnumber mainliners three to one in the next decade.

There are other concerns as well. By the close of the twentieth century, nearly two-thirds of all Protestant congregations had memberships of 120 or fewer. These smaller churches are especially vulnerable as their members age, youth exit, facilities deteriorate, and full-time pastors become too expensive to employ. Currently, smaller churches draw only 11 percent of Americans attending worshiping communities, while more than 50 percent of all America's churchgoers attend larger churches — that is, congregations with 350 members or more in which professionally trained staff lead a variety of spe-

---

1. For a quick and convenient overview of declining membership in one mainline denomination, consider the Presbyterian Church (USA). Between 1960 and 2006, membership in this denomination diminished by more than one million. This depletion is especially acute in urban centers. In 1960, Presbyterian congregations in Manhattan, in New York City, listed some 28,000 members in 61 congregations. More than one-third of these Presbyterians could be found in four large churches. In 2005, Manhattan Presbyterians had dwindled to about 13,000 members in 28 churches. About half of those members were located in the same four large congregations, while 16 (of the 28) churches had memberships of less than 100. Currently, 48 percent of Presbyterian congregations across America have memberships of 100 or fewer. See www.pcusa .org/media/uploads/research/pdfs/denominational_size.pdf.

cialized ministries. One pundit called this trend toward larger, multifaceted congregations the "Wal-Martinization" of Protestantism.

Changes in Membership Affiliation

Membership statistics in the early decades of the current century highlight other demographic realities. In 2004, Baylor University sociologists discovered in a national survey that only 10 percent of Americans claimed no affiliation with a congregation or religious group, and some 22 percent of Americans belonged to ecumenical or mainline Protestant congregations.[2] By 2012, however, a poll by the Pew Forum discovered that nearly 20 percent (i.e. one in five) of Americans checked "none" or no religious affiliation. One-third of adults under the age of thirty are religiously unaffiliated.

Pew researchers noted that the "nones" are this country's fastest-growing religious category. These same scholars found that two-thirds of Americans — affiliated or unaffiliated — say religion is losing its influence in their lives. Further, another researcher, Mark Chaves, has noted that "beginning with those born in the 1960s, more people raised in a mainline church became more unaffiliated than became evangelical" (Chaves 2011, 88).

The Blurring of Vision

As if the above statistics were not sobering enough, leaders in mainline Protestant denominations are wearied from the paralyses brought on by endless divisive conflicts: liturgical controversies, dwindling finances, sexual standards for the ordination of clergy, definitions of marriage, disaffections of the under-thirty generation, crippling biblical and theological illiteracy, evasions of denominational affiliation, inept pastoral leadership, and, as one authority put it, a growing "doctrinal anemia."

2. "The Baylor Religious Survey," Baylor Institute for Studies of Religion. See www.baylorisr.org. For an interpretation of this survey, see Stark 2008. The results of a comprehensive survey (sample size 35,000) taken in 2008 of the American religious landscape can be found in the publications of the Pew Forum on Religion & Public Life. See religions.pewforum.org.

Leonard Sweet, the astute Methodist theologian, claimed that, at the close of the twentieth century, mainline Protestants were undergoing "faithquakes."[3] The tectonic plates of American mainline Protestantism, seemingly so secure as in the years before World War II, were, by century's end, quivering and separating.

Scholars have tried to discern the reasons and contours of this breakup. Dan R. Dick's examination of seven hundred United Methodist congregations found that 63 percent are in various stages of (to use his term) "decay" (Dick, ch. 2). Equally problematic is the reluctance or inability of church leaders to assess the progress or regress of their long-established programs of education, fellowship, and worship. When leaders are disinclined to learn what, in fact, is going on in their faith communities, the prospects for transformation are bleak.

Analyses of this current Protestant malaise now grow at an exponential rate. One group of scholars details how lethargic congregations are unable to imagine how their futures could be different. Others describe how mainline congregations are becoming cocooned communities, out of touch with their "charter story" (the Bible) and exhibiting little missional interest beyond their own survival. Still others find leaders ill-equipped to distinguish a *distinctively* Christian community from merely another voluntary association that meets on Sundays.

I contend, however, there is another narrative, or line of reasoning, by which to interpret this disorientation among many contemporary mainline Protestants. It may not be the only narrative, but it is a plausible one. Here is the main plot: intrusive, potent cultural values of contemporary America have skewed Christianity's classical beliefs and deconstructed the Church's wisest and proven faith-forming practices.

According to this narrative, cultural impulses now present Protestant congregations with a multitude of obstacles. Those impulses include competing worldviews, alienating racial and class alignments, individualized therapeutic agendas, negligible membership obligations, and competing aesthetic tastes in music and liturgies.

---

3. See especially Leonard Sweet, *FaithQuakes* (1994). Sweet wrote the book, he says, "For Christians with the shakes, who know the church is the last hope for saving our families, our cities, our businesses, and the earth."

Such cultural impulses, I maintain, exert their greatest impact at the local level. Alan Wolfe, the seasoned sociologist, reads this narrative even more somberly:

> Tracing the history of Christian thought from the New Testament to the twentieth century, the theologian H. Richard Niebuhr documented the ways in which Christ could become a transformer of culture. But in the United States, culture has transformed Christ, as well as other religions found within these shores. In every aspect of religious life, American faith has met American culture — and American culture has triumphed. (Wolfe, 3)

Other informed commentators on American religious trends, apparently, concur — and it is hard for informed church observers to disagree.[4]

The late Art Buchwald once quipped, "These may be the best of times or the worst of times, but they are the only times we have." In the early decades of the twenty-first century, congregational leaders who seek to reframe their ministries and mission will no doubt bump into cultural values and sociological priorities that run counter to established Christian norms. Such leaders, I believe, will need to re-envision a biblical/theological "frame of reference" in order help their congregations focus their ministries and mission for the twenty-first century.

Two faith-forming and congregation-shaping assignments now appear urgent. First, leaders will need to identify — and name — those socio-cultural impulses currently influencing their congregations' convictions and practices. Second, leaders will need to envision *and* interpret a theologically informed mission that incarnates foundational affirmations *and* practices for Christian communities. This chapter addresses the first task. The second requires the remainder of this book.

---

4. The distinguished sociologist and philosopher James D. Hunter more recently rendered the same conclusion: "For all the deep belief, the genuine piety, the heroic faith, and the good intention one finds all across American Christianity today, large swaths have been captured by the spirit of the age.... Consumerism, individualism, the therapeutic and managerial ideologies have gone far to undermine the authority of the Christian movement and its traditions" (Hunter, 93).

An Immodest Proposal

One way to interpret the disorientation in contemporary Protestant congregations is to trace their immersion in a selected set of socio-cultural values and worldviews that permeate this nation's Baby Boomers and Gen Xers. Again, these are the cohorts of persons who currently lead most mainstream congregations.

To help assess the operative assumptions of these church leaders, I will employ the methodology of the well-known organizational theorist Peter Senge.[5] He claims that unless an organization (read "congregation") becomes a "learning organization," there is little hope of changing that organization. Senge contends there are *mental models*, that is, tacit assumptions or sub-surface impulses that regulate any organization's practices. These mental models are often revealed through metaphors (for example, "Our church is like ...") and narratives ("I remember when ...").

"What is most important to grasp," insists Senge, "is that mental models are *active* — they shape how we act." Mental models act as filters through which organizations process information, decide how to resolve problems, and explain why organizations do what they do. Until an organization recognizes and names its mental models, pathways to reframing and change become obscure and usually counterproductive.[6]

At least six culture-driven mental models have become increasingly embedded in mainline Protestant congregations since the 1950s. Deeply sanctioned in traditional American culture and folklore, I contend these six socio-cultural assumptions can subtly de-

5. Peter Senge, *The Fifth Discipline: The Art and Practice of the Learning Organization* (1990). See especially chapter 10, "Mental Models: Why the Best Ideas Fail."

6. An influential scholar of modern social theory, Charles Taylor, uses the phrase "social imaginaries" rather than *mental models*. By this he means "the ways in which [people] imagine their social existence, how they fit together with others, how things go on between them and their fellows, the expectations which are normally met, and the deeper normative notions and images which underlie these expectations.... [Or-dinary] people 'imagine' their social surroundings, and this is not expressed in theoretical terms, it is carried in images, stories, legends, etc." Such social imagery, Taylor maintains, is shared by groups of people and "provides a common understanding which makes possible common practices." Such pervasive images provide a "sense of how things usually go, but this is interwoven with an idea of how things ought to go" (Taylor, 171-172).

construct the gospel-driven practices of Christian discipleship and witness:

- The quest for *homogeneity*
- The commitment to *individualism*
- The seduction of *consumerism*
- The reality of religious *pluralism*
- The thirst for *spirituality*
- The dominance of *deism*

Singularly or collectively, these mental models — primal cultural energies — provide clues to why so many Protestant congregations are merely conventional and increasingly out of synch with biblical and theological mandates.

1. "Birds of a Feather" — The Quest for Homogeneity

Ancient Greek philosophers thought that human communities were held together by the adhesives of likeness and social commonalities. Thus the saying "Birds of a feather flock together." This self-selection practice has deep roots in American culture. One of the most astute observers of American society, the French visitor Alexis de Tocqueville, wrote as early as the 1830s that America's voluntary associations were bonded by the adhesives of social similarities.

From early on, most American communities gathered in congenial clusters of like-minded persons. In the last half of the twentieth century, political parties, private clubs (many of which excluded persons of different races or religions), fraternities and sororities, Masonic orders, gated communities, redlined suburban neighborhoods, upscale condo associations, elitist colleges, to name a few examples, have followed the established "American way": "like attracts like."

University of Texas sociologist Bill Bishop, in his recent book *The Big Sort: Why Clustering of Like-Minded Americans Is Tearing Us Apart*, claims that Americans over the last three decades have "been reshaping the way they lived. . . . In every corner of society, people were creating new, more homgenous groups. . . . Churches filled with people who looked alike, and, more importantly, thought alike. So were clubs, civic organizations, and volunteer groups. . . . What happened over three decades [was a] more fundamental kind of self-perpetuating, self-reinforcing social division. The like-minded neighborhood supported the like-minded church, and both confirmed the image and beliefs of the tribe that lived and worship there" (Bishop, 6).

Most members of Protestant churches follow this "birds of a feather," self-selective way of operating. As early as 1929, H. Richard Niebuhr's classic study, *The Social Sources of Denominationalism*, explained why American denominations were divided not so much by doctrinal or liturgical differences as by politics, social class, and ethnicity. He noted, of course, that, from the nation's beginnings, American Protestant congregations were defined along racial lines. On the eve of the Civil War, every American denomination split apart as a result of regional, political, and cultural loyalties, not because of differing theologies. Southern Presbyterians and Northern Presbyterians did not reunite until 1984. By 2000, according to sociologists Michael O. Emerson and Christian Smith, only 5 percent of Protestant churches could be classified as multiracial (*Divided by Faith: Evangelical Religion and the Problem of Race in America*, ch. 1).

Beyond the racial, other mental models influence most mainline Protestant congregations where members prefer to associate with fellow parishioners with similar economic views, educational levels, and aesthetic preferences and musical tastes. Even theologically liberal Protestant congregations are not necessarily sociologically diversified.

Worse still, persons who differ sociologically from a congregation's majority can often experience subtle inhospitality and unintentional exclusion from a congregation's decision-making structures. Despite advertising that "Our church is friendly," it is one thing to belong but quite another to bond. R. Stephen Warner in *A Church of Our Own* (ch. 2), claims that since the 1960s the premier challenge for American religious communities has been "to create a social space for those who are different." Ironically, one of the emerging differences between ecumenical congregations and America's independent mega-churches is that the latter are often more socially diverse than the former.

This quest for homogeneity, often exonerated through the metaphor of "our church family," can create serious challenges, if not tensions, for leaders of mainline congregations. The biblical vision reimagines a different orientation. A gospel-driven grace invites all persons of any social background or ethnic/racial origin into a fellowship of believers where the "walls of separation" have been torn down (Eph. 2:14). This ideal of inclusivity is expressed memorably in the apostle Paul's declaration, "There is no longer Jew or Greek … slave or free … male and female; for all of you are one in Christ Jesus" (Gal. 3:28). I contend that mainline leaders are now faced with re-examining the Scriptures' expectations for congregations as inclusive communities. Chapter 5 will address the practices of hospitality and the welcoming of strangers in congregations.

2. "My Way" — The Commitment to Individualism

For many Baby Boomers the hit song "My Way," made famous by Frank Sinatra and Elvis Presley, still resonates. Its lyrics tell the story of a man who, nearing his death, summarizes how he lived: he did things his way and he is proud of it. Yet this "my way" attitude is not new in American society.

Americans have long prized the mental model of rugged individualism. Our mythologies are energized by stories of the resourceful pioneer, the sanctity of individual rights under the U.S. Constitution, Ralph Waldo Emerson's extolling of self-reliance, *laissez-faire* economics, a fierce confidentiality surrounding our personal wealth, and a tight-lipped privacy of one's religious commitments. Individualism stresses the loosening of societal restraints and the freedom to choose one's own lifestyle.

Since World War II the quest for independence has acquired new and potent energy as a small library of studies now attest: sociologist David Riesman's classic study *The Lonely Crowd* (1960); historian Christopher Lash's *The Culture of Narcissism* (1979); sociologist Robert Bellah's *Habits of the Heart* (1985) and *Individualism and Commitment* (1987); political analyst William Hamilton's *Religion and Personal Autonomy* (1992); and *New York Times* columnist David Brooks's *Bobos in Paradise* (2000). Each of these argues that the attitudes of many ordinary, post-World War II Americans have morphed into mind-sets of personal autonomy and self-fulfilling lifestyles. During the same decades, many traditional restraints of family, economic reserve, sexual boundaries, and other social mores bent and gave way.

With this escalating individualism in the foreground, Robert D. Putnam, in *Bowling Alone: The Collapse and Revival of American Commu-*

nity, traced some (though not all) of the depletion of America's "social capital" in public affairs such as political parties and philanthropic giving. He attributes this social tendency to a late-twentieth-century inordinate reinvestment in "private affairs" (Putnam, 46). Concerns for the common good were often displaced, he maintained, by individuals' personal agendas and advancements.

The mental model of individualism carries enormous implications for Protestant congregations. Wade Clark Roof charts many of these implications in *Spiritual Marketplace: Baby Boomers and the Remaking of American Religion* (1999), a book without peer for the ecclesial issues presented here. Roof contends that Americans participate in congregations in the same way they participate in other voluntary associations, namely, *on their own terms.*

Many, if not most, shop around for a suitable congregation where their own self-defined spiritual needs and tastes are best met. Choosing churches out of loyalty to the "brand names" of Protestant denominations has become increasingly passé. Most Protestant folks, Roof found, participate in mainline congregations believing whatever they prefer, attending whenever they choose, contributing what they want, and behaving as they feel. Many think their church exists for their benefit. In such a milieu, congregational leaders must now contend with a wide variety of members' individualized beliefs and lifestyles.

Two illustrations magnify Roof's findings. A cartoon in *The New Yorker* magazine (July 1998) shows a well-heeled couple shaking hands with a jovial priest, clothed in priestly vestments. As the pair are leaving the worship service, the gentleman says, "I guess this is auf Wiedersehen, Padre. Estelle and I are setting up our own little religion." A prominent Atlanta pastor recently told of a member who wanted to know if Presbyterians had a place in their belief system for reincarnation. When the pastor responded that Christianity knows nothing of reincarnation and holds to the resurrection of Jesus as its central claim, the member withdrew and later joined a church elsewhere (Adams, 27).

However one construes the embedded individualism in American culture, the counter-cultural challenges for congregational leaders are formidable. When *every* congregant can act as an arbiter of a church's mission and priorities, consensus and mobilization become harder to achieve. More important, an exaggerated and unaccountable individualism is at deep odds with the lordship of Jesus Christ, the one who claimed, "I am the way" (John 14:6) and who calls his disciples to "Come, follow me" (Matt. 19:21). As we shall see in chapter 6, entering into a community of Christian disciples requires a radically different orientation from the mental model of the "my way" generation.

3. Born to Buy — The Seduction of Consumerism

Novelists often open up topics that theologians skirt around. In *Henderson the Rain King*, Saul Bellow's main character, Eugene Henderson, flashing lots of cash, looks for meaning by going on a trip to Africa, hoping to relieve his suffering and boredom. "There was a disturbance in my heart, a voice that spoke there and said, 'I want, I want.' It happened every afternoon and, when I tried to suppress it, it got even stronger."

As early as 1954, David Potter, a distinguished American historian, once described Americans as a "people of plenty." Our national character, he maintained, has been shaped by a culture of abundance, accompanied by a sense of entitlement to this nation's vast resources. Unique in the history of humanity, Potter observed in the 1950s, was the assumption that every middle-class American child required a bedroom of his or her own (Potter, 193). The economist John Kenneth Galbraith once argued that the modern American economy did not flourish by satisfying the needs of consumers, but by creating the desire for products consumers do not necessarily need. It has been estimated that the average adult American sees between two thousand and three thousand advertisements in a twenty-four hour period. Our closets, garages, electronic gadgetry, bookshelves, and fly-fishing gear attest to the seductive powers of such enticements. On most days we who have some feel entitled to more.

Juliet Schor, a Boston College sociologist, writes often about a "new consumerism." What emerged in the last decade of the twentieth-century, she claims, was an upscaling of lifestyle norms: "Luxury, rather than mere comfort, [became] a widespread aspiration" (Schor 2000, 448-49) In *Born to Buy*, Schor fears that "children's social worlds are increasingly constructed around consuming, as brands and products have come to determine who is 'in' or 'out,' who is hot or not, who deserves to have friends, or social status" (Schor

2005, 10-11). A Harvard professor, Susan Linn, in her book *Consuming Kids*, calculates that the average American child now sees forty thousand television commercials every year (Linn, 28).

Gary Cross, a historian of America's commercial culture, takes another tack. He argues that consumerism is now elevated to an ideology. Across contemporary American society, he writes, there is a growing "belief that goods give meaning to individuals and their roles in society.... Americans define themselves and their relationships with others through the exchange and use of goods." In fact, claims Cross, consumerism is now, arguably, the dominant ideology in America, a worldview more compelling than political ideologies, religions, or class and ethnic distinctions (Cross, ch. 1).

Bumper-sticker wisdom often nails these conclusions: consumerism is both therapeutic ("Depressed? Go shopping!") and stuffed with worldview perspectives ("Those who die with the most toys win!"). Only rarely do Americans see the more subversive bumper stickers: "The best things in life aren't things."

Most Protestant leaders are aware of Jesus' many comments about personal finances and generosity. Far more extensive than references to human sexuality, Jesus regularly confronted his disciples about their management of financial resources. "Take care!" Jesus said. "Be on your guard against all kinds of greed; for one's life does not consist in the abundance of possessions" (Luke 12:15). He had severe words for those who serve wealth (*mammon*) rather than God (see Matt. 6:24 and Luke 16:13).

Most of us middle-class Protestants remain haunted by Jesus' words in Matthew 25:40: "Truly I tell you, just as you did it to one of the least of these who are members of my family, you did it to me." In contrast to an undisciplined consumerism, the Lord expected his disciples to initiate compassionate services directed to the well-being (*shalom*) of others and advocacy for those impoverished and powerless. In a later chapter, on *diakonia* (service), I will return to Jesus' call for a congregation to become "a church for others," just as Jesus himself was "a man for others."[7]

---

7. A growing cadre of scholars points to another outgrowth of consumerism, namely, that popular Americanized religion and Protestant practices themselves may be viewed as commodities. See Vincent J. Miller, *Consuming Religion: Christian Faith and Practice in a Consumer Culture* (2005).

Meanwhile, still another mental model grows across the American landscape: religious pluralism. It, too, presents a puzzling challenge for leaders of mainline Protestant congregations.

4. Paths Up One Mountain — The Reality of Religious Pluralism

In her groundbreaking book A *New Religious America*, Diana Eck of Harvard University wrote this:

> Envisioning the new America in the twenty-first century requires an imaginative leap. It means seeing the religious landscape of America, from sea to shining sea, in all of its beautiful complexity. Between New England churches and the Crystal Cathedral in southern California, we see sacred mountains and the homelands of Native peoples, the Peace Pagoda amid maples in Massachusetts, the mosque in the cornfields outside of Toledo, the Hindu temples pitched atop the hills of Pittsburgh and Chicago, the old and new Buddhist temples of Minneapolis. Most of us of have seen too little of this new religious America. (Eck, 11)

This "beautiful complexity" is not really new for Americans. In September of 1893, representatives from dozens of world religions gathered at the "Parliament of Religions" in Chicago to explain their faith traditions. By the time the centenary anniversary of the Parliament gathered in 1993, nearly all the religious traditions present in the earlier gathering had planted religious communities within a 100-mile radius of Chicago.

Since the 1960s, however, religious pluralism has emerged as a new creed or even ideology for many Americans. *Religious pluralism*, as I shall call this ideology, is not simply an acknowledgement of religious diversities. Rather, the term implies a creed that assumes an inherent sameness in all religious faiths. The leveling of differences, so the argument goes, will, in turn, help reduce friction and confrontations in public spaces and agendas.[8]

Houston Smith's *The World's Religions*, which has sold more than

---

8. For a lively overview of this issue, see Stephen Prothero, *God Is Not One: The Eight Rival Religions That Run the World — and Why Their Differences Matter* (2010).

two million copies since it first appeared in 1958, defended the essential sameness of all the world's religions. This slippery creed, designed in part to sooth social discord and incivility, presents a delicate dilemma for mainline Protestants. On the one hand, contemporary Protestants are expected to affirm this nation's historic ideal of tolerance for the different. As early as 1779, Thomas Jefferson authored his famed "Bill for Establishing Religious Freedom," which made sure that no one religious tradition in his native Virginia trumped or denigrated others. "No man," Jefferson law's said, "shall be compelled to frequent or support any religious worship, place or ministry whatsoever ... nor shall suffer on account of his religious opinions or beliefs." Jefferson's ideal remains an integral part of the American way and the First Amendment to the Constitution guarantees that way.

On the other hand, it is easy to be tolerant when one believes little or nothing. No religious community, including Christian ones, ought to be required to deny or water down its faith claims, identity, and heritage merely to accommodate the need for civic tolerance. Every faith community is left poorer and compromised when a creedless pluralism flattens the dignity of religious differences.

The fact remains, however, that the globalization of economies, ease of emigrations, innumerable seminars and lecture series, the diversity of religious practices and clothing in public spaces, and the worldwide communication systems now present Protestant parishioners with formidable and diverse religious encounters. Interfaith dialogue can no longer be avoided in a congregation's educational programs and discussion groups. Such dialogue, as Jürgen Moltmann recently wrote, "by no means leads to depreciation of other religions, but all others have a right to discover what Christians believe and don't believe" (Moltmann 2010, 3). Little wonder that current church leaders find themselves between the rock of Christian faith commitments and the hard place of promoting religious pluralism.

One sobering assessment of civic pluralism's influence on mainstream Protestants can be found in the research published in *Vanishing Boundaries: The Religion of Mainline Protestant Baby Boomers* (Hoge 1994). Three well-known sociologists interviewed some five hundred Baby Boomers who graduated earlier from Presbyterian confirmation classes in the 1960s. Nine out of ten thought it possible to be a good Christian without attending religious services; eight out of ten thought individuals should arrive at their own beliefs independent of any religious organization; and seven out of ten thought all religions are equally valid ways to find ultimate truth about God. Nearly half of the grown-up confirmands interviewed reported that they had found few good reasons to remain involved in *any* religious community.

The sociologists state candidly their basic conclusion: the congregations that reared these young people offered them no compelling reasons or training about how and why "Christianity is special" (Hoge, 13-18).

In such a religiously diverse society, a Christian who witnesses verbally to his or her faith in a public setting can appear arrogant, invasive, and even un-American. How, then, do Christians, with grace and humility, testify to what makes Christianity so special without denigrating persons of another faith or disrespecting those who profess no religious commitment? Answering the biblical mandate to "go into all the world and make disciples" (Matt. 28:19) can become flat-out intimidating when the cultural mantra "Don't ask; don't tell" governs personal faith exchanges across the American landscape.

In such a cultural context, congregational leaders are now required to re-examine and re-style their congregations' practices of evangelization. It is increasing clear that Christian testimony in a pluralist society is no casual, trouble-free, self-learned practice. This book's chapter on *martyria* — that is, witnessing and advocating — is designed to help equip leaders prepare for Christian witnessing amid the diversities of the twenty-first-century social and political context.

But yet another mental model spreads across America's cultural landscape. *Religious pluralism* actually blows on the coals of an American-styled *spirituality*.

5. "*Spiritual Smorgasbords*" — *The Thirst for Spirituality*

The meaning of the word "spirituality" is slippery. The late Joseph Sittler, a beloved Lutheran theologian at the University of Chicago, once commented that "spirituality" is like an old Barnum & Bailey circus tent: "It covers so many various kinds of animals, events, acts and episodes, that it's hard to pin it down." But that did not keep him from trying. "Spirituality is that effort in life to interiorize and drench the whole of life with the powers of spirit, whether it be with the spirit of man, the spirit of culture, or religiously speaking, the spirit that identifies with the deity, whatever it is" (Marty 2000, 18).

Limitless spirituality options now permeate American society. On one coastline, one hears the eloquent yearnings of the distinguished Jewish theologian Abraham Heschel: "The search of reason ends at the shore of the unknown.... The sense of the ineffable is out of place where we measure, where we weigh.... [Our] mind is like a fantastic seashell ... where we hear a perpetual murmur from the waves beyond the shore" (Heschel, 1). On an opposite coast, the testimony of Bobbi Parish offers another option. In her *Creating Your Personal Sacred Text*, she offers "a step-by step guide to writing your own scripture, using selections from various texts of your choice as well as 'your own words'" (Parish 1991, ch. 1). Such a venture implies, apparently, that this spirituality does not define us; rather, we define it. In Middle America, barrels of *Chicken Soup for the Soul* nourish golfers, dog lovers, and heart attack victims. A transnational website, *Allspirit*, contains hundreds of references (from "Advaita to Zen") extolling spiritual wisdom, specialized practices, and catechizing communities.

Sociologists tracking America's postmodern spiritual questing find a surfeit of options. In *After Heaven: Spirituality in America Since the 1950s*, Robert Wuthnow found that the "traditional spirituality of inhabiting *places* has given way to a new spirituality of *seeking*." "Habitational spirituality" was traditionally centered in congregations where formal worship services, catechetical instruction, and religious practices such as baptism and the Lord's Supper served as the prime ingredients of Christian piety and community cohesion. Such corporate experiences offered security, stability, and certainty. But Wuthnow has detected a substantive shift beginning in the last decades of the twentieth century: "What is significant about sacred places turns out not to be the places themselves" (Wuthnow 1998, 3).

The "habitational spirituality" of organized religion drew boundaries through specific locations and facilities, established rituals and traditional doctrinal affirmations. Stability and certainty were among the benefits. These boundaries, however, are giving way, claim sociologists like Wuthnow. Seekers are willing to forgo institutional security in exchange for a more fluid spirituality. They are more comfortable with processes of "perpetual seeking," where metaphors like "explorer" and "sojourner" seem more fitting. Such seekers are "content with ambiguity, provisional truths, and practical wisdom that suits everyday needs" (Wuthnow 1998, 50). In short, the cultural mantra "Spirituality yes; religion, no!" has now acquired creedal status, especially among the generations behind the Baby Boomers.[9] As one man in his sixties told Wuthnow, "Religion is a structure, an institution. It limits you. Spirituality is something you are."

Clearly, these assessments of spirituality can mystify leaders of contemporary mainline congregations. It is no small task, as one author put it, to "unfuzzy the fuzzy." In contrast to the multiple "designer faiths" available at America's spirituality smorgasbord, Roger Owens, a Methodist pastor and theologian, lists a portfolio of spirit-driven *practices* that constitute Christian spirituality, such as keeping Sabbath, giving testimony, shaping communities, forgiving others, dying well, praying faithfully, celebrating sacraments, educating the young, and interpreting Scripture (Owens, 3-4). Little wonder that leaders can feel disoriented when they try to differentiate the spiritualities of the seeker generations and the classical spiritual practices listed by Owens.

One more mental model embedded in American culture requires addressing, namely the pervasive influence of *deism*. Arguably, deism reigns as the default theology in much of America. To understand why mainline congregations feel tremors in their foundations, we need to tackle this much-honored, overarching worldview prevalent in America's past and present.

6. "Americanized Gospel" — The Dominance of Deism

I deeply admire the documentary films produced by Ken Burns. His portrayal of America's Civil War will go down as one of the finer pieces of film art in our era, and his series on America's national parks is equally acclaimed. In July 2008, a journalist from *The Christian Century* interviewed Burns and inquired about Burns's religious background. Burns replied,

9. I have been helped by two books. One is by Robert C. Fuller, *Spiritual, But Not Religious: Understanding Unchurched America* (2001). See especially chapter 6. The other is by Tex Sample, U.S. *Lifestyles and Mainline Churches* (1990).

I was born an Episcopalian and was at best an haphazard attendee.... I find myself in the tradition of the founders — what
Thomas Jefferson called a deist ... interested less in the organized
forms of religion than a spiritual pursuit.... Standing in awe on the
edge of Yosemite Valley ... or on the rim of the Grand Canyon [one
reaches] out for the hand of someone next to you.... The series *The
National Parks* describes it — "the scripture of nature."[10]

This gifted American artist, aware of the language and practices of
traditional Christianity, gave his personal faith journey a different
spin and called it "deism."

Deism has a long pedigree in American society.[11] Popular among
the nation's founding leaders, the term "deism" is usually employed
to describe a religious worldview that emerged among the Enlightenment philosophers in Europe and England in the eighteenth century.
Disgruntled with the claims of classical Christianity, deists substi-
tuted another theological orientation. They allowed that God existed,
but such a God was transpersonal and did not actively intrude in
human affairs. A well-worn metaphor pictures the deist's God as a
watchmaker who, in creation, wound up the world but then let it
wind down on its own. Orthodox deists, past and present, believe
that human reasoning and experience are sufficient guides for an
individual's social, moral, and political responsibilities. By this line
of reasoning, Christian faith claims regarding divine revelation, the
norm of Jesus Christ's gospel, or the Holy Spirit's interventions are
no longer necessary. Praying is passé. Eucharist celebrations should
be reconfigured. Claims of miracles anywhere or at any time are
deemed fanciful.[12]

As Burns's above comment noted, most of America's founders

10. Quoted in *The Christian Century* (July 15, 2008: 32-33).

11. For a quick review of "deism" and its major advocates see http://en.wikipedia
.org/wiki/Deism.

12. There were, of course, severe and diverse critiques of this American-styled
deism. The mid-nineteenth-century literature of the Romantic movement, nationwide revivals, and the voluminous writings of establishment Reformed, Lutheran,
and Roman Catholic theologians included critiques of this "American gospel." In the
twentieth century, two world wars, the Jewish Holocaust, and the rise of Protestants'
neo-Orthodoxy theologies have further challenged the formal theological reasoning
of deism.

endorsed this religious perspective as reasonable, congenial, and practical. Among them Thomas Jefferson was most notable. Imbued with the Enlightenment's deistic assumptions, Jefferson produced his own version of the New Testament. With a pair of scissors, he cut out all references to miracles and divine revelation, retaining only Jesus' ethical teachings in his published "Jefferson Bible." Here is how the historian Jon Meacham, in *American Gospel*, summarized the theological orientation of the nation's founders:

> For them Jesus of Nazareth was a great moral teacher — even the greatest in history — but was not the Son of God; the Holy Trinity was seen as an invention of a corrupt church.... The mind of man, not the mysteries of the church, was the center of faith. (Meacham, 8)

More revealing are the findings of sociologists at the Institute for Studies of Religion at Baylor University. In 2005 they tried to clarify how Americans understood their God. They finally settled on four clusters, or types, of theological orientations that characterize ordinary citizens on the American landscape: the Authoritarian God (Type A); the Benevolent God (Type B); the Critical God (Type C); and the Distant God (Type D). The latter cohort of Americans think that "God is not active in the world ... and tends toward thinking about God as a cosmic force which set the laws of nature in motion.... As such, God does not 'do' things in the world and does not hold clear opinions about [human] activities or world events." To the surprise of these researchers, the majority of interviewees affiliated with Protestant mainline denominations favored the theological perspective of the "Distant God" over the others.[13]

---

13. The details of the "The Baylor Religious Survey" conducted by the Institute for Studies of Religion at Baylor University can be traced in www.baylorisr.org. Only 0.3 percent of believers in "Distant God" believed that converting others "was an important part of being a good person." The novelist John Updike, no mean commentator on mainline Protestantism, summarizes this "distant" theological orientation with more bite. He describes certain Protestant church members this way: "[They] went to church as faithfully as they played tennis and golf and attended rallies to keep out developers. Yet, their God, for all his colorful history and spangled attributes, lay above the earth like layers of icy cirrus, a tenacious and diffident other whose tendrils failed to intertwine with fibrous blood and muscle" (Updike, 122-123).

Equally surprising are the findings of the largest religious survey ever taken among America's adolescents, conducted between 2001 and 2005 and reported in *Soul Searching: The Religious Lives of American Teenagers* (2005). Christian Smith and his colleagues discovered that most American teenagers opt for what Smith called a "moralistic, therapeutic deism." In such a view, God is little more than a "divine butler" summoned at exam times, football games, commencement exercises, and romance breakups. Otherwise, this deistic God does not engage or interfere with persons' commitments and routines. Smith found these deistic views equally distributed among teenagers attending liberal, evangelical, and mainline churches — as well as no church at all. Smith concludes:

> The language of Trinity, holiness, sin, grace, justification, sanctification, church, Eucharist, and heaven and hell, among most Christian teenagers [is being] supplanted by the language of happiness, niceness, and an earned heavenly reward. It is not that U.S. Christianity is being secularized. Rather more subtly ... Christianity is actively being colonized and displaced by a quite different religious faith.

Smith adds one more sobering comment: "The religion and spirituality of most teenagers actually strikes us as very powerfully reflecting the contours, priorities, expectations, and structures of the larger adult world into which adolescents are being socialized" (Smith, 170-1171).

These findings resonate with the late Flannery O'Connor, Roman Catholic novelist and keen observer of American Christianity. She was continually puzzled by Protestants who, in her opinion, reduce the Christian faith

> ... into poetry and therapy ... and [have] gradually come to believe that God has no power, that he cannot communicate with us, cannot reveal himself to us, indeed has not done so and that religion is our own sweet invention. (O'Connor, 497)

It is not that deism has gone unchallenged. Few theologians in the twentieth century countered deism with the finesse of C. S. Lewis. In a much quoted excerpt from *Mere Christianity* (1952), Lewis mocks the deist claim that Jesus was merely a great moral teacher.

27

Innumerable others, before and after Lewis, have mounted clear rebuttals that most lay leaders can appreciate.[14]

Weighing deism further and expanding the list of other mental models operating in American society risks overload. Rather, we need to focus on a deeper understanding of a gospel-driven vision for all Christian communities. As an elder in a Connecticut Presbyterian congregation recently put it, "A vision is what we want to see happen, but we have to explain why." Only a more compelling vision displaces a lesser one.

Envisioning a Future

Two prominent scholars, Mark Chaves and Nancy Ammerman, have documented practices in many Protestant congregations that significantly shape the churches' ministries and mission. Chaves found leaders who were unable to articulate an overarching vision or overarching mission and then stick with it. Instead, sadly, he found that when a small group of church members, the ones who possessed clout and influence, approached a governing board to introduce programs of their liking, they could usually succeed *without* referencing or deferring to the mission and purpose of the congregation (Chaves 2004, ch. 10).

The other premier chronicler of American congregations, Nancy Ammerman, discovered that a cross section of congregations experiencing decline is "unable to envision how they might be different." She and her team of researchers found that declining congregations made minimal references to their biblical or theological heritages when trying to reimagine their future. Further, fearing the risk of internal conflict that often accompanies institutional change, leaders of these congregations preferred stability and peacefulness to creating a vision for a different future (Ammerman 1997, 323, 335).

These scholars and others point to urgent assignments for

14. C. S. Lewis wrote, "A man who was merely a man and said the sort of things that Jesus said would not be a great moral teacher.... But let us not come with patronizing nonsense about His being a great human teacher. He has not left that open to us. He did not intend to" (Lewis 1952, 36). Many modern Protestant theologians challenge the worldview of deism. For starters, see Jürgen Moltmann, *Jesus Christ for Today's World* (1994) and N. T. Wright, *Simply Christian: Why Christianity Makes Sense* (2006).

twenty-first-century congregational leaders. To identity and offset the socio-cultural mental models currently undermining the theological commitments and mission of mainline Protestant congregations, church leaders will need to …

- *recapture* the language and meaning of any Christian congregation's most precious treasure, the Christian gospel, which is not reducible to the Americanized gospel of deism;
- *examine* the New Testament's ideal of hospitality, which is at odds with current quests for social homogeneity;
- *revisit* Jesus' call for discipleship, which is at odds with the prevailing dictums of individualism and self-autonomy;
- *propose* how the practice of grace-filled witnessing is doable in a society where a civic pluralism expects a reticence about sharing Christian faith journeys;
- *engage* Jesus' mandates for compassionate service of others and advocacy for the poor in a society swamped by consumerism; and
- *celebrate* the triune God's beauty and worthiness in passionate worship in a contemporary society thirsting for the "living water" that gushes up to eternal life (John 4:14).

Each of these assignments requires familiarity with biblical and theological directives; each needs to be integrated into the web of a congregation's most cherished practices; each applies equally to clergy and laity; and each congregation will need to listen afresh to those sober words of the apostle Paul, "Don't let the world around you squeeze you into its own mold, but let God remold your minds from within, so that you may prove in practice that the plan of God for you is good, meets all his demands, and moves toward the goal of true maturity" (Rom. 12:2 as paraphrased by J. B. Phillips).

To engage these assignments, let's begin the next chapter by discussing the normative conviction of the Christian faith: the gospel.

CHAPTER 3

The Gospel in Four Dimensions

> Peter said to them, "Repent, and be baptized every one of you in the
> name of Jesus Christ so that your sins may be forgiven; and you will
> receive the gift of the Holy Spirit. For the promise is for you, for your
> children, and for all who are far away, [for] everyone whom the Lord
> our God calls to him."
>
> — ACTS 2:38-39

In these days of postmodern moods and mental models, the priority
of the Christian gospel may be a well-kept secret in mainline Protes-
tant congregations. Garrison Keillor, the savvy voice of the popular
radio program "A Prairie Home Companion," travels across America
and frequently comments on signs he sees outside church buildings.
In Louisiana, a congregation advertised the coming week's sermon as
"Jesus Saves, Repent for the Kingdom of Heaven Is Near and Christ
Is Coming Soon." In Massachusetts, another church sign read, "Loss
Makes Friends of All of Us as We Weave Patterns in the Journey of
Our Lives." Keillor wryly noted, "It gives one pause to know what
churches are up to."

In her landmark study, Nancy Ammerman found that many fail-
ing and perplexed Protestant congregations had lost contact with
their "charter story" (Ammerman, 322-323). In stark contrast to her
soulful conclusion, I contend that the *primary and urgent vocation* of
any contemporary Christian community remains the same as it
was in the New Testament (hereafter, NT) era: the people of God are
called to be faithful advocates for, and practitioners of, the Christian

gospel. Again, bumper-sticker wisdom shines: "The main thing is to keep the main thing the main thing."

What light is to seeing, the gospel is to congregations. No figure of speech trumps light as *the* metaphor for God's providence and grace. Light is the most stable reality in our universe. By it we measure distance and keep time. Without it, most things can't grow. While light is freely available to all, it is never consumed by those who use it. In the incomparable preface to his account of the Christian gospel, John wrote, "What has come into being in [Jesus] was life and the life was the light of all people. The light shines in darkness, and the darkness did not overcome it" (John 1:3-5).

The Scottish theologian, Thomas F. Torrance, once said that Jesus is "audible light," that is, in Jesus "God's Word and God's Light coinhere in one another ..." (Torrance, 96). This grace-filled, transcultural, life-affirming gospel illumines any Christian community of any size, in any social context, in any era, in any nation. But this gospel is at deep odds with the deism embedded in American culture.

The Gospel as a Shorthand Term

The word "gospel" comes from the Greek word *euaggelion*.[1] It is usually translated in the New Testament as "good news." Obviously, we derive the terms "evangelist" and "evangelical" from this Greek term. In English, the word "gospel" derives from an earlier English form, "good-spiel" or "good-story." The title of the once-popular musical "Godspell" is a variant of this early Anglicized term.

In Christian discourse, however, the word "gospel" is used in several ways. In one way, the term (usually capitalized) refers to the New Testament's four literary narratives — Matthew, Mark, Luke, and John — that contain what we know about the historical Jesus. The biblical scholar N. T. Wright of St. Andrews University in Scotland puts it this way: these Gospels "present a portrait of Jesus of Nazareth which is firmly grounded in real history" (Wright 2006, 99). These

1. Legions of scholars have worked to clarify this familiar term. For a quick and accessible explanation of the word *euaggelion*, see the late William Barclay's *New Testament Words* (1955). More complex and technical issues are addressed in "Gospel" in *A Dictionary of Biblical Interpretation*, ed. by R. J. Coggins and J. L. Houlden (1990).

supremely authoritative narratives, sometimes called the canonical Gospels, are the primary sources of our understanding of who Jesus was and what he taught, suffered, accomplished, and promised. For centuries they have been the irreplaceable and authoritative resources for instruction, direction, and reflection. They remain so for most Christian communities today.

Another use of the word "gospel" requires a longer explanation. Here I rely on a cadre of scholars who say the word functions in the New Testament as a rhetorical term.[2] Apparently, the earliest Christians searched for a fresh way to encapsulate the "story they found themselves in." In the decades following the resurrection and ascension of Jesus of Nazareth and following the outpouring of the Holy Spirit at Pentecost (Acts 2), these early Christians settled on the Greek word *euaggelion*, that is, "gospel." Old words were, apparently, too worn and inadequate. The old wineskins of older vocabularies could not accommodate the new wine of the good news associated with Jesus of Nazareth.

Thus, the term "gospel" was employed as a convenience, a shorthand term. Most, though not all, early Christians knew the historical details of the life of Jesus of Nazareth. Eventually, "gospel" provided a way to interpret the *meaning* of Jesus' life, death, and resurrection without having to reiterate all the particular historical events of Jesus' life.

So the term "gospel" has come to mean much more than mere historical information. It summarizes why of Jesus was the Word that "became flesh and lived among us ... full of grace and truth" (John 1:14).

Similar rhetorical devices are commonplace in communities. For example, Americans employ the shorthand term "September 11," to recall those horrific attacks on the Twin Towers in New York City and the Pentagon in Washington, D.C., in 2001. When we now speak of "9/11," we assume our hearers know the gruesome details of that ghastly day. However, what "9/11" *means* or *implies* has inspired countless editorials, government reports, essays, and novels, all of which seek to *interpret* the catastrophe.

2. For those wanting a fuller explanation of this term, see especially Joseph A. Fitzmyer, "The Gospel in the Theology of Paul," *Interpretation: A Journal of Bible and Theology*, XXXII (1979): 339-350.

In like manner, the early Christians employed the term "gospel" to explain (and declare) the good news of what the sovereign, redeeming God of Israel was up to in the life, death, and resurrection of Jesus (see Acts 8:12; 10:34-43; 15:7; Rom. 1:1; 15:16; 1 Thess. 2:2, 8; 1 Pet. 4:17). Used in this way in the NT, the word *euaggelion* equates with the founding and core convictions of Christian communities. Paul, who may have been the first apostle to adopt the term, reminded the Christians in the Greco-Roman city of Corinth that the basic ingredients of the gospel story were already known to them. "For I handed on to you as of first importance what I in turn had received: that Christ died for our sins in accordance with the scriptures, and that he was buried, and that he was raised on the third day in accordance with the scriptures" (1 Cor. 15:3-4).

Later, to the same group, Paul summarized what the gospel proclaims: "in Christ God was reconciling the world to himself" (2 Cor. 5:19). Paul reminded another Christian community, at Colossae, that "the gospel has come to you ... so it has been bearing fruit among yourselves from the day you heard it and truly comprehended the grace of God" (Col. 1:6).

According to sermons referenced in the Acts of the Apostles, this same gospel illumined and motivated the ministries and mission of the earliest Christian communities. Virtually every page of the New Testament details how the proclaiming of this gospel, under the Holy Spirit's promptings, generated faith and empowered hope even when confronted by skeptics and unsympathetic "cultural despisers." All allegiances, all agendas, all practices, all ethics, all membership qualifications, all institutional priorities flowed out of — and were subject to — this normative, grace-filled gospel.

No human invention, no earthly wisdom, no socio-cultural value system superseded or usurped this bedrock affirmation. When slippage did occur, as in the Christian communities of Galatia, Paul deemed them "bewitched" and scolded them for deserting "the one who called you in the grace of Christ and ... turning to a different gospel — not that there is another gospel" (Gal. 1:6-7).

This same apostle prefaces his seminal exposition of the Christian faith to the Christian community in Rome with verve and confidence: "For I am not ashamed of the gospel; it is the power of God for salvation to everyone who has faith, to the Jew first and also to the Greek. For in it the righteousness of God is revealed through faith"

(Rom 1:16). It is not misleading when Paul summarized his calling and mission when he testified to the Colossians, "I, Paul, became a servant of this gospel" (Col. 1:23).

It is the premise of this book that the premier vocation of any contemporary Christian congregation is to make this gospel clear and believable — first, to all members and, through them, to all persons in their host societies. When congregations circumvent this mandate, they can degenerate into mere voluntary associations, or worse, become spokespersons for others' political, racial, economic, and entertainment agendas. Instead of cut-rate purposes and self-serving programs, mainline congregations today are summoned to a divine mandate: namely, to interpret the belief-claims and demonstrate the faithful practices that emerge from this "good news."

To better appreciate this divine mandate given to all Christian communities, I propose four interwoven explanations that interpret the term "gospel":

- the gospel in its *essential* sense;
- the gospel in its *expansive* mode;
- the gospel as *expressed* in Word and Sacraments; and
- the gospel as *experienced* by ordinary people.

1. The Essential Gospel

By "essential" I mean the core or foundational gospel. In my experiences as a pastor and teacher I've identified three interwoven affirmations that constitute this *essential gospel*:

- Jesus himself is the best of the good news;
- the proclamation of grace is for any person; and
- a life-affirming hope is available for all.

Jesus himself is the best of the "good news." Few New Testament scenes are more instructive for contemporary congregations than when Jesus was brought to Jerusalem as an infant. One elderly Simeon, known in Christian history as "the devout one," had gone up to the temple to pray. At the same time, Jesus' parents arrived for his dedication according to Jewish customs. Simeon, like a beloved grandfather, lifted the child into his arms, looked at him, praised God, and announced,

> My eyes have seen your salvation,
>> which you have prepared in the presence of all peoples,
> a light for revelation to the Gentiles,
>> and for glory to your people Israel. (Luke 2:29-32)

It is not inappropriate to say that Simeon was, in fact, holding the gospel. Beginning with that tender scene, the meaning of the "good news" is indistinguishable from the person at the center of its story. According to some New Testament translators, the introductory words of Mark's gospel account should read, "The beginning of the good news, which *is* Jesus Christ, the Son of God" (Mark 1:1, emphasis mine). This *essential gospel*, in short, is centered in, on, and around Jesus, son of Mary, raised by Joseph, acknowledged as Messiah, host at a divine meal, crucified at Golgotha, raised from the dead, and loved by those who knew him best. It is a message to be proclaimed with urgency and joyful hope.

Ever since that day when Jesus was dedicated in the temple, the earliest Christians searched for adequate language to describe Jesus. Near the snow-capped Mount Hermon, Jesus once asked his closest disciples who they thought he really was. Peter, speaking for them, testified, "You are the Christ, the Son of the living God" (Matt. 16). Later, the writer of the New Testament letter to the Hebrews wrote that Jesus was understood as "the reflection of God's glory and the exact imprint [image] of God's very being" (Heb. 1:1-3).

Throughout the NT, the earliest Christians searched for titles and metaphors sufficient to interpret their understanding of Jesus. For many of those Christians, the quintessential interpretation of the gospel emerged in the apostle Paul's letter to Christians in the Greek city of Philippi:

> Live in such a way that you are a credit to the message of Christ.... Stand united, singular in vision, contending for people's trust in the Message, the good news.... Agree with each other, love each other.... Think of yourselves the way Christ Jesus thought of himself.... When the time came, he set aside the privileges of deity and took on the status of a slave, became *human*! Having become hu-

man, he stayed human.... [Jesus] lived a selfless, obedient life and then died a selfless, obedient death — and the worst kind of death at that — a crucifixion. Because of that obedience, God lifted him high and honored him far beyond anyone or anything, ever, so that all created beings in heaven and on earth ... will bow in worship before this Jesus Christ and call out in praise that he is the Master of all, to the glorious honor of God the Father. (Phil. 1:27–2:1-11, as paraphrased by Eugene Peterson in *The Message*)

Decades later, the Gospel According to John employed a different but equally memorable vocabulary. The gospel comes to humans as *the* Word that was more than mere words. "In the beginning was the Word, and the Word was with God, and the Word was God.... And the Word became flesh and lived among us ... full of grace and truth" (John 1:1, 14). Thus, throughout the NT, the gospel was identified with the grace-filled life, atoning death, and startling resurrection of Jesus Christ, with what some call "the Christ-event."

This gospel was not reducible to ethics or feelings or propositions or wise sayings. Further, this gospel, under the Holy Spirit's prompting, creates the church; that is, no church creates the gospel. Thus, Christians sing this affirmation robustly, "Christ is made the sure foundation, Christ the head and cornerstone."

The gospel as the proclamation of grace is for any person. Grace is God's love in action. Grace is not earned like a salary but is an unmerited gift, a gift that keeps on giving, a love that loves even when there is little to love. The gospel proclaims that, at God's initiative, grace reconciles alienated humans with God and with one another. Jesus' grace-driven announcement that "anyone who comes to me I will never drive away" (John 6:37) lies at the base of Christians' confidence and hope.

Modern analyses of divine grace initiatives pale before the incomparable parable Jesus told about a father and his two sons, usually called the parable of the "Prodigal Son" (Luke 15). Martin Luther called this parable "the gospel within the gospel." In this story Jesus called his listeners to reimagine what the God of Abraham, Isaac, and Jacob might be pursuing not only among the people of Israel, but in the whole human family.

Layers upon layers of gospel affirmations are at play in this famed parable. Here are but a few: when ordinary humans are powerless to alter our futures, when we are haunted by guilt and paralyzed with regret for past choices, when we struggle with our depleted selves, when we face our creeping finitude, then — *then* — God, like a watchful parent, whom Jesus called "Abba, Father," offers a surprising affirmation of acceptance. The alienated one — the "other" — is embraced and returned to the community to which he belonged since birth.

Then comes the capstone comment. In response to the elder son's complaint of neglect, the father says, "Son, you are always with me, and all that is mine is yours. But we had to celebrate and rejoice, because this brother of yours was dead and has come to life; he was lost and has been found." (Luke 15:31-32). Reconciliation opens options for life. Refusal of reconciliation flirts with lingering death. Little wonder that a wide segment of Americans sing, "Amazing grace, how sweet the sound."

The gospel is life-affirming hope for all. The gospel is good news because it is the story of God's intention to bring meaning-filled life and hope to ordinary humans. At the dawn of creation the Scriptures say the life-breath of God initiated humans' power to live (Gen. 2). In God, says the psalmist, there is a "fountain of life" (Ps. 36). Jesus promised to a new disciple, the woman at the well in Samaria, "living water... gushing up to eternal life" (John 4:10, 14). The Pentecost narrative tells of God's empowering Spirit "pour[ed] out ... on all flesh" (Acts 2). These claims and promises were sealed as reliable at the Easter event when God raised the dead Jesus and, as many have noted, creation started again.

Metaphor after metaphor describes the life-giving wholeness that this gospel brings. Here are just a few New Testament chapters that highlight these multiple images. Jesus is

- the light in a society that prefers darkness (John 1);
- bread in a hungry world, wine for human thirst (John 6);
- living water for a human's parched existence (John 4);
- the shepherd who searches for strays and ushers them into the fold (John 10);
- a Savior in solidarity with humans who feel God-forsakenness (John 6);
- the Messiah who calls us friends (John 15); and
- the Lord who is present wherever any "two or three are gathered in [his] name" (Matt. 18).

Simultaneously, this Jesus-derived gospel brings

- dignity and hope to the poor and alienated (Mark 5);
- release for all who are captive to despair and who are hopelessly imprisoned (Matt. 25);
- challenge to those who love only themselves (Luke 6); and
- warnings to those who "tear down barns and build bigger ones" (Luke 12).

In summary, and most important, this gospel is

- a gift from the self-revealing God and not a human discovery;
- a gift from God that no human earns or deserves; and
- a gift given to be shared with all others.

All of the above dimensions of this *essential gospel* might well be summarized in Jesus' words to his followers: "I came that they may have life, and have it abundantly" (John 10:10).

2. The Expansive Gospel

Every human community derives its identity out of *memory* and *hope*. Christian congregations are no exceptions. As people of God and stewards of the gospel, they are privileged to engage a *particular* memory and practice a *particular* hope. In Scripture, "covenant" and "kingdom of God" are the preferred terms Christians use to summarize their corporate memory and their gospel-inspired hope.

The Gospel and God's Covenant The term "covenant" basically means "promise." According to the entire biblical narrative, God is absolutely faithful in keeping his promise to redeem and direct the lives and communities of ordinary humans. Covenanting is the basic way God in his freedom chooses to belong to humans. Beginning with the early Hebrews, Abraham and Sarah, God declared, "I will establish my covenant between me and you, and your offspring after you … an everlasting covenant, to be God to you and to your offspring after you" (Gen 17:7). Later, God reminded Moses, "I will take you as my people, and I will be your God" (Exod. 6:7).

Not only were Abraham's descendants "blessed to be a blessing," but through the Abrahamic covenant "all the families of the earth shall be blessed" (Gen. 12:1-3). By any measure, that covenant was "good news" not only for those chosen Hebrews, but for all humankind.

The writers of the Old Testament (hereafter, OT) never tire of rejoicing in God's faithfulness to uphold his promises. One psalmist, rehearsing Israel's experiences in Egypt and Sinai, sings out, "Remember the wonderful works that [God] has done.... He is mindful of his covenant forever" (Ps. 105:5, 8). Isaiah, the Hebrew prophet most often quoted in the New Testament, proclaims, "The spirit of the Lord God is upon me ... he has sent me to bring good news to the oppressed, to bind up the brokenhearted.... For I the Lord ... will make an everlasting covenant with them" (Isa. 61:1, 8). And one dares not overlook the remarkable story of that unenthusiastic missionary, Jonah. He preached a one-sentence sermon and, outrageously, the entire Gentile city of Nineveh responded to Yahweh's inclusive covenant. Meanwhile, Jonah pouted and protested. He thought it was better to die than to witness the squandering of God's grace and covenantal promises on Gentile reprobates.

I imagine that when Simeon, the devout one mentioned earlier, held the infant Jesus and spoke of God's "light" to the Gentiles and "glory" for Israel, the echoes of God's awesome covenant for all humankind resonated.[3] Those same echoes are amplified forever in Jesus' announcement at the Last Supper. In his shed life-blood and broken body, the ancient Abrahamic covenant was renewed and expanded. "This cup," Jesus said, "is the new covenant in my blood" (Matt. 26:28). Thereafter, all subsequent people of God, those "blessed to be a blessing," will be nourished by the grace abounding in bread and wine. Christians in any congregation remain impoverished and deprived when they ignore this *expansive gospel's* grounding in this covenantal heritage.[4]

At the same time, another biblical term — the "kingdom (or reign) of God" — enriches and expands the term "gospel." This "king-

3. In the opening verses of his epistle to the Romans, the apostle Paul connects the gospel to that which God "promised beforehand through his prophets in the holy scriptures" (Rom. 1:2).

4. Methodists worldwide often begin each new year with a festive liturgy known as the "Covenant Service," which celebrates belonging to God and each other.

dom" language appears more than one hundred times in the Gospels. The term has commanded the attention of countless scholars and requires some explanation here, however abbreviated.

The Gospel and the Kingdom of God According to Mark's account, Jesus launched his public ministry in Galilee "proclaiming the good news of God" and saying, "The time is fulfilled. The kingdom of God has come near; repent and believe the good news" (Mark 1:14). Luke blends the gospel and the kingdom like this: "[Jesus] said to them, 'I must proclaim the good news of the kingdom of God to the other cities also; for I was sent for this purpose.' So he continued proclaiming the message in the synagogues of Judea" (Luke 4:43-44).

In the most basic sense, the announcement of the "reign of God" meant a new and inextinguishable sovereignty had entered human existence and encompassed worldwide societies. As one theologian put it, "Anyone who stresses the lordship of God means the rule of God in the present."[5] Such a claim posed an enormous affront to the caesars of Rome and to every other ruler or secular power, past or present.

This reign or kingdom was not unheard of earlier in Israel's history. Years before the psalmist affirmed, "All your faithful shall bless you. They shall speak of the glory of your kingdom [and] make known to all people ... the glorious splendor of your kingdom" (Ps. 145:10-12). This promised kingdom, Christians believe, was sealed and delivered with Jesus' crucifixion and resurrection, when a new and different worldview began. Human history was not to be interpreted as an endless cycle of repeated events, but as a purpose-driven narrative moving toward a divinely appointed "day" when all things will be made new, an era when human hopelessness and meaninglessness would be finally dislodged (Rev. 21).

At the same time, this new kingdom signaled the inauguration of a new social order and a new value system in which all would enjoy justice, all would flourish, and all would "learn war no more" (Isa. 2). It is the gospel-based vision that God is "in mission" to redeem and

5. The distinguished New Testament scholar Paul S. Minear linked the lordship of Jesus and the kingdom of God in this way: "When Jesus' disciples called him 'Lord,' they pointed to a single event with a triple implication: God had made him Lord by raising him from the dead; God had raised them with Jesus to be servants of this Lord; God had begun a new creation transforming the world into a Kingdom under the sovereignty of this King" (Minear, 83).

restore what God had originally intended at creation for ordinary people and human societies.

Just as the covenant-laden gospel affirmed the faithfulness of God's grace and redemption, God's new kingdom reassured Jesus' disciples of wiser, more liberating and hopeful ways to live, even if it meant that their witness and lifestyles might become counter-cultural. When the disciples worried and fretted about their futures, Jesus taught them to pray, "Our Father ... your kingdom come, your will be done on earth as it is in heaven" (Matt. 6:10).

The contemporary theologian Jürgen Moltmann interprets this biblical vision of hope and the kingdom of God like this:

> God's present, liberating, healing activity points beyond itself to the kingdom of freedom and salvation.... As parables of the kingdom, Jesus' parables are also parables of the new creation in the midst of the everyday life of this exhausted world. Finally, with the resurrection of Christ, the new creation begins. (Moltmann 1993, 99)

Accompanying this new "reign of God" is a radical realignment of tired social constructs. Class cleavages, gender prejudices, ethnic and racial denigrations are chasms to be reconciled as the prophet Isaiah once predicted, that is, where society's "wolves" and "lambs" will live together peacefully (Isa. 11). In that society, political and economic power, under God's reign, will be used for the empowering and flourishing of others, not for hoarding more power and financial leverage. Again Moltmann is insightful:

> *God's kingdom is experienced in the present* in companionship with Jesus. Where the sick are healed, and the lost are found, where people who are despised are accepted and the power discover their own dignity, where people who have become rigid and fossilized come alive again, and old tired life becomes fruitful once more — there the kingdom of God begins.... Just because in companionship of Jesus the kingdom of God is experienced in the present, its completion is hoped for in the future. Experience and hope strengthen one another mutually. (Moltmann 1994, 19-20)

Surprisingly, many contemporary Protestant denominations call congregations to function as "provisional expressions of the kingdom of God." That is, contemporary congregations are expected to become communities where God's "new reign" is already exhibited. Participating in a congregation is to be a "foretaste" of participating in the "kingdom's coming earth."

In this "new reign" many, if not most, of the mental models in modern societies listed in the previous chapter are to be radically altered. While more about the kingdom of God will be addressed in chapter 8, the mandate for congregations remains unambiguously clear: when churches remain ignorant of their covenantal heritage or when they become blasé about their vocation as servants in the "reign of God," they risk obsolescence in God's divine mission to renew God's creation.

Under the light of the *expansive gospel*, it ought to be obvious that contemporary Christian communities are not entrepreneurial enterprises. As members of the church we are not free to invent our own heritage or design our own futures. Admittedly, it will become a daring and daunting responsibility for mainline leaders to assess their congregations' ministries and mission in light of this *expansive gospel* — especially when the mental models of their host societies remain so prominent and competitive.

3. Expressions of the Gospel

Protestant theologians usually refer to the Scriptures and the sacraments of baptism and Lord's Supper as divinely instituted "means of grace." All are utterly dependent on the presence of the Holy Spirit for their efficacy. All are infused with mystery and hope. All are the indispensable media by which the gospel is made obvious and believable.[6]

The Gospel and the Word of God From the earliest references in Genesis to the visions in the Revelation to John's gospel, God chooses to address humans by speaking. Over and over the Scriptures affirm, "And God said...." It is a founding conviction of the people of God,

---

6. I am indebted to Daniel Migliore's text *Faith Seeking Understanding: An Introduction to Christian Theology*, 2nd ed. (2004), especially chapters 2 and 12. The book provides a masterful summary of the doctrines of Word and sacraments for mainline Protestants.

both Jew and Christian, that God communicates *and* acts in ways that ordinary humans can understand.

The Scriptures employ ordinary words and common metaphors (such as shepherd, king, light, water, father, mother) to indicate who God is and what God wills for humans. God's Word is not the specialized language of philosophers or the secret code words of religious elites. John Calvin, the influential Reformer of the sixteenth century, believed that the triune God *accommodates* to our human limitations in order to be better understood. It is the testimony of countless peoples, past and present, that when they read the Scriptures, they sense God is speaking.

The late theologian Karl Barth spent a lifetime exploring what the "Word of God" means for modern believers. For him "Word" and "gospel" were interchangeable. Barth claimed the Bible is the *written* Word bearing witness to Jesus as the *incarnated* Word, when "the Word became flesh and lived among us ... full of grace and truth" (John 1:14). When this Word or gospel is proclaimed — that is, witnessed to by ordinary people as well as preachers — those testimonies can become, through the intervention of the Holy Spirit, a living Word of the living Lord.[7]

The people of God, Jew and Christian, are people of the Word. The unforgettable language of Psalm 119, with its multiple synonyms, so testifies:

> Oh, how I love your law [Word]! ... I have more understanding than all my teachers, for your decrees [words] are my meditation.... Your word is a lamp to my feet and a light to my path.... The unfolding of your words gives light; it imparts understanding to the simple.... Trouble and anguish have come upon me, but your commandments [words] are my delight.

The prophet Isaiah put it this way: "The grass withers, the flower fades; but the word of our God will stand forever" (Isa. 40:8). "Everyone then who hears these words of mine and acts on them will be like a wise man who built his house on rock" (Matt. 7:24). "Heaven and earth will pass away," Jesus said, "but my words will not pass

---

7. For those who are eager and inquisitive, see Karl Barth, *Evangelical Theology: An Introduction* (1964). This book grew out of lectures Barth presented in America in 1962.

away" (Matt. 24:35). The earliest Christian leaders called together the emerging and widening community of disciples and declared, "'It is not right that we should neglect the word of God....' [And] the word of God continued to spread" (Acts 6:1-7).

These few biblical references to the Word of God underscore, however, an escalating crisis in most Protestant congregations. Evidence pours in about the growing unfamiliarity with even the most elementary knowledge of the Bible's contents. Recently, Stephen Prothero of Boston University tracked the disparity between Americans' veneration of the Bible and their unfamiliarity with its contents. According to polls, most Americans cannot name any of the four Gospels or name the first book of the Bible. Only one-third of Americans know that Jesus (not Billy Graham) delivered the Sermon on the Mount. The pollster George Gallup, who worried that the United States is becoming "a nation of biblical illiterates," also found that "born-again Christians are only marginally better informed" (Prothero 2007, 6-7). In a later chapter, I will address more fully this crippling disconnect. The fact remains, however, that the gospel is unintelligible when divorced from the witness and words of the Bible. Providentially, the faithful God provided another witness to the gospel when Jesus instituted the Christian sacraments of baptism and Lord's Supper.

The Gospel and the Sacraments If the Word will not be heard appreciatively, Christian communities, from their beginnings, received other gifts as media to express this gospel. In baptism, the gospel is *visualized*, and in the Lord's Supper, it is *tasted*. Since their inauguration, Christian theologians have called these sacraments "visible signs of an invisible grace," "visible words," or "testimonies to the embodiment of the love of God in Jesus Christ." While the New Testament does not precisely define the word "sacrament," baptism and the Eucharist (as the Lord's Supper is often called) are indispensable, biblically based resources for congregants' pilgrimages of faith.

"The sacraments," writes Daniel Migliore, are "enactments of the gospel by means of which the Spirit of God confirms to us the forgiving, renewing, and promising love of God in Jesus Christ and enlivens in us in faith, hope, and love" (Migliore, 280). John Calvin, a Protestant Reformer of the sixteenth century, wrote in the same vein: "The sacraments bring the clearest promises; and they have this characteristic over the word because they represent them [i.e.

the promises of God] for us as painted in a picture from life.... The sacraments, therefore, are exercises which make us more certain of the trustworthiness of God's Word.... [They] lead us by the hand as tutors lead children" (Calvin, 1280-1281).

Baptism — The New Testament records that Jesus himself was baptized and instructed his followers to follow his model. "Go and make disciples of all nation," he said, *"baptizing* them in the name of the Father and of the Son and of the Holy Spirit" (Matt. 28:19).

The sacrament of baptism is multidimensional. In its most immediate sense, it visualizes the cleansing from sin and sin's powers by the grace of the triune God. In another sense, baptism signals a new identity in the believer. Baptism simultaneously celebrates a believer's resurrection into a new way of life and, at the same time, ensures one's entrance into a new community in which his or her discipleship will be nourished and fellowship with other believers enjoyed.

Finally, baptism, like Jesus' baptism, signals the promise of a lifelong anointing by the Holy Spirit, who endows every believer with gifts to be employed in a congregation's ministries and mission in the world.

The Lord's Supper — From their beginnings, Christian communities believed the gospel was to be proclaimed to all the human senses, not only spoken to the human ears. And they had good precedent for that belief. The psalmist had said centuries earlier, "O taste and see that the Lord is good" (Ps. 34:8). Perhaps, Jesus had this belief in mind when he hosted an unforgettable meal in an "upper room" for his disciples. When bread was broken and wine poured out, the ultimate expressions of divine love were forever clarified. With Judas present, Jesus instructed his disciples to perpetuate this same meal. "Do this to remember me," he instructed.

With the Lord's Supper, Jesus instituted Christianity's most cherished ritual and liturgical foundation.[8] At the same time, this holy sacrament was — and is — an irreplaceable proclamation of the gospel. When the gospel cannot be heard through words, it still can be *tasted* by persons of any age, in any condition of health, of any social

---

8. The term "Eucharist" derives from a Greek term meaning "thanksgiving." In the traditional liturgical prayer known as the "Great Prayer of Thanksgiving," the people of God are "reminded of all of God's lavish gifts in creation, and preservation of the world, and most of all of Christ's life, death, and resurrection for our salvation."

status or educational attainment. In the Lord's Supper, writes Daniel Migliore, "the past, present, and future of God's creative and redemptive work is proclaimed" (Migliore, 292-293).

This meal of meals, charged with "Paschal mystery," is usually preceded by the "Great Prayer of Thanksgiving" that rehearses God's covenantal love throughout Israel's past. This holy communion, however, is no mere commemorative event like America's Memorial Day or Fourth of July. Rather, in the Lord's Supper, Jesus Christ promises be present here and now through the power of the Holy Spirit.

Moreover, at this meal participants signal their solidarity with all believers of any class, nation, or age. It is the celebratory feast of the kingdom of God, a foretaste of the coming "marriage supper of the Lamb," at which persons of all kinds and stations will gather to praise God for God's wondrous salvation (Rev. 19). This foretaste is what theologians mean when they say the Eucharist is an "eschatological" happening. That is, the Lord's Supper is the preliminary celebration that points to a future time when all of the people of God will gather together into God's eternal kingdom to glorify the triune God and enjoy God forever.

In these two Spirit-infused sacraments, the gospel is visualized and tasted. The sacraments are mandated for every Christian congregation because they publicly identify why and how disciples of Jesus Christ belong together as God's people. When "Word and sacraments" are circumvented or neglected, or replaced with other agendas, the gospel itself can be subverted and congregations can degenerate into mere social gatherings where "members only" folks occupy their leisure hours.

4. The Experienced Gospel

Most Protestant communities, especially those in the Wesleyan tradition, teach that human experiences of the gospel help shape its meaning. The Methodist *Book of Discipline* says that the "living core of the Christian faith ... [is] vivified in personal experience." Mountains of testimonies — real and reliable — attest to this gospel as life-transforming. Below are but a few accounts of persons whose faith journeys vivify the gospel. They are also testimonies that continue to enliven the faith of this author.

A Student and a Poet Early in my college days, a gifted English professor introduced us gawky freshmen to the writings of John Donne. A contemporary of William Shakespeare, Donne was an accomplished poet and essayist before he converted to the Christian faith. Later, in 1615, he became an Anglican priest. His gifts for writing about his faith fused with his passions: "Burn on, sweet fire, for I live by that fuel." In 1623, despondent over the deaths of his wife and five of his twelve children, he poured out his broken heart in sermons, essays, and poems that still illumine, especially for me, the gospel.

Donne's "Hymne to God the Father," written after his recovery from a severe illness, remains etched on many hearts, including this author's:

> Wilt thou forgive that sinne where I begunne,
> Which was my sin, though it were done before?
> Wilt thou forgive that sinne, through which I runne,
> And do run still: though still I do deplore?
> When thou has done, thou has not done,
> For I have more.

> Wilt thou forgive that sinne which I have wonne
> Others to sinne? and, made my sinne their doore?
> Wilt thou forgive that sinne which I did shunne
> A yeare, or two: but wallowed in, a score?
> When thou hast done, thou hast not done,
> For I have more.

> I have the sinne of feare, that when I have spunne
> My last thred, I shall perish on the shore;
> But sweare by thy selfe, that at my death thy sonne
> shall shine as he shines now, and heretofore;
> And, having done that, Thou hast done,
> I feare no more.

(Donne, 490-91)

Since those early college days when I was "taken in" by the same divine grace honored in Donne's poetry, the gospel has remained for me redeeming and enduring.

The Essayist and a Congregation In 1999, the gifted contemporary essayist and university professor Anne Lamott chronicled her journey into the Christian faith in *Traveling Mercies*. She grew up during the 1960s in the San Francisco Bay area in a tight-knit but unbelieving family. Presbyterians, her father supposedly said, were only a little above the snake handlers in Kentucky. Excelling as an athlete and student, she drifted into adulthood while something deep inside her was unraveling.

An inner emptiness gnawed at her center, and, as the song goes, she "looked for love in all the wrong places." Church stuff, she said, both teased and disgusted her. Yet, she writes, ever since her childhood days she sensed that some transcendent God pursued her. To tell about this other-worldly beckoning, Lamott employed a memorable metaphor. God seemed like some cat, she said, persistently trying to enter into her house. One night, hung over from pills and alcohol, and hemorrhaging profusely, she sensed the presence of the Divine One at her bedside. But her wording is much superior to mine:

> I became aware of someone with me, hunkered down in the corner.... The feeling was so strong I actually turned on a light to make sure no one was there. But after a while in the dark again, I knew beyond a doubt it was Jesus. I felt him as surely as I feel my dog lying nearby as I write this.... Finally I fell asleep, and in the morning He was gone.... But then everywhere I went I had the feeling that a little cat was following me, wanting me to reach down and pick it up, wanting me to open the door and let it in. But you know what would happen: you let a cat in one time, give it a little milk, and then it stays forever. So I tried to keep one step ahead of it, slamming my houseboat door when I entered or left.... One week later, when I went back to church, I was so hung over I could not stand for the songs, and this time I stayed for the sermon which I just thought was so ridiculous.... But the last song was so deep and raw and pure that I could not escape. It was as if the people were singing between the notes, weeping and joyful at the same time, and I felt like their voices or SOMETHING was rocking me in its bosom, holding me like a scared kid, and I opened up to that feeling — and it washed over me. I began to cry and left before the benediction, and I raced home and felt that little cat running along at my heels, and walked down the dock past dozens of potted flow-

ers under a sky as blue as one of God's own dreams, and I opened the door to my houseboat, stood there for a minute, hung my head and said, "Fuck it, I quit." I took a long deep breath and said out loud, "All right you can come in." (Lamott 1999, 48-51)

That was, Anne Lamott testified, "the beautiful moment of my conversion." She then quoted the great English Christian poet George Herbert to summarize her own new birth:

And here in dust and dirt, O here,
The lilies of love appear.

In a later interview, in 2002, Lamott reported, "I don't know much but I understand how entirely doomed I am without God."

A Philosopher and Parent In contrast to dramatic, spicy conversions, the distinguished Yale University philosopher Nicholas Wolterstorff testifies to a different vivifying process. While growing up in a Dutch immigrant community on the prairies of southwest Minnesota, he says he grew into the gospel, with a faith characterized by "simplicity, sobriety, and measure." In an essay first published in *Finding God at Harvard* (1996), Wolterstorff recounts "the grace that shaped my life." I do an injustice if I do not use his own wording:

My induction into the [Christian] tradition, through words and silences, ritual and architecture, implanted in me an interpretation of reality — a fundamental hermeneutic. Nobody offered "evidences" for the truth of the Christian gospel.... The gospel was report, not explanation. And nobody reflected on what we as "modern men" can and should believe in all this. The scheme of sin, salvation and gratitude was set before us, the details were explained; we were exhorted to live this truth.... Every family meal — and every meal was a family meal — was begun and concluded with prayer, mainly prayers of thanksgiving. Before the prayer following the meal there was a reading ... sometimes from devotional literature and often from the Bible-story book.... The piety in which I was reared was a piety centered on the Bible, Old Testament and New Testament together.... [Our] Christian experience was appropriating the Bible, the experience of allowing the Bible to shape one's imagination and emotion and perception and interpretation and action. The practice of the tradition taught without telling me that the Bible had to be interpreted; one could not just read it and let the meaning sink in. The center from which all lines of interpretation radiated outward was Jesus — Jesus Christ.... The affirmation of what is good in creation, society, and self was undergirded by a deep sacramental consciousness: the goodness surrounding us is God's favor to us, God's blessing....

Several experiences have evoked in me a great deal of reflection and reorientation. I was confronted with the faces and voices of the people in Palestine and South Africa suffering injustice. And I have felt confronted by the Word of the Lord telling me that I must defend the cause of these suffering people. My tradition yielded me the category: it was a call.... Slowly I began to see that the Bible is a book about justice; but what a strange, haunting form of justice! Not our familiar modern Western justice of no one invading one's right to determine one's life as one will. Rather the justice [for] the widow, the orphan, and the alien. A society is just when all the little ones, all the defenseless ones, all the unprotected ones, have been brought back into community. Biblical justice is the shepherd leaving the corral to look for the hundredth one and throwing a feast when the one is found. (Monroe, 152, 155)

In this passionate testimony, "gospel," "covenant," and "kingdom of God" are wed. But Wolterstorff's faith is not without pain. Echoing his earlier *Lament for a Son* (1987), he concludes his Harvard testimony by mentioning the tragic death of his beloved son who died senselessly on a slippery mountain path in Austria:

My whole tradition had taught me to love the world, to love the world as a gift, to love God through and in the world — wife, children, art, plants, learning.... But it didn't tell me this: It didn't tell me that the invitation to love is an invitation to suffering. It let me find out for myself.... The gospel had never been presented to me as best explanation, most complete account; the tradition had always encouraged me to live with unanswered questions. Life eternal doesn't depend on getting all the questions answered.... So I shall struggle to live the reality of Christ's rising and death's dying. In my living, my son's dying will not be the last word. (Monroe, 156-157)

The Journey of a Theologian Jürgen Moltmann, born in 1926, taught Christian theology at the University of Tübingen, in Germany, from 1967 to 1994. Widely known around the world for his *Theology of Hope*, Moltmann is one of the Western world's most influential contemporary Protestant theologians. By his own account, his faith pilgrimage began as a young soldier in Hitler's Nazi Germany.

Without any religious upbringing in the city of Hamburg, Moltmann was a mere lad of seventeen when he was conscripted to man an anti-aircraft turret. One night, during an Allies firestorm bombing of Hamburg, a bomb tore to pieces his friend who was standing alongside of him. Moltmann, however, remained unscathed. "That night I cried out to God for the first time, 'My God where are you?'"

Moltmann has since testified in several places that his lifelong journey into the gospel and into a lifetime given to theological reflection began on that awful night. Vividly, in *Jesus Christ for Today's World*, Moltmann recounts his faith journey. Again, a longer quote is unavoidable:

> The German Reich had collapsed. German civilization had been destroyed at Auschwitz. My own home town of Hamburg was in ruins; and in my own self things looked no different. I felt abandoned by God and human beings, and the hopes of my youth died. I couldn't see a future ahead for me. In that situation an American chaplain [in a prisoner of war camp in Belgium] put a Bible into my hand, and I began to read it. First of all the psalms of lament in the Old Testament: "I have fallen dumb and have to eat up my suffering within myself.... I am a stranger as all my fathers were" (Psalm 39). Then I was drawn to the story of the passion, and when I came to Jesus' death cry, I knew: this is the one who understands you and is beside you when everyone else abandons you. "My God, why have you forsaken me?" That was my cry for God too. I began to understand the suffering, [the] assailed and God-forsaken Jesus, because I felt that he understood me. And I grasped that this Jesus is the divine Brother in our distress. He brings hope to the prisoners and the abandoned. He is the one who delivers us from the guilt that weighs us down and robs us of every kind of future. And I became possessed by a hope when in human terms there was little to hope for. I summoned up the

courage to live, at a point when one would perhaps willingly have put an end to it all. This early companionship with Jesus, the brother in suffering and the liberator from guilt, has never left me since. The Christ for me is the crucified Jesus. (Moltmann 1994, 2-3)

Moltmann eventually ended up as a prisoner of war in a compound known as Camp Norton, near the Scottish village of Kilmarnock. "In Kilmarnock the miners and their families took us in with a hospitality that shamed us profoundly.... We were accepted as people ... and that made it possible for us to live with the past of our people, in the shadow of Auschwitz, without repressing anything, and without becoming callous."

As his advocacy for the gospel gained worldwide influence, Moltmann accounted for his faith journey in yet another way:

For a long time I looked for you [God] within myself, and crept into the shell of my soul, protecting myself with an armor of inapproachability. But you [God] were outside — outside myself — and enticed me out of the narrowness of my heart [and] into the broad place of love for life. So I came out of myself and found my soul in my senses, and my own self in others. The experience of God deepens the experiences of life. It does not reduce them, for it awakens an unconditional Yes to life. The more I love God the more gladly I exist. The more immediately and wholly I exist, the more I sense the living God, the inexhaustible well of life, and life's eternity. (Moltmann 1992, 98)

The Playwright in Manhattan It ought not to be surprising that whenever the gospel is obscured in congregations, it emerges, under the unpredictable providence of the Holy Spirit, in quite secular venues. Margaret Edson, a kindergarten teacher with a love for the poetry of John Donne, wrote the play W;t, (sic) in 1993. It was subsequently performed in New York, where it won a Pulitzer Prize in 1999. Later, Emma Thompson starred in W;t's memorable television performance. With two friends, my wife and I caught a live performance in a theater in lower Manhattan.

The play involves the slow unraveling of the defenses of a fictional Vivian Bearing, a distinguished professor of seventeenth-century English poetry and the editor of the definitive edition of John Donne's works. Confined to a cancer unit at a university hospital and slowly succumbing to cervical cancer, the self-assured professor wades deeper and deeper into uncharted waters.

After enduring a series of brutal and humiliating examinations by sundry medical personnel, Bearing edges into physical and emotional depletion. At this point her beloved teacher, professor emerita Ashford, pays a visit to Bearing's bedside, finding her pale and writhing in pain. The elder professor is appalled to see her prized student so stricken. In one memorable, poignant scene, the elder professor slips off her shoes and swings into bed alongside of Vivian in order to warm her former student's chilled body.

> "Shall I recite to you? I can recite something from Donne."
> "Noooo," moans Vivian.

Instead of quoting past metaphysical poets, the elder professor begins to read from a book she had just purchased for her grandson. Vivian drifts in and out of consciousness as the older professor reads from the child's story *The Runaway Bunny*.

> "Once there was a little bunny who wanted to run away," the story begins. "If you run away," the bunny's mother says, "I will run after you. For you are *my* little bunny."
> "If you run after me," responds the bunny, "I will become a fish in a trout stream and I will swim away from you."
> "If you become a fish in a trout stream," says the mother, "I will become a fisherman and will fish for you."
> "If you become a fisherman," counters the bunny, "I will be a bird and fly away from you."
> "If you become a bird and fly away from me," says the mother, "I will be a tree that you come home to."

In the midst of this contemporary parable of God's irresistible grace, Vivian's life continues to slip away. The older professor says, "It is a little allegory of the soul. No matter where it hides, God will find it. See, Vivian?"

After a chaotic scene of medical code-blue theatrics, the stage grows pitch dark and desolate. Death arrives. Then, for one dazzling moment, the unclothed, elegant, resurrected body of Vivian Bearing appears, bathed in transcendent light, healed and renewed by divine Mystery.

We left the theater in weighty silence. Genesis tells us that the Spirit broods over all creation. That evening only a calloused soul could deny the gospel hovered over Manhattan.

A Seminarian and Her Professor Tex Sample, in his book *Ministry in an Oral Culture* (1994), recounts an incident while teaching at a seminary in Missouri. With a newly minted Ph.D. from the East and a classroom of adoring students, Sample tells of poking fun at those older Protestant hymns he considered mushy, individualistic, escapist, syrupy. He launched into the song "In the Garden," singing it in a nasal voice, mocking words and tune. After class, while he was still on a roll, a thirty-year-old female student waited and cornered him.

> Tex, my father started screwing me when I was eleven, and he kept it up until I was sixteen and found strength to stop it. After every one of those ordeals I would go outside and sing that song to myself: "I go to the garden alone, while the dew is still on the roses, and he walks with me and talks with me, and he tells me I am his own." Without that song I don't know how I could have survived. Tex, don't you ... ever ... ever ... ever make fun of that song in my presence again. (Sample 1994, 78)

Philosophers claim that the meaning of words depends on how and where they are used. All descriptions of the gospel, like this student's, are laced with specific contexts and conditioned by immediate human experiences.

Of course, any description of a person's encounters with the gospel can come up limp. Most do. Admittedly, not all faith accounts are equally compelling. But aesthetically deficient media do not negate the gospel's truth and salvific power. "It is one thing to sing 'In the Garden' as privatistic sentimentalism," observed Sample. "It is quite another when it sustains the survival of people who struggle to make it through one more day" (Sample 1994, 78-79).

Stories, like those told above, make the gospel vivid and thereby more believable. At the same time, similar stories told in contemporary Christian communities usually, with the Spirit's presence, inspire in those communities a renewed confidence to engage those who have yet to experience this life-affirming gospel.[9]

The Gospel Revisited

One might sum up and interpret the term "gospel" — the good news — like this:

- This good news from God is ultimately realized in the life, death, and resurrection of Jesus of Nazareth and calls for our response.
- This good news encompasses the memories of the people of God (covenant) and funds their hope for a new and different society (the reign of God).
- This good news is expressed preeminently in the Word of God in the Holy Scriptures and in the sacraments that Jesus instituted.
- This good news is continually made vivid and convincing through the testimonies and mission-driven practices of ordinary Christians in everyday pursuits and vocations.

By now it ought to be obvious how radically different this gospel, in all four dimensions, differs from the "Americanized gospel" of deism noted in chapter 1. The deist's god is distant, an "unmoved Mover" and a muted god. In stark contrast, Jews and Christians "do not live by bread alone, but by every word that comes from the mouth of God" (Deut. 8:3; Matt. 4:4). Again, the best of those words is that Word — Jesus of Nazareth — who "became flesh and lived among us . . . full of grace and truth" (John 1:14).

Practicing the Gospel

This book contends that the primary vocation of any Christian congregation is to become informed stewards of — and gracious witnesses for — this gospel.

---

9. For a fascinating digest of diverse accounts of Christians who "experienced God" — from the apostle Paul to the rock musician Bono — see John M. Mulder and Hugh T. Kerr, eds., *Finding God: A Treasury of Conversion Stories* (2012).

Such a calling, however, will require faith-forming practices in the everyday lives and communities of the people of God.

A non-practiced, merely cerebral gospel is no compelling gospel at all. With this claim in mind, *the remainder of this book will address five gospel-driven, faith-forming practices that identify and define a congregation's vocation.* But note well: these five *faithful practices,* as I shall call them, are expected of *every* Christian disciple, young and old, educated or untutored, talented or halting. Five key words identify them:

- *koinonia,* or belonging,
- *mathētēs,* or discipling,
- *martyria,* or witnessing,
- *diakonia,* or serving, and
- *leitourgia,* or worshiping.

Each of these faithful practices will require a chapter to explain why and how each emerges out of the gospel. I will strive to explain why each is incongruent with many of the secular mental models in contemporary American culture. And each of these faithful practices will be in the service of the vision spun out by the renowned Methodist theologian Albert Outler.

> Give us a church whose members believe and understand the gospel of God's healing love of Christ to hurting men and women. Give us a church that speaks and acts in consonance with its faith — not only to reconcile the world but to turn it upside down. Give us a church of Spirit-filled people in whose fellowship life speaks to life, love to love, and [where] faith and trust respond to God's grace. And we shall have a church whose witness in the world will not fail and whose service to the world will transform it. (Outler, 56)

In preparation for coming chapters, however, a brief introduction about the meaning and boundaries of the term "practice" is necessary.

CHAPTER 4

On Practices

"Be doers of the word, and not merely hearers...."

— JAMES 1:22

Spread across the pages of the New Testament is the claim that believing the gospel in all its dimensions is never disengaged from practicing that gospel.

The biblical way of faithfulness connects believing and doing in a circuitry of interaction. As Jesus once taught, "Everyone who *hears* these words of mine *and acts on them* will be like a wise man who built his house on rock.... Everyone who *hears* these words of mine *and does not act on them* will be like a foolish man who built his house on sand" (Matt. 7:24-29. Emphasis mine). Human conduct, especially those repeated behaviors, has always served as a reliable indicator of subsurface beliefs and attitudes. "Even children make themselves known by their acts" (Prov. 20:11).

However, this symbiotic interaction of "faith" and "works" takes on greater complexity in the shared practices of a congregation. Repeated weekly rituals, worship services, sacrament celebrations, fellowship dinners, coffee hours, educational programs, youth conferences, budget priorities, and cross-cultural mission trips are tell-tale signs of how believing and doing interface in congregational life.

Dorothy C. Bass maintains that such practices in congregations are more than mere indicators of a way of life (Bass 1997, 5). They embody the markers of a congregation's real identity, and they sustain the community's purpose. Most important, such practices manifest how, *if at all or to what extent*, a congregation participates in the gospel-driven mission of God who, through Christ, is "reconciling the world to himself" (2 Cor. 5:19).

Currently, a wide variety of scholars are trying to clarify the meaning of the slippery term "practice."[1] Sometimes the term "practice" means little more than simply the things we do repeatedly, as when we practice our piano lessons or golf swings. Sometimes something more broad is indicated when we say that a person practices medicine or has a law practice. Currently, the term "best practices" has come to mean those repeatable activities that collected wisdom regards as the most effective ways to produce desired institutional outcomes.

Communally sanctioned and driven practices are the bearers of tradition and core values. They highlight identity, reveal priorities, and signal missional preferences. To clarify the symbiotic relationship of embedded meanings and public behaviors, some scholars employ the term *praxis*, or *praxes* in the plural.

In *praxis*, the *why* of a practice is intentionally blended with the *how* of the behaviors. Some philosophers call *praxis* "informed action."[2] Ray Anderson, a theologian at Fuller Theological Seminary, moved *praxis* a step further when he coined the term *Christopraxis*. "Christopraxis," he wrote, "is the medium through which the Christian community embodies and enacts its fundamental vision of the gospel. . . . Christopraxis is the ministry [in a congregation] of making disciples" (Anderson 48, 53).

---

1. An elaborate discourse about the nature and logic of practices now influences Christian theology, liturgy studies, and spiritual disciplines and has helped to redefine the traditional field of study known as Practical Theology. For a brief but insightful and current discussion of the concept of faithful, Christian practices in congregations, see Craig Dykstra and Dorothy C. Bass, "A Theological Understanding of Christian Practices" in *Practicing Theology: Beliefs and Practices in Christian Life*, ed. by Miroslav Volf and Dorothy C. Bass (2002). Under the editorship of Phyllis Tickle, a small library of established Christian practices — such as prayer, Sabbath keeping, fasting, pilgrimages, and tithing — is now available and accessible to laity. Brian McLaren initiates this series with his insightful book, *Finding Our Way Again* (2008).

2. The term *praxis* is often illustrated by observing ordinary human friendships. A theory of friendship is not neatly divisible into preconceived abstractions and standardized behaviors. Rather, practicing friendship involves reciprocal processes of motives and actions, of feelings and behaviors, of inward commitments and outward behaviors. Friends improvise activities according to changing circumstances and do so without jeopardizing their friendship.

In Anderson's view, a congregation's *Christopraxes* are intentionally designed to continue Christ's own ministries of witness, compassion, reconciliation, and justice seeking. Another theologian calls such *praxes* "habitations of the Spirit." Methodist William H. Willimon offers yet another perspective: "The Christian faith is that set of practices appropriate to a group of people who have been caught off-guard, blindsided by a living God" (Cole, 230).

Throughout the coming pages, however, I shall use the term "faithful practices" to signify those biblically mandated, Spirit-driven, missional responsibilities of a Christian community. I will assert that such practices emerge from — and are faithful manifestations of — the gospel.

Naming a Congregation's Faithful Practices

One basic premise of this book is this: the gospel revealed in Jesus Christ requires Christian congregations to develop particular, biblically-mandated, time-honored, Spirit-infused practices. More specifically, I contend that five faithful practices are now the essential markers of faithful Christian communities. They vivify the gospel to a wider public. Or, as some theologians put it, they celebrate and testify to the ongoing presence of God in human history in a particular locality.

Through each and all of these behaviors, a Christian community seeks to reflect the lifestyle of the risen Lord. These faithful practices are public "signs and seals" of a congregation's character.

This list of five is not original with me. Many who analyze contemporary Christian communities identify and address them.[3] However, because the usual labels for these practices have become skewed and worn out, I will revert to the original Greek terms in the New Testament (NT).

Again, the five essential faithful practices I propose for Christian congregations are these:

3. The United Methodist bishop and theologian Robert Schnase once published an imaginative text for "fruitful congregations" that lists five practices: radical hospitality, passionate worship, intentional faith development, risk-taking mission and service, and extravagant generosity. See his *Five Practices of Fruitful Congregations* (2008). Maria Harris, a Christian educator, structured a church's educational curriculum around these five practices. See her *Fashion Me a People: Curriculum for the Church* (1989).

- *Koinonia,* or *belonging*
  This term is usually translated as "fellowship." Its core value is belongingness or bonding. It points to the practices of Christian hospitality in congregations who gladly accept and embrace those who are "other." It is at deep odds with the mental model that idolizes exclusiveness and homogeneity in American communities.

- *Mathētēs,* or *discipling*
  This term highlights the practices associated with the lifestyle of a disciple of Jesus. "Apprentice" is a useful synonym. Disciples in the New Testament are lifelong learners, engaged in lifelong faith formation. We derive the proper name "Matthew" from it. *Mathētēs* implies that Christian congregations are meant to be disciple producers. They are not voluntary organizations content with endorsing designer faiths and merely accommodating cravings for socializing. Not surprisingly, the disciplines inherent in *mathētēs* can contradict the American societal ideals of individualism and autonomy.

- *Martyria,* or *witnessing*
  Among the last instructions given by Jesus to his disciples was this: "You will receive power when the Holy Spirit has come upon you; and you will be my witnesses" (Acts 1:8). This term, *martyria,* means "witness" or "advocate." Our English word "martyr" derives from it. As the earliest Christians said, "We cannot keep from speaking about what we have seen and heard" (Acts 4:20). Christian *martyria,* or testimony, is usually addressed to those *outside* the community of faith. It, too, is in tension with a pluralistic society that promotes "Don't ask; don't tell" etiquette codes. Chapter 7 will address this practice in contemporary Protestant congregations.

- *Diakonia,* or *serving*
  This term translates into English as "service" or "ministry." We derive the word "deacon" from it. *Diakonia* emphasizes those responsibilities expected of Christian communities who are called to serve those who are abandoned, hopeless, powerless, and hungry. "I am among you," Jesus said, "as one who serves" (Luke 22).

In sharp contrast to the "new consumerism" in American society, the practices of *diakonia* center a congregation's ministries around acts of compassion and concerted efforts at justice seeking. Chapter 8 will examine these ministries more fully.

- *Leitourgia*, or *worshiping*
  We get the word "liturgy" from this New Testament word, which in turn is derived from the Greek term for "work" or "service." "Liturgy" is the "work of the people" — hence, we hold "worship services." I use *leitourgia* in chapters 9 and 10 to designate a congregation's privilege and obligation to design and structure worship services responsibly. "God is spirit, and those who worship him must worship in spirit and truth," Jesus said (John 4:24). As we shall see, Christian worship seeks to address ordinary humans' quest for the transcendent in postmodern societies. Authentic worship, centered in Word, sacraments, and prayer, is vastly different from the mere entertainment sometimes found in religious circles. Finally, I shall contend that the faithful practices of *leitourgia* in congregations are expected to take place in three venues: the gathered community, families, and individuals.

The Prototype for Faithful Practices

The DNA of these five faithful practices is traceable to the New Testament book of the Acts of the Apostles. In his second chapter, after describing the Spirit-inspired transformations at a Pentecost celebration, the New Testament writer Luke lays out the foundational practices of the earliest Christian community. These practices have become paradigmatic for all other faithful Christian communities. They emerged among a heterogeneous, linguistically diverse, international group of new believers who, after the resurrection and ascension of Jesus, had assembled in Jerusalem for the Jewish harvest festival of Pentecost.

In response to being filled with the Holy Spirit and hearing the apostle Peter's proclamation of the gospel, these new converts asked the apostle what they were to *do*. And Luke recorded what happened next.

Life and Practices Among the Earliest Believers — Acts 2:37-47

[37]Now when they heard this, they were cut to the heart and said to Peter and to the other apostles, "Brothers, what should we do?" [38]Peter said to them, "Repent, and be baptized every one of you in the name of Jesus Christ so that your sins may be forgiven; and you will receive the gift of the Holy Spirit. [39]For the promise is for you, for your children, and for all who are far away, everyone whom the Lord our God calls to him."

[40]And he testified [*martyria*] with many other arguments and exhorted them, saying, "Save yourselves from this corrupt generation." [41]So those who welcomed his message were baptized, and that day about three thousand persons were added. [42]They devoted themselves to the apostles' teaching [*mathētēs*] and fellowship [*koinonia*], to the breaking of bread and the prayers [sacrament and *leitourgia*].

[43]Awe came upon everyone, because many wonders and signs were being done by the apostles [gifts of the Holy Spirit]. [44]All who believed were together and had all things in common; [45]they would sell their possessions and goods and distribute the proceeds to all, as any had need. [46]Day by day, as they spent much time together in the temple [*leitourgia*], they broke bread at home and ate their food with glad and generous hearts [*koinonia*], [47]praising God and having the goodwill of all the people [*martyria*]. And day by day the Lord added to their number those who were being saved.

On that unforgettable day of Pentecost, the baptisms of a diverse group of persons became a sign and seal of their new identity. What followed was equally defining: they were welcomed into Jesus' beloved community and ushered into a new lifestyle and mission. This pivotal passage lays out the biblical paradigm for faithful practices in any Christian congregation in any era and in any society.[4] To the

---

4. This account describes the internal community of the earliest Christians and should be supplemented with the equally descriptive and radical account in Acts 4:32-37, which reads:

Now the whole group of those who believed were of one heart and soul, and no one claimed private ownership of any possessions, but everything they owned was held in common. With great power the apostles gave their testimony to the resurrection of the Lord Jesus, and great grace was upon them all. There was not a needy person among them, for as many as owned lands or houses sold them

extent that these faithful practices are prescriptive for contemporary Christian congregations, let's conclude by briefly noting several assumptions that lie at the center of each of them:

- Each one of these faithful practices emerges as a fitting response to the gospel. At the same time, each one is critiqued by that same gospel.
- Each of these faithful practices is expected of Christians of all ages and is best nurtured within a hospitable, loving community. Example and imitation are the Christian faith's proven pedagogical methods. As lifelong efforts, these practices shape the identity and mission of a congregation and, under the Holy Spirit's empowering, are always "works in progress." Faithful practices are institutional habits in the making.
- Each of these faithful practices is related symbiotically. Each one illumines and nourishes the others. No one practice matures in isolation. Majoring in one, such as worship or fellowship, is no excuse for neglecting the others.
- Each of these practices requires that leaders become bilingual. That is, congregational leaders must interpret *both* the language of the biblical world where the gospel originated *and* the idioms of contemporary cultures. These faithful practices, whether in rural, urban or suburban environments, need "user friendly" explanations for ordinary parishioners of all ages, all educational levels, and in all stages of discipleship.
- Finally, leaders of contemporary mainline congregations may become surprised and perplexed when they recognize how countercultural these faithful practices can become.

This abbreviated discussion of how *faithful practices* are related and employed in contemporary congregational life can be further clarified, hopefully, by considering the graphic representation on page 64.

---

and brought the proceeds of what was sold. They laid it at the apostles' feet, and it was distributed to each as any had need. There was a Levite, a native of Cyprus, Joseph, to whom the apostles gave the name Barnabas (which means "son of encouragement"). He sold a field that belonged to him, then brought the money, and laid it at the apostles' feet.

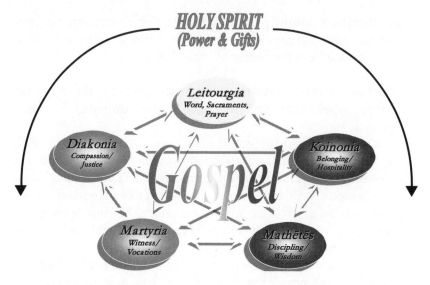

"And remember," Jesus promised, "I am with you to the end of the age."

CHAPTER 5

Practicing the Arts of Belonging
....
Koinonia

They devoted themselves to the apostles' teaching and fellowship, to the breaking of bread and the prayers.

— ACTS 2:42

When it comes to emotional energy, few words in the English language can compete with "home." Popular ballads, Broadway dramatists, and contemporary hymn writers employ the word "home" to tap the deep yearnings of ordinary humans to belong. Musician Paul Simon sings it this way:

> Homeward bound
> I wish I was
> Homeward bound
> Home, where my thoughts escaping
> Home, where my music's playing
> Home, where my love lies waiting
> Silently for me....

In the popular twentieth-century musical Les Misérables, a waiting father, Jean Valjean, comes center stage to sing a prayer for his future son-in-law, "Bring him home." One of America's most beloved gospel hymns, "Precious Lord, Take My Hand," composed by Thomas Andrew Dorsey in a shroud of grief, ends with the soul-stirring phrase, "Take my hand [and] lead me home." "The longing for home," novelist Frederick Buechner once wrote, "is so universal a form of longing that there is even a special name for it, which is of course homesickness" (Buechner 2006, 229).

When one tallies the opinions of prominent social scientists such as Robert Bellah, Wade Clark Roof, and Robert Wuthnow, the quest to belong to community may be the defining societal feature of our time. The exponential expansion of smart phones and the growing use of text messaging, blogging, Twittering, Facebook, Skype, and YouTube may, in fact, attest to that quest.

The Pew Research Center found that half of American teenagers send fifty or more text messages a day, and one-third send more than one hundred a day. Another survey found that 54 percent said they text friends at least once a day, but only 3 percent said they talk to friends face-to-face on a daily basis. Researchers are still trying to measure whether texting and instant messaging helps or diminishes the intimacy and emotional dimensions of regular, extended face-to-face engagements. Jesse Rice, in *The Church of Facebook: How the Hyperconnected Are Redefining Community* (2009), found that congregations' efforts to synchronize parishioners electronically do not necessarily generate Christian communities.

Beyond the availability of new technologies for communication in the twenty-first century lies a deeper issue: belief in the gospel of Jesus Christ and belonging to Christian community are inseparable. Dietrich Bonhoeffer, in his premier treatise on the church, *Life Together* (1939), insisted that Christians "belong to one another only through Jesus Christ.... The longing of Christians for one another is based solely on this message" (Bonhoeffer 1939, 31-32).

With that theological affirmation in mind, I want in this chapter to address the biblical concepts summarized by the Greek word *koinonia*. Afterward, I intend to outline several congregation-based ministries that seek to incorporate the contemporary practices of *koinonia*, namely hospitality, caring, and organizing.

Koinonia in Biblical Perspectives

Koinonia is one biblical word among several that characterizes post-Pentecost Christian communities. In the New Testament (NT), it is usually translated "fellowship" or "partnership" or "belonging." It derives from a root term meaning "common." In the foundational second chapter of the Acts of the Apostles, it is said that the earliest disciples "devoted themselves to the apostles' teaching and fellowship [koinonia]. . . . All who believed were together and had all things in common [koinos]." Paul writes that Corinthian converts were "called into the fellowship of [God's] Son, Jesus Christ our Lord" (1 Cor. 1:9). Supportive practices such as extending "the right hand of fellowship" and eating together are often mentioned.

In his letter to the Christians living in the metropolis of Ephesus, Paul scolded Gentile members for their exclusivist attitudes toward their Jewish fellow members. "Remember," he writes, "that you were at that time without Christ, being aliens from the commonwealth of Israel, and strangers to the covenants of promise, having no hope and without God in the world. But now in Christ Jesus you who once were far off have been brought near by the blood of Christ. For he is our peace; in his flesh he has made both groups into one and has broken down the dividing wall, that is, the hostility between us" (Eph. 2:12-14).

The distinguished biblical scholar Paul Minear of Yale University once traced the many images that describe the churches mentioned in the New Testament. He found nearly one hundred different metaphors, a gallery of pictures, that point to the assumption of belongingness. Images such as "the people of God," "members of the household of God," and the "Body of Christ" are prominent throughout the NT. "The association with the body image produced a Christological definition of the people who made [the church] more explicitly universal, more corporate, more personal, more existential, and more spiritual." A "dynamic sense of solidarity," Minear concluded, lies at the center of all practices in the community of Christ's disciples (Minear 2004, 229, 245).

From the Church's beginnings, the gospel-based sacraments of baptism and the Lord's Supper embodied affirmations about koinonia. In baptism, persons were initiated into the communal life of a congregation; celebrations of the Lord's Supper, where hospitality was assured, kept them there. In both sacraments, then and now, koinonia is made effectual and lasting only by the power and presence of the Holy Spirit. Both sacraments are open to all persons regardless of gender, race, education, aesthetic preferences, age, or social class. Both rituals usually conclude with a Trinitarian benediction: "The grace of the Lord Jesus Christ, the love of God, and the communion [koinonia] of the Holy Spirit be with all of you" (2 Cor. 13:13).

Beyond these sacraments, virtually every other major theological doctrine in the Judeo-Christian tradition presumes a fundamental human need to belong: covenant, atonement, reconciliation, and the mandate to love.

But there is more. At the deepest level, Christians affirm that the human instinct to belong derives, ultimately, from God. The Christian classical affirmation of God as Father, Son, and Holy Spirit is one attempt to address the inherent relationality of the triune God. Some have expressed this relationality as an "eternal dance" in which the divine rhythms flow with self-giving love. As one theologian put it, "The God of the Bible establishes and maintains life in communion.... God is the covenantal God. God's will for life in relationship with and among the creatures is an expression of God's faithfulness to his own eternal life, which is essentially communal" (Migliore, 79). Thus, when the Genesis narrative announces that humans were created "in the image God," another pivotal affirmation is at play: humans' communal instincts derive directly from their Creator, the ultimate source of the human capacity for all relationships.

The faithful practice of *koinonia*, however, is almost always tested when congregations engage their missional callings in their host societies. When the earliest Christians' mission required engagement with the alien values and structures of the Greco-Roman societies beyond the regions of Israel and Judah, a new hybrid of the people of God emerged. Beginning with that wide diversity of people present at Pentecost, most New Testament accounts note that the first-century Christian churches were, surprisingly, socially diverse communities.

When those early churches were at their best, their experience of the gospel prompted them to devalue deep-seated societal boundaries. When slippage did occur, as it did in the congregations of Galatia, the apostle Paul leaned hard on them: "As many of you as were baptized into Christ have clothed yourself with Christ. There is no longer Jew or Greek ... slave or free ... male and female, for all of you are one in Christ Jesus" (Gal. 3:27-28).

With these biblical and theological perspectives in mind, I want to propose three indispensable, contemporary faithful practices that embody *koinonia*. While not the only ones associated with *koinonia*, they are, biblically speaking, obligatory for every maturing Christian and for every faithful congregation:

- *Koinonia* and the practice of hospitality — From stranger to friend
- *Koinonia* and the practice of caring for others — From isolation to hope
- *Koinonia* and the practice of organization — From ambiguity to cohesion.

1. Koinonia *and Hospitality — From Stranger to Friend*

Most congregations assume they are friendly. Most have signs proclaiming that "All Are Welcome." There is a difference, however, between friendliness and hospitality. Hospitality requires the embracing of the stranger.[1] Christian hospitality refuses to allow another to continue as an alien. Hospitality is not a programmatic strategy to maneuver outsiders to become like their hosts. If there is to be any change in behavior, outlook, or appearance at all, it must always come according to the stranger's choice and timing. Hospitality requires a mature understanding of the grace of God.

Neither is hospitality a simple matter of refined manners or cultured civility. Rather, hospitality is the offer of freedom for "the others" to find their own way and to discover the presence of God in their lives while among supportive friends. In hospitality, the "other" is welcomed home. Hospitality is the antidote to the human malady of homesickness. In this sense, wrote the late Henri Nouwen in *Reaching Out*, the practice and perfection of hospitality is the "most basic movement in the spiritual life" (Nouwen, 1975).

The practice of hospitality, I believe, is within reach of most, if not all, members of a congregation. Here are some ways hospitality is enacted:

- listening,
- interpreting,
- escorting, and
- dining.

---

1. Miroslav Volf's *Exclusion & Embrace: A Theological Exploration of Identity, Otherness and Reconciliation* (1996) is a masterful treatment of contemporary tribalism. See also Tim Dolan's "So You Think You Are Friendly," *Congregations Magazine* (2011): 14-18.

Listening as Hospitality The German theologian Dietrich Bonhoeffer, while a prisoner of the Nazi regime in World War II, wrote an unforgettable comment about the art of listening:

> Christians ... forget that listening can be a greater service than speaking. Many people are looking for an ear that will listen. They do not find it among Christians, because these Christians are talking [when] they should be listening. But he who can no longer listen to his brother will soon be no longer listening to God either.... One who cannot listen long and patiently will presently be talking beside the point and be never really speaking to others, though he be not conscious of it. Anyone who thinks that his time is too valuable to keep quiet will eventually have no time for God and [or] his brother, but only for himself and for his own folly. (Bonhoeffer 2005, 97)

Congregants can learn the art of listening by cultivating phrases like, "I hear you" or "Go on, I'm listening" or "Tell me what you are going through" or "Let me repeat what I think I've been hearing" or, better, "That must have hurt a lot." The best physician I ever knew always concluded his examinations by sitting down and, looking right at me, asking, "Is there anything else you want to tell me?" He listened for anxieties half-hidden between my words. Grace-filled listening affirms another's humanity and intrinsic worth. Many will recognize hospitable listening as the essential ingredient in the practice known as "spiritual direction."

As Mary Rose O'Reilley notes, for many trained in academic and corporate cultures, much listening can descend into *critical* listening. We often pay attention only to muster a counter-argument. But the listening linked with hospitality strives for an openhearted, nonjudgmental reception of the other. When we "begin to hear not only what people are saying, but what they are trying to say, you sense the whole truth about them. And you sense [another's] existence, not piecemeal, not this object or that, but as a translucent whole" (O'Reilley, 17).

Interpreting as Hospitality Not long ago my wife and I were invited to worship in a Christian community in an economically depressed neighborhood on the outskirts of Cape Town, South Africa. A student, who was supported financially by our former congregation, had invited us to "come and see" where she served as pastor. We were ushered to chairs in the front row. The service began when women, dressed in white blouses and black skirts, danced down the aisle, singing exuberantly a hymn of praise.

When the gathering initiative finished, one elderly woman came and sat beside us. She shared her liturgy book so that both of us could follow along. But the language was Xhosa, of which we understood nothing. With her forefinger she would follow along the pastor's reading, pointing to the prayers and Scriptures. Every time she came to the name of Jesus in Xhosa, she said to us in broken English, "Jesus! Lord!" Rarely have we ever felt such acceptance in a strange place. The common faith that filled us was a greater bond than the formidable cultural and language issues that separated us. It was a living enactment of the apostle Paul's instruction to the Christians in Rome: "Contribute to the needs of the saints; extend hospitality to strangers" (Rom. 12:13).

Helping members to decipher a congregation's practices is not easy. Hospitality requires hosts to become bilingual. To bridge the gap between insiders' lingo and outsiders' blank stares, ordinary members must explain what appears enigmatic to guests. In a language and vocabulary suitable for the outsider, hospitality requires making plain why something is said or enacted. Without such interpretations, exclusion can become even more severe.

Mainline congregants now live in a society increasingly puzzled by established Christian vocabularies, symbols, and rituals. In such a context, interpreting for the outsider is more than a courtesy. It is an expression of grace and acceptance. Here are a few questions I (and other pastors) have been asked: Why do worshipers stand sometimes and sit at other times? Why is water poured on the heads of infants? Why is a bit of bread and sip of wine called a feast? What is all the talk about blood? Why do Christians sing old songs? Why are worship services structured and precisely timed like TV shows? Why do churches always ask for money? Why do clergy wear different clothes? Authentic hospitality encourages questions. Ordinary Christians ought to be able to answer them.

Welcoming as Hospitality Most mainline congregations I visit rarely recognize how difficult it is for outsiders to enter their worship places and coffee hours. Many of these congregations put the responsibility of entrance on the strangers — asking them to wear a name tag or inviting visitors to stand and introduce themselves or requesting them to sign a registration card. Yet some mainline congregations are retooling their practices of hospitality. One example will have to serve for many others. Once, while visiting a mainline congregation outside San Francisco, I observed what has now become for me a model of hospitality at worship services. Before pronouncing the benediction, the pastor issued a warm invitation for any visitor to come forward to the chancel area after the service. She remained "up front" rather than going to the main doors to greet regular worshipers.

Curious, I moved to a front pew to listen. As the inquirers assembled, she introduced herself to each person (there were seven) and engaged each one directly. Addressing the whole group, she asked if anyone had a question about what had gone on in the worship service. One asked what her clerical stole meant; another asked about the "children's sermon"; and another asked if she and the congregation "believed in the Bible." Giving each question dignity and import, she answered each person clearly and with splashes of humor.

Moving toward conclusion, she explained that the congregation's purpose was to teach the Christian faith and to equip persons to live faithful and meaningful lives "all week long." Several members waited alongside the pastor. I later learned these were deacons who had been coached on how to escort the guests to the coffee hour and introduce them to other parishioners.

In an atmosphere of gracious hospitality, the deacons solicited and noted the names, phone numbers, and addresses (including emails) of the visitors. As the guests began to leave, the deacons gave each a "Welcome Bag." It contained a few chocolate-chip cookies, an informational brochure about the church, as well as a deacon's name and phone number. Before departing, the deacons promised to contact the visitors during the coming week to invite them back.

Energizing this welcoming ministry practice are two essential Christian affirmations: hospitality flourishes when strangers are free (rather than pressured) to choose to participate or not; and, more important, hospitality is an incarnational practice — that is, the demonstration that God usually comes to people through other people of

God. We'll explore both of these affirmations more fully in a later chapter on *martyria*, or witnessing.

Dining Together as Hospitality Hospitality reaches a new level when ordinary people, like those new Christians in Acts 2, "break bread" together. Eating together incorporates multiple Christian arts and practices. At table, strangers are made welcome; common human needs as basic as hunger and thirst are satisfied; all class differences are leveled; table talk means conversation enjoyed; serving becomes a pleasure; imaginations are kindled; chores are transformed into simple acts of charity; and the goodness of God's bounty is joyfully acknowledged. In moments almost inexplicable, the demarcation line between host and guests evaporates.

In Frederick Buechner's novel *Love Feast*, Gertrude Conover hosts a "spur of the moment" Thanksgiving dinner. The guests are a strange combination of local residents, secretaries, nuns, students, and a traveling evangelist, Leo Bebb. After a generous and tasteful dinner, Bebb says, "The Kingdom of Heaven is a love feast where nobody's a stranger. Like right here.... What would happen if we'd find home is each other?"

Surveying the New Testament, one is struck by the frequency of Jesus eating with his disciples as well as with strangers. On almost every other page Jesus transgressed ancient religious taboos and social protocols by eating with others. He drank with a Samaritan woman (John 4), fed a diverse group of five thousand (Matt. 14), dined with a tax collector named Zacchaeus (Luke 19), and welcomed an ashamed Peter to breakfast (John 21).

Not to be overlooked is the imagined feast that breaks out when the prodigal son returns, even when a pouting elder brother refuses to participate in such nonsense (Luke 15). More important, since that day in the "upper room" when Jesus convened the disciples to celebrate the Passover (Luke 22), Christian disciples have celebrated one extraordinary meal as the supreme symbol of hospitality, a hospitality inclusive enough to take in Judas. As most mainline Protestant liturgies put it, Christians "from east and west and from north and south" are invited to sit at table and participate "in the joyful feast of the kingdom of God." As one biblical scholar noted, "Jesus requires his disciples to be guests in his presence so they can learn to be hosts for others" (Koenig, 118).

2. Koinonia and Caring for Others — From Isolation to Hope

Multiple studies of modern congregations highlight a well-known finding: people often exit Christian communities through the "back door" because the members of the congregation are deemed uncaring or unresponsive or even hurtful. In moments of human crises — sickness, a death in the family, unemployment, isolation that attends depression, yielding to addictions, loneliness, to name a few — the Christian community is sometimes perceived as distant and irrelevant. Yet most leaders in mainline Protestant congregations acknowledge the need for a pastoral-care system extensive enough to care for all members, not just a select few. Protestant congregations with successful strategies for caring for every parishioner usually include several models:

- a pastor-centered caring system;
- a laity-led caring program; and
- pastoral care through small groups.

Pastor-Centered Caring Using data from a nationwide survey about pastors in the United States, Jackson Carroll tallied how lay persons in congregations perceived their pastors' core responsibilities. While 66 percent thought that conducting worship was a pastor's priority, 42 percent expected their pastors to visit in homes and hospitals, and 32 percent said they would turn to their pastors in times of crisis (Carroll 2006, 119).

The survey confirmed what most mainline congregations already know: the pastor reigns as the primary agent of care in Christian communities. In contemporary Western society, she or he remains one of the few public figures who have ready access to the private crises of families and individuals. Pastors are privileged companions in the life-defining moments of birth, marriage, illness, and death.

Parishioners' sense of belonging — *koinonia* — is often mediated and nurtured by a pastor's caring and presence. Two illustrations will have to suffice.

Heidi B. Neumark, a Lutheran pastor who once served a Hispanic and African American congregation in the South Bronx section of New York City, has preserved some of her experiences in pastoral care in her inspiring book *Breathing Space* (2003). Among her many encounters with hurting parishioners, one particular visitation stands out. Pastor Neumark called on hospitalized Michelle, an African American. Here is how the pastor remembered the visit:

> Michelle's eyes were covered with gauze protection because she had lost the ability to blink. She had a feeding tube down her throat and was hooked up to a respirator. She was awake enough to feel considerable discomfort. Her hands were hot and limp, with no strength left to squeeze. I sang softly to her, her most requested hymn ... the one we'd sung together countless times, "Precious Lord, Take My Hand." ... I don't believe she cared about the color of the hand holding hers. It was the skin contact, the touch, the tenderness, a human hand that mattered most.... I also recognized, with gratitude, this hymn as one of Michelle's gifts to me.... She took my hand and began to pat it, comforting and ministering to me. (Neumark, 163)

The memoirs of faithful pastors overflow with similar stories. Once, at a small gathering of pastors, a recent retiree told us about the retirement party his congregation had thrown for him. We all knew him as a gifted preacher, and many of us cribbed from his published sermons. A long line of parishioners, he reported, waited patiently to greet him. When he went home that evening, he said to his wife, "You know, only one person said anything about my sermons. They simply thanked me for visiting them in the hospital, going to lunch during a family scandal, or conducting a funeral for a child or parent."

Yet "the cure of souls" (to use an ancient phrase) by solo pastors has a downside. As congregational membership grows, say beyond two hundred members, a solo pastor is unable to service the multiple crises that members often encounter. Some other system must be devised to alter the dependency on a solo pastor. One way to resolve this organizational dilemma is to add another professional to the pastoral staff. Another way is to call forth the gifts of the Holy Spirit already resident among the members of the congregation.

Laity-Led Caring Several well-known laity-led caring systems are current in mainline congregations. I mention only two. The "Stephen Ministry" caring program is one of the most successful and enduring.

Begun in the mid-1970s, this distinguished program is a "complete system for training and organizing lay persons to provide one-to-one care to hurting people in and around your congregation." Its basic assumption is that caring for the congregation is not the sole responsibility of the pastor.

Rather, this program assumes that every congregation includes many persons who are gifted, willing, and open to being called into a caring ministry. To date, this program has trained more than 500,000 lay persons in 10,000 congregations in 150 denominations. Its training curricula, publications, and equipping focus is without peer in American congregations.[2]

A second strategy for pastoral care calls for reconfiguring the office of deacon in mainline congregations. Shortly after I arrived as the pastor of a center-city Presbyterian congregation, I discovered that the primary responsibilities of the ordained deacons were to wash communion glasses, count the offerings, and deliver the chancel flowers to a few shut-in members. One day a deacon called my office and asked if she might go along on a hospital visit. She said the seriously ill patient was a longtime friend.

Going up the stairs to the hospital room, the deacon asked if she might pray when we got to the room. I said, "Of course." After a brief and quiet greeting, I asked the patient if it would be okay for Margaret (not her real name) to pray for her and her physicians. When the patient nodded approval, Margaret instructed me to lay my hand on the patient's foot, while she put her hand on the patient's forehead. When we joined hands, Margaret prayed, passionately, lovingly over her dear friend. In a mysterious, ineffable moment, God became fearfully present and grace abounded. When we left the room, we both were caught up in deep awe.

"Margaret," I softly said, "I don't know what to say. Is it possible that you have the Holy Spirit's gift of healing?" We paused in the stairwell.

"Yes I do," she quietly replied.

"How long have you had this gift?"

"About two or three years," she said.

"Why did you not tell me?"

Her answer took me aback. "Because you never asked me."

2. See especially the Stephen Ministry website: www.stephenministries.org.

That staircase conversation started a quiet transformation in our congregation. I learned to arrange hospital visits so Margaret and others could go with me. It seemed that when I prayed over sickly folks they stayed pretty much the same. But when Margaret prayed, they very often did better.

Soon Margaret began to recruit persons in our congregation who exhibited the Spirit's gifts for healing and caring and wisdom. We revisited the biblical narratives regarding the office of deacons (see Acts 6 and 1 Tim. 3) and decided to redesign our system of pastoral care. Our goal was to ordain deacons as the congregation's *primary* caregivers.

Eventually, all who were called by the congregation into the office of deacon were expected to undergo six months of practical training and spiritual preparation. Pastoral skills were taught and practiced; the spiritual disciplines of prayer and biblical reflection were accentuated; boundaries of confidentiality and limitations were emphasized; and the Spirit's gifts were encouraged and honored.

As differing gifts surfaced, three kinds of deacons evolved: the *crisis deacons* were mature Christians equipped to enter into all sorts of human predicaments; the *caring deacons* shepherded those with chronic and long-term disabilities; and the *administrative deacons* created a training curriculum, trained newcomers, and administered the day-to-day details of caring for an entire congregation.

The new system did not satisfy every parishioner. Compromises were inevitable, especially among the older members, and it took nearly three years to refine and implement. In the end, however, a much more effective caring system emerged and an entire congregation witnessed afresh the gifts of the Holy Spirit promised at baptisms and resident in ordinary members.

Small-Group Caring Caring ministries via small groups are now standard practice in most congregations. A recent national survey of more than 32,000 United Methodist congregations found that small group ministries were one of four key areas that fueled vitality in congregations large or small (Garcia, 15). The volume of literature and experiences about congregation-centered small groups is large, but two selections are especially instructive. One is a first-rate publication of the Evangelical Lutheran Church in America (ELCA) by David Mayer and others titled *Starting Small Groups and Keeping Them Going* (1995).

A team of ELCA authors offers several guidelines to help small groups in churches to remain faithful to the gospel and update the Christian tradition of "house churches."

First, a faithful small group requires a "vertical dimension," that is, the group gathers in the name of Jesus and centers its meeting on prayer and biblical reflection. *Second*, small groups provide ample opportunity to share the joys and failures of individual faith journeys. Caring comes easier with belonging. Without this component, groups either intellectualize about faith issues or devise tasks to perform.

Third, small groups must relate to the church. Group leaders are especially responsible to ensure that splinter groups or gripe sessions or subversive political lobbying do not emerge. Small groups are not substitutes for corporate worship with the entire congregation.

Fourth, to remain faithful to the gospel, small groups must invite and welcome the stranger. "Faithful small groups are never secret meetings of the initiated, but joyful gatherings of pilgrims inviting others to share the journey" (Mayer, 7-8).

Finally, effective lay leaders of small groups are not self-appointed volunteers. Rather, they need to be carefully selected, publicly "called" and, once appointed, trained in those relational strategies that promote openness, inclusiveness, confidentiality, and compassion.

Once, while visiting a Presbyterian congregation in Indiana, I observed an impressive model for small group ministries. Located near a major university with a wide diversity of parishioners, I attended a small group meeting of adults that convened twice a month in various parishioners' homes.

After gathering around a dining-room table, where only soft drinks were served (no food), the leader led us in a discussion of a biblical passage, a text that would usually be addressed the following Sunday by the pastor. The group then moved to the living room, where the leader asked participants to "check in." Each reported on previously mentioned issues: managing their work, navigating family issues (especially children), and rehearsing church responsibilities. Finally, the leader, reminding the group of the time constraints, asked, "What is happening in your life that you would like the people of God to pray for?"

Again, ordinary and extraordinary issues surfaced. One friend usually volunteered to pray on behalf of the petitioner not only then but throughout the coming week. The session ended with all saying the Lord's Prayer.

Afterward, traveling in the car, the pastor explained how small groups in their congregation had become the primary vehicle for pastoral care. Along the way, he outlined the key ingredients necessary for their successful small groups:

- members covenanted to attend sessions twice a month, usually for six months at a time, after which a new covenant would be offered;
- pastors selected, appointed, and then trained the groups' leaders;
- reflections on selected biblical passages were intended to enhance a maturing discipleship;
- personal stories and concerns were encouraged, but within boundaries of confidentiality;
- revisiting personal and family issues mentioned previously was encouraged at follow-up meetings; and
- visitations to hospitals or following up on family needs or scheduling luncheon conversations often occurred among participants.

In a later conversation, this pastor said the single most important ingredient of their small group ministry was the thorough training of the lay leaders who shepherded the groups. When I asked for the resource that best helped with his role of equipping others for this caring ministry, he enthusiastically endorsed Bill Donahue's *Leading Life-Changing Small Groups*, the well-known textbook used by the Willow Creek congregation near Chicago.[3]

The small group movement in Protestant congregations has not escaped the scrutiny of sociologists. In two major studies Robert Wuthnow discovered that some two-thirds of Americans participated in some kind of support group during the last half of the twentieth century. While these groups ranged from book clubs, Alcoholics Anonymous, and therapy groups, most small groups, he found, were

3. There are several excellent resources for appreciating the ministry of small groups. One is by Theresa F. Latini, *The Church and the Crisis of Ministry: A Practical Theology of Small Group Ministry* (2011). See especially her "Interview Guide" for selecting small group leaders, pp. 220-221. Another is by Thomas Kirkpatrick, *Small Groups in the Church: A Handbook for Creating Community* (2005).

located within and around congregations where Bible study, prayer, and practices of spirituality were prime agendas (Wuthnow 1994a, 1994b).

Wuthnow documented four outcomes of this small group movement in American congregations. *First*, where small group ministries thrive, the pastor was not necessarily considered the congregation's sole caregiver. In fact, small group ministries sometimes inaugurated new strategies for the pastoral care of members.

Second, Wuthnow found that participation was motivated by a quest for emotional support and for a buffer to isolation and loneliness. "Community is what people say they are seeking when they join small groups," he noted. Wuthnow maintained that the small group movement changes the Protestant understanding of belonging to a community and redefinines the American style of spiritual practices.

Third, Wuthnow found that small groups can promote a subtle "me first" religion, in which "each believer becomes capable of deciding which combination of beliefs to emphasize and does so mainly by drawing on personal experience rather than paying any special attention to the clergy or to the collective, historic wisdom of the church" (Wuthnow 1994a, 358).

Finally, Wuthnow suggested that the small group movement in recent American Protestantism is another expression of the American penchant for disestablishment when religious organizations become too structured. "Small groups," he said, "lie at the intersection of individual needs and institutional structures" (Wuthnow 1993, 1238).

3. Koinonia and Organization — From Ambiguity to Cohesion

All human communities require some kind of organizational structure and practices. Without them, "mission drift" seeps in and benign ineffectiveness reigns. Congregations are no different. At their best, a congregation's organizational structures and practices exist to serve Jesus' mandate to "go into all the world and make disciples." To facilitate that vocation, *some* organizational design is required. Conventional wisdom lists at least three essential components of that design:

- governance
- stewardship
- communication

Clearly, these components usually come under the oversight of congregational leaders and deserve some comment, however abbreviated.

Koinonia *and* Governance Most Christian congregations employ established organizational procedures and denominational directives in order to administer and fulfill their mission. One seasoned observer of congregations put it this way: "Governance is a crucial part our life together for two reasons. One reason is that life is messy …and disordered houses do not stand…. The other reason is equally vital: governance is necessary for the positive flourishing of life…. Communities, in order to be communities, must be ordered, cared for, led" (Robinson 2011, 11).

The apostle Paul, impatient with the hassles in the congregation at Corinth, admonished them to manage their ministry "decently and in order" (1 Cor. 14:40). That admonition stands as a preface to the thick organizational manuals published by mainline denominations in our own day. The Methodist *Book of Discipline*, the Lutheran *Model for Congregations*, and the Presbyterian *Book of Order* are examples of these manuals for a congregation's operations.

Prominent in these manuals are directives to guide the congregation in a multitude of organizational necessities: procedures for electing pastors and officers; directives for how finances are to be managed with transparency; and the delineations of the responsibilities of various councils and committees. Particularly explicit are the pastor's roles, responsibilities, and authority. Customarily, such manuals also clarify the procedures for a congregation's relationship with higher denominational judicatories. And for mainline congregations, they usually seek to implement the Protestant vision of combined lay and professional leadership.[4]

No governance issue is more critical in congregations than the

---

4. Penny Edgell Becker's seminal study of congregations in conflict concluded that most messy conflict is rooted in different visions of the church's identity, mission, and member commitment. Such conflicts, she found, often swirl around two questions: "Who are we?" and "How do we do things here?" (*Congregations in Conflict: Cultural Models of Local Religious Life.* Cambridge University Press, 1999, ch. 1).

leadership role of pastors. No longer can a pastor lead twenty-first-century mainline parishioners *merely* by the virtue of her or his ordination, office, and education. Little wonder that heavy reassessments are underway, especially in Protestant seminaries.

One helpful introduction to pastoral leadership can be found in a collection of essays titled *Leadership in Congregations,* edited by Richard Bass. It brings together ten years of research and reflection about pastoral leadership in American Protestant congregations and tracks how current patterns and practices are changing. One typically insightful essay, "Forming God's People," claims that leading a congregation means "giving structure to a vision." That structuring, writes Mark Branson of Fuller Theological Seminary, involves interpretation, partnerships, strategies, and framing "inviting" questions. Leaders, he insists, must learn to ask questions, not simply make pronouncements. Here is one question he deems pivotal: "What kind of people do we need to be for this vision to make sense?" (Bass 2007, 107). Branson's question is a variation of another favorite query promoted by a wise pastor of my acquaintance: "Why are we doing what we claim we are doing?"

Koinonia *and* Stewardship The topic of stewardship falls appropriately within the realm of the practices of *koinonia.* Belonging implies obligations. Christians' responses to God's grace and generosity encompass a wide swath of responsibilities, and most contemporary studies treat the topic of stewardship in an expansive and comprehensive way. For example, Douglas John Hall, in his important book *The Steward: A Biblical Symbol Come of Age* (Eerdmans, 1990), insists that Christian stewardship covers a broad range of issues such as environmental concerns, parenting, health issues (i.e. the AIDS epidemic, health care, and famines), political agendas, and economic priorities.

Leaders in one Presbyterian congregation in Maryland appealed to its members with this comprehensive view of stewardship:

> Stewardship is the grateful response to God's grace and goodness. It requires consideration of how our choices affect others, of how we can be good caretakers of the created world, and of how we can best serve God as disciples of Christ. Presbyterians believe stewardship is caring for all of God's creation every day.... It means care for our minds and bodies in healthful ways.... It means using our

time and talents for God's purposes. Good stewardship of God's world requires us to take an active role in ... the political process. ... Stewardship is what we do every day of our lives.[5]

For this book's purposes, however, I want to confine the discussion about stewardship to one particular dimension of Christian stewardship, namely, the arena of the management of personal and corporate finances in mainline congregations.

In any era, belonging to the "household of God" requires members to contribute financially in order to fulfill their congregation's ministry and missional responsibilities. The early Christian community noted in Acts 2 linked fellowship (*koinonia*) with the distribution of financial resources so that the physical needs of all were met. Acts 4 records that believers sold properties and possessions and laid the proceeds "at the apostles' feet" for later distribution. Apparently, leaders in the earliest Christian communities were called not only as "stewards of the mysteries of God" (I Cor. 4:I), but as managers of community financial resources.

In contemporary American society, where consumerism reigns, managing a congregation's financial resources is a complex task for at least three reasons. First, most Americans participate in a society that imposes stiff norms regarding the public exposure of personal expenditures. From childhood, Americans, especially middle-class ones, are taught never to disclose salaries or prices paid for automobiles or homes, or how much individuals are invested or in debt. Such "privatization of money," observes sociologist Robert Wuthnow, leads most Americans to act "radically alone" when distributing their personal financial resources. Wuthnow found that 92 percent of persons surveyed never or hardly ever talk about charitable giving outside their family circles; and, surprisingly, they were least likely to talk about personal finances and giving with their fellow church or synagogue members (Wuthnow 1994c, 139). Most American church and synagogue members, Wuthnow found, are silent about their financial contributions, and they expect those contributions to remain private.[6]

---

5. This call to stewardship was circulated at Saint Mark Presbyterian Church in North Bethesda, MD.

6. See especially chapter 6 in Robert Wuthnow, *Poor Richard's Principle: Recovering the American Dream Through the Moral Dimension of Work, Business, and Money* (1996).

Second, American congregations are undoubtedly distressed when curtailment of church contributions occurs. Two prominent sociologists, Christian Smith and Michael Emerson, headed up a team of researchers in 2007 to try to explain why American Christians are often ungenerous. They found that 20 percent of American Christians give nothing to churches, and the remaining 80 percent typically contribute 1.5 to 2 percent of their incomes after taxes.

In their book *Passing the Plate: Why Christians Don't Give Away More Money*, the authors offer nine hypotheses for what they call a riddle: "Why is it that American Christians give away so relatively little of their money?" Among the nine possible explanations for such reluctance are (1) lack of awareness or teaching about tithing; (2) their presumed lack of sufficient resources; (3) the practice of unplanned and inconsistent ways of giving; and, surprisingly, (4) the reluctance of pastors to wrestle with the theological and moral teachings regarding financial decisions and obligations in sermons. The "bottom line," these researchers conclude, is that stewardship challenges in mainline congregations appear to be entering a new era of societal inhibitors and financial complexities (Smith and Emerson, 2008, ch. 3).

Third, the inescapable annual responsibility of raising funds for a congregation's ministries and mission rests on the shoulders of congregational leaders. Since the last third of the twentieth century, however, this responsibility has become more taxing.

Based on research involving five hundred congregations, two well-known analysts of the giving patterns in American congregations point to a sobering future. "If the patterns of the past quarter-century continue uninterrupted, by the middle of the next [twenty-first] century many of the church structures we are familiar with will no longer be receiving significant financial support from church members." These same analysts noted the tendency across theological orientations "for congregations to focus upon themselves--their own life and activities — while showing less commitment to the larger mission of the church" (Ronsvalle, 1010, 1012). The same financial downsizing is felt in denominational headquarters of mainline Protestants. The presiding bishop of the Evangelical Lutheran Church in America reported, "In 2008, after adjusting for inflation, the value of mission support had declined by a half since the founding of this church in 1988" (quoted in *The Christian Century*, Nov. 2, 2010, p. 16).

So where might church leaders turn for insights and resources to help manage these stewardship challenges? Our *first* move requires consulting the Scriptures.[7]

According to the Hebrew heritage, the giving of one's resources was an imitation of the gracious giving acts of God. Giving at least the tithe (10 percent) was a tangible expression of one's commitment to God and a reflection of the justice and mercy that God intends for all of creation. Jesus affirmed that ancient tradition but carried the responsibilities of stewardship further.

Addressing his disciples as well as a large crowd Jesus said, "Take care! Be on your guard against all kinds of greed; for one's life does not consist in the abundance of possessions" (Luke 12:15). By the end of his discourse about the stewardship of material possessions, he warned, "From everyone to whom much has been given, much will be required; and from the one to whom much has been entrusted, even more will be demanded" (Luke 12:48).

New Testament scholar Richard Hays traces the continuity between Jesus' stewardship expectations and the apostle Paul's exhortations to those Christian communities he helped establish. To the Corinthians, Paul insists there should be a "fair balance" between those who have abundance and those who are in need (2 Cor. 8:13-15). Such a practice of sharing is the minimal expression of conforming to Christ's example of self-emptying, which ought to lead the Philippian community to "look not to [their] own interests, but to the interests of others" (Phil. 2:4).

A *second* resource leaders can turn to for help with stewardship challenges is their own denominational headquarters. During the first decade of the twenty-first century every mainline denomination accelerated its efforts to provide consultants, promotional publications, strategies for "campaign management," and websites to shore up congregational leaders. At the same time, a small industry of private entrepreneurs has emerged to offer plans, procedures, and promises to help address dwindling financial resources in current mainline congregations.[8]

7. An excellent and brief survey of the biblical exhortations for Christian disciples to share their financial possessions can be found in Richard Hays's *The Moral Vision of the New Testament*, (1996, 464-68).

8. One seasoned and proven program has been developed by Herb Miller. He approaches financing congregational ministries by teaching stewardship on a biblical

Third, there is a growing consensus around several "best practices" that inspire greater generosity and responsibility among members of a congregation.[9] I mention only a few that many leaders have found effective:

- Contributions, biblically speaking, are measured by proportions not amounts. The biblical mandate for tithing or percentage giving is both fairer and clarifying. Jesus honored a widow's meager two copper coins above the large sums contributed by wealthier persons (Mark 12:41-43).
- Wise advice is available from Indiana University's notable Center on Philanthropy.[10] The center finds that people do not, generally, give to causes. Rather *people give to people with great causes.* That is, a trusted person's advocacy for a great cause is more persuasive than merely published information about a worthy cause. In this light, leaders, as well as other respected members, need public opportunities to share how their own faith and stewardship practices relate. Personal testimonies are necessary complements to the best stewardship sermons by a pastor.
- Transparency and openness about a congregation's finances are required for leaders. Secrecy breeds discontent and distrust. Parishioners may differ over financial priorities, but all have a right to know about all financial commitments and transactions to which they have contributed.
- *Finally,* stewardship of our financial resources requires continual monitoring and prayer. Here is how the devout and late Scottish theologian John Baillie once addressed God in a morning prayer:

Give me open hands, O God, hands ready to share with all who are in want the blessings which Thou hast enriched my life. Deliver

---

basis rather than from a fund-raising perspective. Miller's ministry has proven itself in small-town churches as well as large congregations in urban areas. Begin with his book *New Consecration Sunday Stewardship* (2007), then check out his publication *Nuggets*.

9. There is abundant literature about financial management in congregations. One good place to start is Michael Duvall's *Creating Congregations of Generous People* (1999). See also www.GenerousGiving.org.

10. For access to the findings of Indiana University's Center on Philanthropy, see especially their website at www.philanthropy.iupui.edu/lake-institute-on-faith-and -giving.

me from all meanness and miserliness. Let me hold my money in stewardship and all my worldly goods in trust for Thee; to whom now be all honour and glory. (Baillie, 63)

Koinonia *and Communications* While it is evident that all communities must communicate with their members clearly and effectively, twenty-first-century technology has revolutionized the way congregations tell their stories.

While face-to-face contact remains the preferred method of witness, and while weekly bulletins and the venerable monthly church newsletter in "hard copy" continue to disseminate important information, newer electronic methods of communication have become a necessity for congregations who want to stay in touch with members. One large survey found that four out of five American congregations now have an "established presence" on the Internet. Social media is now deeply embedded in the everyday lives of most Americans.[11] Websites, blogs, Twitter, Skype, Facebook, YouTube, and other tools of the Web 2.0 generation are becoming the preferred means of networking.[12]

Podcasted sermons, online classes with PowerPoint presentations, and nationwide webinars are now available "24/7." Technological innovations have already transformed the way congregations educate their members.

Email, already considered antiquated by some, remains indispensable in most congregations. Recently, while visiting a congregation in Norfolk, Virginia, I watched a pastor, who had recently returned from a hospital visit, enter a few strokes on her computer and instantly send emails to two-thirds of the congregation. She urged

11. According to one researcher, the first text message was sent twenty years ago. It read "Merry Christmas." In 2011 more than 8 trillion texts were sent worldwide, or about 15 million a minute. According to the Pew Research Center, 68 percent of American adults use Facebook, and 16 percent use Twitter. Among people ages 18-29, 82 percent use Facebook and/or Twitter compared to 67 percent of those ages 50 to 64.

12. Not every pastor is completely seduced. One Lutheran pastor wrote in *Word and World* (Summer 2010) that she decided not to sign up for Facebook, though she acknowledged its potential usefulness in ministry. She felt that Facebook offers a mediated form of relationship, which can keep us from being really present with one another. "There are some places you need to bring your body. Places like births and baptisms … worship and weddings, deathbeds and funerals…. Any time a casserole is needed, it is a safe bet that a message on Facebook won't do the trick."

them to pray for the stricken parishioner and promised to update the congregation as the member recovered. When I asked her if this electronic connection worked for an older generation in the congregation, she replied, "Not yet, but we are gaining on it."

More recently, a national network called "Care Pages" created a "keep in touch" ministry with hospitalized parishioners. Personal messages and prayers can be forwarded to patients, who may then reply if they are able. Of course, patients and families must authorize the use of this blog-like program (see www.carepages.com).

In her helpful book *Reaching Out in a Networked World*, Lynne M. Baab outlines multiple ways congregations can employ new media technologies in a society where the communal life of villages, defined neighborhoods, and rural distances no longer prevails. "In order to help congregation members grow in their participation in the life of faith, the congregation's leaders need to persist in using every possible means of communication about the things that really matter to the congregation," she writes. Churches' biggest challenge in this area of communication, however, is to project a "coherent expression of what they value and who they are" (Baab, 164).

Effective websites, Baab maintains, reflect the values and identity of congregations. Unfortunately, she finds that most congregations emphasize buildings and facilities, leaders' personalities and responsibilities, or bland institutional histories instead. These staple items, she contends, need to be supplemented (or replaced!) with positive links to other local organizations and ministries, with creative use of the arts, and with invitations to ask questions and explore spiritual options. Unless a highlighted "mission statement" is accompanied by stories of parishioners engaged in that mission, the mission statement remains, she says, fictional.

Beyond the opportunities to employ websites to witness to a congregation's ministries looms the challenge of a networked society and networked religion. A leading scholar, Heidi Campbell of Texas A & M University, maintains that in a society that is increasingly individualized and decentralized there are growing numbers of persons who are less tied to traditional religious communities and belief patterns. If the societal trend in North American is "belief but not belonging," then the Internet's "networked religion" can be viewed as a challenge or opportunity. "The features of religion online closely mirror changes with the practice of religion in contemporary society" (Campbell 2012, 65). Campbell suggests congregational leaders will ned to understand how many contemporary persons, especially young people, live in two spiritual spaces: church on Sunday and their Internet communities on Monday.[13] In a groundbreaking study of congregations published in 1987, James Hopewell argued convincingly that a congregation's identity and mission is conveyed through the stories members tell about themselves and their congregations. Such narratives signal what a congregation *really* believes and practices.

A typical American congregation, Hopewell found, is a collage of stories. In both private and public arenas, a congregation *is* what it communicates via these narratives. With Hopewell's insight acknowledged, no synthetic medium of communication, hard copy or electronic, is a fit substitute for the personal telling of one's faith story to another. In both private and public arenas a congregation *becomes* what it communicates. How it communicates is as critically important a responsibility of a congregation's leadership.

Summing Up the Practices of Koinonia

Few descriptions of the biblical practice of *koinonia* are the peer of the sermon of John Winthrop aboard the flagship *Arabella* in 1630. While still at sea and bound for a new home in a New World, Winthrop the "govenour" addressed those doughty Puritans who were about to found the Massachusetts Bay Colony. Winthrop wanted to prepare his followers for their daunting mission that lay ahead in a land soon to be named "New England." Though a lay leader, Winthrop focused his vision on an Old Testament text from Micah 6. Many of us still find his often-quoted sermon a stirring definition of *koinonia*:

> Now the only way to avoid shipwreck and to provide for our posterity is to follow the counsel of Micah to do justly, love mercy and walk humbly with our God. For this end, we must be knit together

13. For an overview of emerging networked religion, see Lorne L. Dawson and Douglas E. Cowan, eds., *Religion Online: Finding Faith on the Internet* (2004). Heidi Campbell's research is expanding. Begin with her *Exploring Religious Community Online: We Are One in the Network* (2005). To appreciate the extent of "religion surfers" via the Internet, see the Pew Internet and American Life Project at www.pewinternet.org.

in this work as one man; we must entertain each other in brotherly affection; we must be willing to abridge ourselves of our superfluities, for the supply of others' necessities; we must uphold a familiar commerce together in all meekness, gentleness, patience and liberality; we must delight in each other, make others' conditions our own, rejoice together, mourn together, labour [and] suffer together, always having before our eyes our commission and ... our community as members of the same body. So shall we keep the unity of the Spirit in the bond of peace, [for] the Lord will be our God and delight to dwell among as, as his own people.... For we must consider that we shall be as a City upon a hill, the eyes of all people are upon us.... We shall be made a story and a by-word through the world. (Hollinger, 13-16)

CHAPTER 6

Practicing the Arts of Discipleship
....
Mathētēs

They devoted themselves to the apostles' teaching.

— ACTS 2:42

In the Greek language of the original New Testament (NT), the word *mathētēs* means "disciple." We derive the name "Matthew" from it. It carries the overtones of an apprentice, or one who learns from a mentor and one who does what one is taught. A disciple in the New Testament is one whom Jesus summoned, whereas an apostle is a disciple who is sent out on a mission. In this chapter, I employ the words "disciple," "discipling," and "discipleship" interchangeably.

Not long ago, a friend inherited the pastoral leadership of a mainline congregation in eastern Pennsylvania. The senior pastor had been called to another congregation, and my friend, the associate pastor, was left "holding the bag."

While awaiting the arrival of the new senior pastor, my friend gathered a select group of leaders for a close reading of the New Testament book of Acts. By the conclusion of their four-month time of discernment, they had decided to address three questions to every committee, program, and leader:

- What kind of disciples are you deploying into the world?
- What kind of community is necessary to deploy those disciples into the world?
- What kind of leaders are necessary to guide those communities to deploy disciples into the world?

Members of that Pennsylvania congregation redefined their identities, priorities, and mission by addressing those three candid questions. Membership responsibilities, it was implied, were to be subordinated to disciple formation.

These congregants soon discovered that disciple making requires supportive communities with trained leaders. Finally, they decided to be intentional about preparing Christians to live faithfully in families and societal structures outside their congregational gatherings. At last check, the three questions above continued to guide this thriving congregation.

Most leaders in Protestant congregations acknowledge that the gospel is "good news" for all persons. The young and untutored, as well as the mature and informed, are the beneficiaries of God's gracious promises and Word. If it were not so, the Christian faith would be unbearably elitist.

At the same time, the gospel produces an appetite to grow in faith and love. If this were not so, Christianity would become too superficial for tough ethical choices and too irrelevant for discerning God's call to missional responsibilities in changing societies.

Jesus left his followers with an unambiguous mandate: "Go … and make disciples of all nations" (Matt. 28:19). The operative words are "make disciples." More than two decades ago (1988), the Lutheran World Federation affirmed that directive: "The primary objective of the participation of the church in the mission of God is, as expressed by Christ in his missionary mandate, to make disciples." The United Methodist Church endorses the same objective: "Our mission is to make disciples of Jesus Christ for the transformation of the world."

"Making disciples" in mainline congregations is not without challenges. To begin with, the word "disciple" may be an unwelcomed term in this postmodern society. In many circles, to be called a "disciple" is not a compliment. It can carry overtones of persons blindly following some guru who demands "dumbed-down" followers who submit with unquestioning loyalty.

Moreover, the American mental model of individualism and "doing things my way" can grate against the expectations of Christian discipleship. Jesus' call to "come and follow me" and his invitation to "take up your cross and follow me" feel out of sync with modern modes of autonomy.

With these uncongenial possibilities admitted, most congregational leaders recognize their call to educate the young and to advocate a biblically based faith for all believers. To help leaders manage their congregations' discipling ministries, this chapter will

- *address* broad themes in the NT's teachings about Christian discipleship;
- *outline* three indispensable practices inherent in Jesus' call to discipleship; and
- *offer strategies* that can help contemporary congregations reframe the mandate that Jesus gave to his followers to "go and make disciples."

The New Testament's Focus on Discipleship

Throughout the pages of the four Gospels, the word "disciple" is the term of preference for Jesus' followers.[1] This word occurs 269 times in the New Testament. For many, the word "apprentice" is a useful synonym. According to the apprentice mode, the teacher is not only the interpreter of texts but a model for practices to be learned. Disciples are expected not only to master texts but to engage them. Thus, apprentices learn by observation, imitation, reflection, and repeated practicing of ideal ways.

Jesus' disciples were not self-appointed students enrolled in some rabbi's colloquium. Rather, Jesus himself summoned them to "come and follow" and afterward ushered them into a disciplined, covenanted, and wiser way of life.

Even more notable, Jesus called very ordinary persons. His first disciples were, at first blush, without compelling credentials or societal promise. Yet, as an outgrowth of their personal commitment to him and their partnering in his mission, Jesus encouraged his disciples to *revisit* the heritage and faith traditions of the people of God; *develop disciplines*, such as private prayer, corporate worship, and

---

1. Accessible studies of the biblical dimensions of discipleship are plentiful. See shorter treatments by New Testament scholars, especially James D. G. Dunn's *Jesus' Call to Discipleship* (1992), N. T. Wright's *Following Jesus: Biblical Reflections on Discipleship* (1994), and Charles Melchert's *Wise Teaching* (1998).

serving others; *practice* the lifestyle prescribed in the "wise sayings" in the Old Testament Law and the Sermon on the Mount; *perfect* their skills for befriending strangers and loving the unlovely; and *advocate* for more just treatments of powerless. He never implied that such expectations were easily or instantly fulfilled.

These expectations carry at least three important assumptions. *First*, discipling is not the equivalent of merely installing information in the heads of members. Rather, discipleship is a lifelong process of faith formation. Discipling is not simply mastering scriptural texts or deciphering creeds, worthy as those pursuits are. Rather, Christian discipleship shapes a person's identity, an identity fashioned, ultimately, not by what one knows but by whom one loves.[2]

A *second* assumption follows. All discipleship is measured against "the measure of the full stature of Christ" (Eph. 4:13). As Jesus once reminded his followers, "The disciple is not above the teacher, but everyone who is fully taught will be like the teacher'" (Luke 6:40). *Third*, all practices of discipleship are discerned and empowered by the Holy Spirit, the one, Jesus promised, who will "guide you into all truth" (John 13:13).

Mathētēs Practices in Contemporary Mainline Congregations

As early as the 1970s, leaders in several mainline denominations in North America sensed something was amiss. While living through the social upheavals of the Vietnam War, the Civil Rights and feminist movements, ecological alarms, a globalized economy, and the emergence of America's pluralistic religious options, concerned denominational leaders watched as mainline congregations suffered ecclesial vertigo. Denominational loyalties frayed, memberships declined, youth sought allegiances elsewhere, and financial contributions steadily dwindled.

At the same time, some mainline church members headed for the more structured worldviews of fundamentalism, while others floated into a secular drift or meandered through the territories of

2. For a lively discussion of discipleship as formation, see James K. A. Smith, *Desiring the Kingdom: Worship, Worldview, and Cultural Formation* (2009).

"other gods." As one might expect, these sobering trends have received extensive analyses.[3]

Seeking to understand this crisis of confidence, an ecumenical group of scholars launched a massive study in the late-1980s to look into the content and quality of faith circulating in mainline Protestant congregations. The faith journeys of some 11,000 individuals in 561 randomly chosen congregations were systematically surveyed. The sobering results were published in 1990 in a thick book titled *Effective Christian Education: A National Study of Protestant Congregations.*[4]

This monumental study sounded an end-of-century wake-up call for mainstream Protestants. It found that the average Protestant congregation harbored large numbers of persons who failed to internalize and manifest a life-shaping Christian faith. Here are a few of the study's conclusions: a majority of church members rarely read the Bible or prayed regularly; two-thirds never encouraged others to believe in Jesus Christ; more than half of the adults said they rarely encountered and helped the poor or hungry; more than two-thirds believed that obeying rules and following the commandments were sufficient for their salvation; more than half reported they never gave time to help children or youth to grow in the Christian faith; and a staggering 80 percent of high school youth indicated that they felt "at risk" when surrounded by such destructive behaviors as alcohol use, binge drinking, drug use, aggression, suicidal thinking, and sexual intercourse. Not surprisingly, the single most important influence in nurturing faith in a younger generation was found to be families' faith practices. Surprisingly, and in stark contrast, the impact of congregational programs on children and youth was discovered to be minimal and often ineffective.

When scholars subsequently inquired about the reasons for such sobering outcomes, at least two explanations emerged. One was the dominance of "membership cultures" in mainline congregations, and the second was the growing phenomenon of biblical illiteracy. We need briefly to consider each of these explanations.

3. See Robert Wuthnow, *Christianity in the Twenty-first Century: Reflections on the Challenges Ahead* (1993). For recent trends, see David Roozen, "A Decade of Change in Congregations, 2000-2010," which is available online via the Hartford Institute for Religion Research: www.hartfordinstitute.org.

4. This massive work has been summarized in David S. Schuller, ed., *Rethinking Christian Education* (1993).

Membership Cultures in Congregations Remembering this and other end-of-the-century research, religious analysts during the first decade of the twenty-first century detected a drift in many Protestant mainline congregations. Membership chores and a "culture of membership" were displacing, or becoming a substitute for, the teaching the practices of Christian discipleship.

A survey of several studies published in *The Christian Century* in 2007 found that merely fulfilling membership duties in mainline churches rarely produced a maturing discipleship (Robinson 2007, 23-25). Recently, while speaking at a weekend consultation in a mainline congregation in New England, I listened to a gifted but puzzled pastor confess, "Most of what I do in worship, in sermons and teaching, is *ancillary* [his word!] to why people attend here. They come mostly to check up on their friends and provide us with a few financial resources to keep their children off drugs and out of each other's beds." It was more a lament than a description.

Growing Biblical Illiteracy As early as 1970, Christian educators such as James D. Smart drew attention to the implications of the steady decline of biblical literacy among American Protestants. In *The Strange Silence of the Bible in the Church*, he pointed to unnerving trends. "A church" wrote Smart, "that no longer hears the essential message of the Scriptures soon ceases to understand what it is for and is open to being captured by the dominant religious philosophy of the moment, which is usually some blend of cultural nationalism with Christianity. All distinctions become blurred when the voices of the original prophets and apostles are stilled" (Smart, 10).

More recent researchers confirm Smart's earlier disquiet. Findings by the Gallup Organization, George Barna Research Group, and the Bible Literacy Project, in Front Royal, Virginia, provide data about biblical illiteracy growing at an exponential rate. As noted in chapter 3, Stephen Prothero of Boston University has found that most Americans cannot name the first book of the Bible, and only half of American adults can name even one of the four Gospels. Another pollster claims that nearly two-thirds of Americans under the age of thirty do not know who came first, Moses or Jesus.

Bibilcal illiteracy is not confined to Americans in general. One major mainline denomination, the Evangelical Lutheran Church in America (ELCA), regularly surveys its members through its Congregation Life Surveys. In 2001, researchers were surprised to discover that more than half of their members never attended a Bible study. Nearly half reported that they read Scripture only several times (or never) in the previous year.[5]

In another denominational survey taken in 2006, researchers found that only 18 percent of Presbyterian Church (USA) members read the Bible "almost weekly."

Evangelical Christians do not necessarily score better than mainliners. Gary Burge, a professor at the evangelically inclined Wheaton College, monitors the biblical knowledge of incoming students. He was surprised to find that one-third of the entering students could not sequence properly the following: Abraham, the Old Testament prophets, the death of Christ, and Pentecost. Only 20 percent knew to look in the book of Acts to read the stories of Paul's travels (Burge, 45-49).[6]

Biblical illiteracy matters immensely for mainline congregations. "Biblical words are, in fact, the common language we speak as Christians, part of the tool kit with which we build ourselves and our communities of faith," observes the sociologist Nancy Ammerman. Among the people of God of every age, the Scriptures have served as the normative guide for discipleship and worship. As the psalmist proclaimed for all of God's chosen people, "Your [God's] word is a lamp to my feet and a light to my path" (Ps. 119:105).

In the face of such sobering appraisals regarding membership cultures and biblical illiteracy, Jesus' call to discipleship now emerges as an assignment of the highest priority for congregational leaders. To fulfill that assignment, congregation-based ministries in disciples' faith formation — Christian education — will require substantial reframing.

Three Essential Practices of Discipleship

Analysts of modern organizations maintain that the redevelopment of an organization begins by *reframing the discourse* used in that or-

5. As a corrective to this trend, the ELCA has recently launched the "Book of Faith" initiative, which envisions a grass-roots approach to encourage church members to "open Scripture and join the conversation."

6. For a survey of the literature about biblical literacy, see Kristin Swonson, "Biblically Challenged: Overcoming Scriptural Illiteracy," *The Christian Century*, Nov. 3, 2009.

ganization. Richard R. Osmer is among the growing cadre of contemporary scholars seeking to reframe the initiatives for Christian discipleship in congregations for the twenty-first century. Osmer is an internationally prominent practical theologian and educator at Princeton Theological Seminary. His thick and tautly drawn book *The Teaching Ministry of Congregations* is not an easy climb, but the view from the top is worth the effort.

Osmer synthesizes current biblical studies, Protestant theological insights, current sociological research, and relevant educational theories. He begins this much-consulted textbook by unpacking the apostle Paul's strategies for nurturing faithful discipleship in those first-century congregations mentioned in the NT. Afterward, he analyzes data he collected in three congregations: one in the United States, one in South Africa, and one in South Korea. With biblical precedents and on-site data in full display, Osmer proposes a fresh "frame of reference" to encircle the discipling ministries in contemporary congregations by drawing on the traditional metaphors of "pilgrim" and "pilgrimage."

Disciples, Osmer contends, might be better understood as "pilgrims." Expanding this metaphor, he notes that pilgrims follow faithful pilgrimages over proven paths and journey toward desired destinations. Further, because most pilgrimages are beset with hazards and detours, pilgrim-disciples need to belong to communities for instruction and support.

Borrowing language from contemporary theologians, Osmer further expands the pilgrim metaphor: Christian disciples are pilgrims, he proposes, who participate in the divine-human "Theo-drama." By that he means that Christian discipleship is analogous to playing "our part" in the divine drama already underway in the theaters of creation, redemption, and the "new creation of God's reign."

Unlike the remote, apathetic god of deists, the triune God, witnessed to in the Scriptures, *continuously* loves, renews, and faithfully leads "disciples as pilgrims" into a worldwide stage.

Within this pilgrimage/Theo-drama frame of reference, Osmer prescribes three interwoven, distinctive practices: catechesis, exhortation, and discernment. These practices can serve as useful guides for any church leader who steps forward to reimagine and reframe a congregation's faith-forming ministries. While substituting other terms for his trio, I will employ Osmer's seminal research in an effort to provide a "frame of reference" for re-envisioning mainline Protestant educational ministries.

I. *Disciple As Learner* —
Disciples Are Called to Be Lifelong Students and Interpreters

At least two assignments for twenty-first-century mainline congregations are now urgent if discipleship is to flourish. The *first* is a sustained, high-quality educational effort to study and understand the variety of texts in the Bible as the written Word of God. To facilitate that learning, every mainline denomination currently produces excellent Bible study curricula for congregational implementation. Here are just four: The United Methodist Church's *Disciple Bible Study*; the Evangelical Lutheran Church in America's *The Bible, The Book of Faith*; the Presbyterian Church (USA)'s *Feasting on the Word* curriculum; and the Christian Reformed Church in North America's WE: *The Epic Story.*

Each of these studies is carefully crafted, but each requires more than casual study effort. For example, in the superb Methodist program *Disciple*, participants are expected to commit to meeting weekly for thirty-four weeks in classes lasting for two hours. Each member is also expected to set aside forty-five minutes each weekday for class preparation.

The Kerygma Program (established in 1977) and the Bethel Series (taught in more than six thousand congregations) rank among the most prominent and successful trans-denominational curricula.[7] Most, if not all, of these curricula integrate biblical reflection, the practices of discipleship, and missional service in contemporary societies. All of the above curricula have websites that explain their teaching strategies and describe a variety of age-appropriate materials. The assumption motivating such curricula is clear: without familiarity with the Bible's content, the gospel becomes increasingly incomprehensible and easily distorted.

7. The stated goal of Kerygma is to "learn the basics and complexities of the Bible; develop skills for interpreting Scripture; and apply the Bible to personal and corporate life in today's world" (see www.kerygma.com). The Bethel Series' mission is similar: "to lead members of a local church into a disciplined study of Scripture in such a way that they encounter the living Christ" (see www.bethelseries.com).

The *second* assignment for disciples, that of *interpreting* Scripture, is a lifelong and sometimes daunting enterprise. Scholars use the term "exegesis" when they systematically try to draw out the meaning and contexts of biblical texts. Disciples, not just pastors, seeking the meaning and implications of biblical texts can be helped greatly by consulting some of these scholars who write for non-specialist readers. Listed below are a few bibliographic recommendations that can help leaders address the growing biblical illiteracy in Protestant congregations. They are easily ordered online and are worthy additions to the library of any disciple or congregation. Each will require, however, more than casual reading:

- For general, accessible introductions to the Bible see Gordon Fee and Douglas Stuart, *How to Read the Bible for All Its Worth* (2003); or J. W. Rogerson, *An Introduction to the Bible* (1999).
- G. B. Caird's *Language and Imagery of the Bible* (1988) is a classic treatment of the ways figurative language (parable, poetry, metaphor) is used in the Bible. It is a slower, but rewarding, read.
- For a single-volume commentary on every book of the Bible, see the massive *Eerdmans Commentary on the Bible*, ed. by J. D. Dunn (2003). For general information, maps, and cultural contexts of the Bible, see *Baker Illustrated Bible Handbook* (2011), edited by J. Daniel Hays and J. Scott Duvall.
- Because the Psalms are so foundational in the life of a disciple's faith, two commentaries are especially instructive. One is *Reflections on the Psalms* by C. S. Lewis (1958); the other is *The Case for the Psalms: Why They Are Essential* by N. T. Wright (2013).
- The New Testament book of Acts traces the witness and stresses of the earliest Christian communities. Contemporary disciples will be invigorated by reading the commentary *Acts* (2010) by William H. Willimon, United Methodist scholar and bishop.

2. *Disciple as Follower* —
   Disciples Are Called to Lifelong Faith Formation

In Christian disciples' lifelong pilgrimages initiated and sustained by the gospel, the way and ways of Jesus Christ remain the model of a life pleasing to God. One method to describe such pilgrimages is to track the multiple meanings and implications of the verb "to follow" in the NT. To a wide variety of persons, Jesus' consistent pattern was to say, "Come and follow me." Such an invitation involved a commitment to Jesus himself.

Discipleship begins and ends in devotion. Following such a Master was no laid-back pilgrimage. Once an upright young man chafed at Jesus' moral challenge to "sell his possessions and give the money to the poor...then come and follow me" (Matt. 19:21). Other disciples wrestled with Jesus' expectations for extravagant loving. "If you love those who love you," he said to his disciples, "what credit is that to you?" (Luke 6:32).

Not infrequently, Jesus cautioned his would-be followers to count the costs of discipleship. For some, following Jesus meant a change of vocation. Jesus' directive to Peter to "feed my sheep" required a lifelong fisherman to begin a new calling of shepherding others (John 21:15-22).

Finally, when the disciples rejoiced to see the resurrected Jesus one evening in a Jerusalem house, they were confronted with the *ultimate goal and model* of their coming pilgrimage: "As the Father has sent me, so send I you" (John 20:21). In this one summation, Jesus, the risen Savior, becomes both model and Lord. His continued presence was assured when he "breathed on them and said to them, 'Receive the Holy Spirit.'"[8]

I do not, of course, believe that any particular congregation can ultimately determine a person's faith and faith journey. As Marjorie J. Thompson put it, "Only God, whose Spirit is free to create and recreate, has ultimate power to shape us" (Thompson 1996, 12). With that provision gladly acknowledged, *following* Jesus' "way, truth and life" in the twenty-first century usually involves two ongoing commitments. One is the shaping of *moral practices*. The other is the development of *life-affirming relationships*. Each of these deserve attention, however abbreviated.

Shaping Moral Practices How Jesus interpreted and summarized the Old Testament Law and Ten Commandments to his followers is a

---

8. Methodist Leonard Sweet, a professor of evangelism at Drew University, has written a twenty-first-century update about following Jesus. See I Am a Follower: The Way, Truth, and Life of Following Jesus (2012). It is colorful, thoughtful, and timely.

topic of much comment by biblical scholars. Two conclusions, however, surface as undeniably clear. First, in the Sermon on the Mount, Jesus declared that he came "not to abolish" the Old Testmanet law "but to fulfill it" (Matt 5:17). And second, Jesus insisted that all of the law and the prophets flow from the greatest commandment: to love God and one's neighbor (Matt. 22:37). These affirmations, like compasses, help keep every disciple's pilgrimage headed in a faithful direction.

With these affirmations in mind, congregations are called, under the Spirit's empowerment, to advocate particular moral practices among disciples of all ages. Here are a few that Osmer emphasizes:

- *compassion*, the capacity to express sympathy, encouragement, and solidarity;
- *fairness*, the practice of ensuring that all persons and points of view are treated equally and openly;
- *fidelity*, the responsibility to honor commitments and promises;
- *reconciliation*, the courage to engage in conflict resolution while refusing to engage in violence of any sort, physical or verbal; and
- *forgiveness*, the willingness to risk starting afresh and mending relationships (Osmer, 265-280).

Shaping Life-Affirming Relationships While Richard Osmer and others have pointed to multiple arenas in churches where followers of Jesus can gain tutoring and emulate models, no congregation-based program exceeds the influence of families. There is an unchallenged consensus that a disciple's lifestyle and attitudes toward others are *initially* and *primarily* shaped in family units.

Families serve as the "basic training center" for disciples. In *Family the Forming Center*, Marjorie Thompson highlights what psychologists have known for years, namely, that children's earliest experiences with other family members shape their identity and ability to interact with others. More specifically, the life-affirming attitudes toward others that the followers of Jesus are called to exhibit are first practiced in the "sacred shelters" of their families. Here are a few grace-filled attitudes that are family-initiated:

- *acceptance* of differences in family members prepares a disciple to act respectfully toward all others;

- *affirmation* of family members' gifts and callings shapes a disciple's ability to discern and encourage the gifts and vocations of others;
- *accountability* in family circles prepares a disciple to learn how to "speak the truth in love" (Eph. 4:15) with grace-grounded humility;
- *forgiveness* in families, where unacceptable behaviors are distinguished from another's innate worthiness, prepares a disciple to live as an agent of reconciliation and hope;
- *hospitality*, where "the other" is brought inside a family's circle of care, prepares a follower of Jesus to welcome the "different" into faith communities;
- *generosity* in families, where tithing is practiced by all members, introduces a disciple into a lifetime of stewardship.

Thompson concludes her wise book with a timely insight. When churches enable families to succeed in their essential vocation to live out the Christian faith through such life-affirming practices as listed above, "the church sets the family free for mission instead of using up family resources for institutional maintenance" (Thompson 1996, 143).

3. Disciple as Discerner — Disciples Are Called into Lifelong Discernment

To discern means "to judge" or "sift" or "render a decision." Twenty-first-century disciples, engaged in a lifelong pilgrimage within a secularized society, inevitably encounter life options that are complex and, sometime, contentious. Choosing to live and act wisely requires every disciple to discern what responsibilities are worth pursuing and what behaviors or associations are to be avoided.

Christian discernment, however, has a different foundation than that wisdom derived solely from the world's resources. Embedded in Christian discipleship is an honoring of Israel's "wisdom tradition" located in the Law from Moses and in the OT's wisdom literature. Aware of the wise teachings of Jesus in the Sermon on the Mount, the apostle Paul insisted that discernment by Christian communities is continually reframed through the message of the cross of Jesus (see especially 1 Cor. 1–2).

As Osmer puts it, "Those who have the Spirit and discern the un-veiling of God's secret wisdom in the cross are in a position to discern what God is doing in the world" (Osmer, 48). That is, discernment by disciples, whether in the first century or in ours, is conditioned by a maturing understanding of the gospel. With this abbreviated background in mind, where do the practices of discernment come alive in contemporary mainline Protestant congregations?

Discernment and Private Prayer Prayer is the vehicle by which the people of God discern God's will and ways. "Make me to know your ways, O Lord," prayed the psalmist; "teach me your paths" (Ps. 25:4). Similarly, Jesus instructed his disciples to pray that the Father's "will be done on earth as it is in heaven" (Matt. 6:10). What Jesus expected of his followers, he himself demonstrated. In that critical moment in Gethsemane's garden, Jesus longed for an alternative way forward and prayed that the cup of suffering on a cross would "pass from me." But in the end he said, "My Father ... not what I want but what you want" (Matt. 26:39).

The apostle Paul, at outset of his letter to the Christians in Rome, said that he remembered them "without ceasing" in his prayers and later appealed to them not to conform "to this world" but "be trans-formed" so that "you may discern what is the will of God — what is good and acceptable and perfect" (Rom. 12:1-2). These biblical texts remind me of a morning prayer offered by John Baillie of Edinburgh, Scotland, in his enduring book *A Diary of Private Prayer.* He prayed that God would

> take this day's life into Thine own keeping. Control all my thoughts and feelings. Direct all my energies. Instruct my mind. Sustain my will. Take my hands and make them skillful to serve.... Take my eyes and keep them fixed upon Thine everlasting beauty. Take my mouth and make it eloquent in testimony to Thy love.... Make this day's work a little part of the work of the Kingdom of my Lord Christ, in whose name these prayers are said. (Baillie, 41)

Discernment and the Gifts of the Holy Spirit Analogous to Jesus' baptism by John the Baptist (Mark 1, Matt. 3, Luke 3, and John 1), every baptized Christian, according to the NT, is endowed with a gift(s) by the Holy Spirit. These specialized grace-gifts, often called *charism* (singular) or *charismata* (plural), have generated a large body of literature.[9] Biblical scholars tally some two dozen *charismata* in the Christian communities charted in the NT. Usually listed are persons with *words of wisdom, gifts for healing*, prophetic gifts (that is, those who speak for God), gifts for administration, diverse *kinds of tongues* and gifts for *interpretation of tongues* (1 Cor. 12:8-10).

Charismata, freely given at the pleasure of the Holy Spirit to followers of Jesus, are to be employed for the benefit of both the ministries within the Body of Christ and God's mission in contemporary societies. Discerning the reality of these grace-gifts in ourselves and in others is a delicate undertaking. Some congregational leaders use "gift assessment tools" to help parishioners identify their gifts.[10] Some even make use of instruments like the Myers-Briggs Type Indicator personality inventory.

Perhaps the most reliable procedure is to invite "partners in Christ" to identify the Spirit's grace-gifts in one another. Whatever the instruments employed, discipleship training in a congregation remains incomplete if disciples' *charismata* are unnamed, underdeveloped, or ignored.

Discernment with Others in Leading Congregational Ministries One might profitably read the entire Acts of the Apostles just to learn how, by the Spirit's leading, the earliest followers of Jesus discerned their futures when appointing leaders and clarifying their mission. From the election of Matthias to replace Judas (Acts 1:15-26) to the endorsement of Paul's calling to "bear witness in Rome" (Acts 23:11), multiple practical issues needed resolution. These followers addressed and resolved such issues by open interaction of leaders and people, by consulting and interpreting Scripture, by public and personal prayers, and by reaching a consensus about the Holy Spirit's leading.[11]

9. See especially the work by Gordon Fee, *God's Empowering Presence: The Holy Spirit in the Letters of Paul* (1994). Fee has abbreviated this magisterial book in *Paul, The Spirit and the People of God* (2007).

10. See especially the ELCA's Spiritual Gifts Assessment Tool at www.elca.org/faithpractices/assessments.

11. For a rich analysis of this discernment process among Jesus' followers in the first century, see Luke Johnson, *Scripture and Discernment: Decision Making in the Church*

Since those heady days of the earliest churches, countless congregations have tried to follow their precedent-setting procedures. One contemporary example will have to suffice.

Once, when I was serving as a pastor, our elders decided to appoint a part-time person as our Minister of Evangelism. We agreed on the qualifications such a person would need and proceeded to develop a "position description." We intended that she or he would organize partners to visits prospective members, design and organize new members' classes, introduce new members into small covenant groups with a six-week commitment, and track every new member's participation for at least a year.

To discern how we might proceed, a small team of elders gathered to pray that the Spirit would lead us to the appropriate person. After a couple of sessions, we agreed to approach Mary Smith (not her real name). We knew her to be a gifted, outgoing, confident Christian businesswoman who had attended Midwest churches all of her life. So two of us called on her in her home. We asked her to look at the job description, explained how we saw in her the gifts to lead this ministry, and asked her to prayerfully consider the opportunity. To our surprise, she teared up and said softly, "How strange! I have been praying to do something different with my life for weeks now." A few days later she accepted the appointment, visited several other congregations for "on the job training," and thereafter led a distinguished and creative ministry for nearly a decade.

Discernment and Mission The premier model for leaders who are called to discern a different future for their congregations can be found in Acts 15. In the history of the church, this "council of Jerusalem" remains a prototype for leaders for who are called to reconsider established practices, shift resources, and envision a different future.

About 50 CE, the original apostles and others discerned with clarity and consensus that the gospel was indeed for all persons (i.e. Gentiles) and that former norms of identity (such as circumcision) and holiness (such as selective eating partners) were no longer prerequisites for belonging to the people of God. Not inconsequentially, these early church leaders wisely communicated their

---

(1996). For a practical guide, see the work of D. R. Miller and C. M. Olsen, *Discerning God's Will Together: A Spiritual Practice for the Church* (2012).

reasoning and decision in writing to the Gentile Christian communities around the Mediterranean basin and urged compliance in those fledgling churches. That precedent-setting gathering set the procedures and parameters for councils of the church down to our own day.

These practices remain timely as a model for corporate discernment by the people of God: praying for the Holy Spirit's leading; appreciating the social context in which a congregation ministers; distilling the biblical and theological heritage to gain insight for the mission of God's people; providing adequate time for sharing, differing, and silence; listening to testimonies arising from persons on the perimeters of establishment structures; and communicating with persons and communities affected by the decision and counsel.

In our day, I suggest, discernment strives for consensus. While not an easy goal to attain, mission fulfillment in voluntary organizations like American congregations depends on consensus, especially among leaders.

Strategies for Growing Mature Disciples

Across the history of American Protestantism, church leaders have often adopted organizational strategies developed in educational institutions and business organizations. Currently, organizations of all sorts generate "strategic plans" to establish attainable and measurable goals. "Strategic actions" set out to accomplish those goals.

However, unlike secular institutions, Christian congregations are not free to generate goals apart from Jesus' mandates. And no goal for a Christian community is more explicit than Jesus' directive to "go into all the world and make disciples" (Matt. 28:19).

With that distinction emphasized, the term "strategic action" is not inappropriate when congregational leaders strive to fulfill Jesus' divine commission. Where the gospel is well known, where *koinonia* abounds, and where kingdom of God behaviors are embraced, plotting out "strategic actions" can be useful. To that end, I nominate seven "strategic actions" that can help grow mature disciples. They are briefly described below and are, obviously, not exhaustive. Along the way, and in keeping faith with one of the purposes of this book,

I will mention a few accessible resources to help implement these strategies.

1. Sponsor friendships

Discipleship is relational before it is instructional. *Koinonia* prepares the way for *mathētēs*. That is, discipling is initiated and enhanced when human relationships in families, circles of friends, and hospitable communities are available and gracious. Acknowledging the axiom that *God comes to people through God's people*, Christian discipleship rarely matures apart from a community of faith. A Christian education program that intentionally grows disciples will provide repeated opportunities where mature Christians graciously interact with others, especially newer and younger faith-apprentices.

A gifted pastor and congregational development authority, E. Stanley Ott, puts a high premium on the "with me" strategy for developing disciples. "The with-me principle is a simple expression of the profound biblical truth that God is a God *with* us.... We, in turn, ask people to be with us, to share fellowship with each other and with God Himself" (Ott, 15). Ott regularly summarizes his disciple-making strategy with his "with me" mantra: "I do, you watch; we do; you do, I watch; you do."

Our family vacations at a lakeside cottage in northern Michigan. Our next-door neighbors are two devout Christian chemistry professors on the faculty at Michigan State University. During most of the year, they serve as teachers and mentors for a middle-school group in their home congregation. For more than a decade now, they have invited their church school class to the lake for a week in the summer. Their days are filled with morning prayers and Bible study, water-skiing, beach combing, preparing meals together, and fishing for smallmouth bass. Their evening gatherings are enlivened with stories, prayers, and singing. In such a gracious environment, professors become friends as well as mentors, and teenagers make lifelong Christian friends with one another.

It is not so strange that several of the classes' graduates are now chemistry majors in colleges and universities and belong to congregations that prize friendship.

2. Teach Adults

One savvy observer of mainline congregations puts it like this: "Jesus taught adults and blessed children. We teach children and bless adults." Dan R. Dick's survey of seven hundred United Methodist congregations found that in "decaying" churches (his word), adult "learning is subjective, sporadic, and hit or miss.... In vital congregations, classes are formed around essential [biblical] content ... [and] participants move from class to class. In unstable congregations, *fellowship exerts influence over content*" (Dick, 62, emphasis mine).

Of course, emphasizing adult education opportunities does not relieve leaders of providing excellent educational experiences for younger disciples, children and youth. But if adults do not understand the biblical and theological foundations of the Christian faith, it is not likely that their children will fare much better. Over the many years of producing the *Kerygma* curriculum, its designers found that adults learn best when

- they take responsibility for their own learning;
- they are treated as individuals in settings where differences are respected;
- they are not in competition with the leaders; and
- they gain a sense of satisfaction in the progress of their learning (Eason, 30-31).

Several congregations of my acquaintance have instituted an academic model to organize their educational ministries for adults. They gear up a sequential building-block curricula with introductory courses for the less-informed (e.g. Bible 101), intermediate level courses (e.g. Bible 201, Old Testment prophets, or Pauline letters), and upper-level studies (e.g. Bible 301, Ethics In the NT). This same sequencing can be applied to courses for the disciplines of discipleship, such as "Learning How to Pray," "Learning from the Prayers of Great Christians," and "Linking Faith, Parenting, and Work."

In order to reach, potentially, all parishioners, churches offer these courses at different times during the week and re-offer them over several years. Such a curricular strategy signals a reimagined way of *mathētēs*. It is also an antidote to Dick's above-mentioned concern that fellowshiping can subvert thoughtful biblical inquiry.

3. Listen to Youth to Reconfigure Youth Ministries

According to an authority on youth ministries, Kenda Creasy Dean, Protestant congregations with thriving youth ministries have four practices in common: (1) they create a hospitable space for young people to explore Christian vocations; (2) they ask self-awakening questions; (3) they reflect theologically on self and community; and (4) they explore and establish missional opportunities. These practices are possible in every Christian community regardless of size, staffing, and location. One might well turn these four practices into questions and inquire where, if at all, these four elements are evident.[12]

4. Visit Other Congregations

Learning by imitation applies to congregations as well as to individuals. Networking with other successful congregations may be the most efficient way for leaders to gain insight and inspiration for shaping discipleship ministries.

Better than merely reading a book or hiring a consultant, conferring with other creative congregations enables leaders to appraise and reimagine their own educational ministries. I know of one congregation where a group of educators grew increasingly uneasy with the ways they were preparing children for worship. They heard of another congregation two hours away where children's educational and worship ministries flourished. A team of visiting inquirers spent a Saturday listening, questioning, and absorbing, while a host team proudly described and demonstrated their ministry with young children.

The ride home in a van gave the inquirers time to process what changes were needed and what planning was required. Within a couple months, their children's worship ministry was transformed.[13]

12. See especially Kenda Creasy Dean, *Almost Christian: What the Faith of Our Teenagers Is Telling the American Church* (2010). Many have also found a gold mine of ideas in Mark De Vries, *Sustainable Youth Ministry: Why Most Youth Ministry Doesn't Last and What Your Church Can Do About it* (2008). One reviewer calls this book "a hug and a kick in the pants."

13. The source of this children's worship ministry was S. M. Stewart and J. W. Berryman's *Young Children and Worship* (2000).

Networking inspires as well as informs. Continued isolation can grind down and dishearten.

Congregations teaching other congregations can also occur in denominational meetings. Most congregational leaders attend regional denominational gatherings several times a year, in which networking can flourish. In the late 1990s I belonged to a presbytery (similar to Methodist districts, Lutheran synods, or Reformed Church classes) that set aside ninety minutes at each meeting to allow one congregation to teach the others. Over several years, a variety of effective ministries and practices were explained and promoted. Among the programs presented and marketed were middle-school youth ministry, stewardship programs, the pros and cons of "blended worship" services, and tools to help evaluate educational ministries.

While one pastor dubbed these sessions "the Presbyterian show-and-tell hour," most congregational leaders appreciated the "home grown" expertise and even the marketing.

5. Prayerfully Select Leaders

Asking for volunteers to teach or lead is risky. Requesting anybody to "fill a slot" is an invitation to stagnation or worse. When the responsibility of leading a congregation-based ministry is not linked with an appointee's gifts, the results can be disheartening. Not every member is sufficiently suited to teach elementary-aged children or mentor a youth group or serve as treasurer or manage properties. A member who happens to be a consistent attendee or a generous giver is not automatically gifted to serve as a council member or deacon.

The New Testament points to another strategy. The "parts of the body" metaphor used by the apostle Paul in the Corinthian letters emphasizes the variety of Spirit-endowed gifts distributed among the people of God (1 Cor. 12). The Protestant tradition is rightly proud of its "priesthood of all believers" principle: No one person, including the pastor, possesses every grace-gift necessary for a congregation's ministries and mission. Rather, each member's gifts and talents are needed, and each member's gift complements the others.

However, it remains the role of a congregation's leaders to discern prayerfully which parishioner is best equipped to lead a particular ministry, to invite that person to consider serving, and to then provide training so that parishioner succeeds rather than founders. Echoes from Jesus may resonate here: "You did not choose me," he said, "but I have chosen you" (John 15:16).

6. Train Every Leader

Most every organization theorist underscores the dictum *effective leaders train others to lead.* That axiom has deep biblical roots. Jethro, Moses' father-in-law, urged Moses to appoint partners and "teach them ... and make known to them the way they are to go and the things they are to do" (Exod. 18:21-23).

Many of us pastors schooled in the middle of the twentieth century remember with affection reading *The Training of the Twelve,* a devotional classic by the nineteenth-century Scottish pastor and theologian A. B. Bruce. Carefully and comprehensively, Bruce outlines the way Jesus "trained the twelve" over a three-year period. "[Jesus] speaks of the training given to these men [and women] as if it had been a principal part of His own earthly ministry" (Bruce, 12-13). In a tender scene recorded in the book of Acts, a departing Paul reminded tearful elders from Ephesus how he had trained them and "did not shrink from doing anything helpful" (Acts 20:20). Later, those same Ephesian leaders were given the directive to "equip the saints for the work of ministry" (Eph. 4:11).

Most congregational leaders recognize the need to train church school teachers, youth directors, deacons, and lay pastors.[14] Less obvious, perhaps, is coaching of the elected leaders. Once, while attending a gathering of pastors and denominational executives, we launched into a brainstorming session about how elders or council persons might better be equipped for their important callings. What emerged — eventually! — was a daunting curriculum scheme that, nevertheless, held considerable promise and practicality. Here are some of its notable features:

- Ask newly elected council members or "ruling elders" to commit to an additional six months *prior* to beginning their usual three-year term.

---

14. For an excellent resource for "equipping the saints," see Sue Mallory, *The Equipping Church* (2001).

- Present each new officer with a position description and an out-lined course of study with required readings;
- Meet twice a month in order to address such topics as the congregation's history, its biblically based vision and mission, its current program priorities and organizational patterns, its processes for decision making, its financial resources and budget priorities, *along with* training in the arts of handling conflict and differences, listing denominational resources and expectations, and defining the respective roles of pastor, administrative staff, and governing council;
- Provide resources that help maintain those spiritual disciplines that nurture faithfulness in the Christian faith and life; and, finally,
- Celebrate this new calling with an overnight retreat during which all are prayed for, encouraged, and commissioned.

It was assumed that a congregation's pastor and other seasoned leaders would, initially, need to create and teach this program. But it was also emphasized that curriculum materials generated in one congregation could be shared with others.[15]

7. Assess Progress

Ministries aimed at growing mature disciples require periodic appraisal. Perhaps "charting progress" may be a more comfortable term for mainline congregations. Whatever terms are employed, an organization that will not learn about itself will be unable to discern and shape its future.

Effective leaders ask, "How do we know that we are doing what we claim we are doing?"[16] How and where to proceed with such assessments is no small assignment for leaders. Inquiries about the faith journeys of mainline members is, admittedly, a delicate respon-

15. For one example of a curriculum for this kind of training, see Steven P. Eason, *Making Disciples, Making Leaders: A Manual for Developing Church Officers* (2004).

16. An excellent introduction for assessing congregational ministries can be found in Jill M. Hudson, *When Better Is Not Enough: Evaluation Tools for the 21st Century Church* (2004).

sibility for church leaders, especially in a society that prizes a "Don't ask; don't tell" approach to religious experiences.

Yet without really knowing what parishioners are actually experiencing in worship services or learning at weekly gatherings, leaders will remain ill-informed when planning future disciple-growing programs. Anecdotes and random observations, while insightful, are not sufficient for serious reviews. Other means and methods are required if leaders are to shape a congregation's future.

However simplified here, sociologists gather data in one of two methods or both. The *first* is through *qualitative* inquiries. There is a worn-out saying among sociologists that "If you want to know what's going on among the folks in Paducah, ask 'em." Questionnaires, focus groups, and interviews are established methods for gathering insights about what is going on inside the hearts and minds of parishioners.

Reliable *qualitative* assessments begin and end with asking appropriate, open-ended, nonjudgmental questions. Answers, when analyzed and tallied, reveal patterns and insights that the "hard data" of statistical information miss. Most Protestant denominations have research offices and centers that can help with the tools needed for these assessments. Local colleges and universities are other places where assistance with designing research tools can be found. Educators, who routinely evaluate their students' progress, make excellent consultants, as do church members who are skilled in designing business market surveys.[17]

The *second* way to assess progress is the more common *quantitative* method. In this process, a congregation's priorities are measured by "hard data." For example, attendance figures in various programs tracked over a period of time become indices of patterns and future possibilities. Budget analyses usually reveal a congregation's priorities. For example, when personnel expenditures exceed two-thirds of a congregation's total budget, it becomes likely that educational and missional opportunities will lessen. Finally, tallying trends in financial commitments and attendance in particular congregations can

17. While not an easy read, John Swinton and Harriet Mowat have assembled an excellent manual about the purposes and methods of qualitative research for use in congregations. See their *Practical Theology and Qualitative Research* (2006, esp. chapters 1-3).

usually be compared to other churches via denominational research offices.

Both of the qualitative and quantitative sociological methods of inquiry will require leaders' courage and tact. Both methods can provide confidence and footing for planning a congregation's future. And with some soliciting among members, churches can often find expert advice already available in the community.

Beyond Mathētēs

This overview of the practices of gospel-driven discipleship began with leaders in one congregation asking each ministry area, "What kind of disciple are you deploying into the world?" Those leaders were fully aware of members' biblical and theological tentativeness. They knew firsthand of their friends' slippages in practicing the disciplines of the Christian way of life.

But they also knew that Jesus' disciples, who *learn* the Scriptures, *follow* Jesus' lead, and *discern* their gifts, *are also called* to be witnesses for the gospel and advocates of reconciliation in their communities and society. In light of that daunting call to deployment, I turn to another faithful practice in contemporary congregational life, namely, the arts associated with the practices of *martyria*, or witnessing.

CHAPTER 7

Practicing the Arts of Witnessing:
Testimony and Advocacy
....
Martyria

> *"You will receive power when the Holy Spirit has come upon you; and you will be my witnesses in Jerusalem, in all Judea and Samaria, and to the ends of the earth."*
>
> — ACTS 1:8

> *And day by day the Lord added to their number those who were being saved.*
>
> — ACTS 2:47

The Greek word *martyria* in the New Testament is usually translated "witness." The English word "martyr" derives from it. Scholars note that the etymological root of *martyria* is similar to "pointing." Sometimes *martyria* carries the more expansive concept of "witness" as a creed or faith summary.

The novelist and essayist Frederick Buechner, in *Telling Secrets*, describes an incident when he was a visiting lecturer at Wheaton College, near Chicago. While discussing such mundane topics as weather and movies over lunch with two students, one of them asked the other, as naturally as he would ask the time of day, what God was doing in his life. "In the part of the East where I live, if anybody were to ask a question like that, even among religious people, the sky would fall, the walls would cave in, the grass would wither," Buechner said. "I think the very air would stop my mouth if I opened it to speak such words among just about any group I can think of in the East because their faith itself, if they happen to have any, is one of the secrets that they have kept so long that it might almost as well not exist" (Buechner 1991, 82).

Buechner's discomfort is not without *some* foundation. For some, the word "witnessing" carries baggage akin to unwelcomed confrontations. On a larger scale, any person with a history-informed memory acknowledges that Christian witnessing in the name of God often escalated into ugly coercion and unspeakable violence against Jews, Muslims, Native Americans, and Mormons, to name only a few. The founders of the American republic viewed the wars of religion in Europe with disgust and noted that aggressive religious commitments bred violence and alienation in the body politic. To counter such threats, an ethic of toleration was written into the Constitution and the Bill of Rights, policies that disestablished and de-privileged one religious community over all others.

Buechner's discomfort may also be grounded in the swelling diversity of religious commitments in contemporary North American society outlined earlier (ch. 2). Pluralism as an ideology has refined the meaning of religious "political correctness" in public arenas.

For many postmoderns, religious preferences, like one's personal financial and political affairs, are strictly private and best kept closeted. "Don't ask; don't tell" is the mantra. I am reminded of a cartoon in *The New Yorker* by W. Miller in which the three proverbial monkeys are lined up in a row. One called "politics" has his fingers in his ears; one labeled "finance" places his hands over his eyes; and one named "religion" fixes his hands over his mouth.

Buechner's discomfort may arise for still another reason. The growing ignorance about the biblical and theological foundations of Christianity, outlined previously, has left many lay persons in mainline congregations with inferiority complexes. The rapid expansion of biblical and theological scholarship intimidates all but a few well-schooled specialists and some seminarians. As a result, religious advocacy is more and more relegated to trained, professional clergy who, in turn, operate mostly within the confines of their houses of worship or on television stations that specialize in religion.

This baffling socio-cultural milieu unsettles many ordinary mainline Protestants. Nevertheless, Jesus' mandate to "to be my witnesses" in this post-industrial society has ratcheted up the challenges for leaders of congregations. Addressing these challenges, however introductory and abbreviated, is the focus of this chapter. As will become apparent, it is entirely appropriate to employ the term "advocate" as a synonym for "witness."

Emphasizing the Obvious

The gospel message requires messengers. Even the most casual reader of the New Testament (NT) discovers that a Christian congregation's indispensable gift — the gospel — was entrusted to under-credentialed persons like fishermen, tax collectors, women, laborers, and political zealots. The bedrock conviction emerging from the pages of the Bible amounts to this: for those inside and outside the believing Christian community, where the gospel has not yet taken root, *God usually comes to people through God's people.*

Without compromising the Holy Spirit's freedom to act as God chooses, God's revelation was — and is — mediated through ordinary humans in a language that ordinary persons employ. According the Scriptures, God's earliest self-disclosure was communicated to persons such as Abraham, Moses, David, and Israel's prophets and poets. Within that Jewish heritage, Christians believe that Jesus of Nazareth is the normative witness about God, the "Word made flesh … full of grace and truth" (John 1). In response, Christians were — and are — called to become advocates of that Word in every aspect of human life and society.

The apostle Paul called Christians "a letter of Christ … written not with ink but with the Spirit of the living God" (2 Cor. 3:3). Ordinary disciples, he maintained, hold the "treasure [the gospel] in clay jars [or earthen vessels] … [so that] Jesus may be made visible in our mortal flesh" (2 Cor. 4:7-11). Eastern Orthodox communities often refer to Christians as "living icons." Martin Luther once observed, in *Freedom of a Christian* (1520), that "[a]s our heavenly Father has in Christ freely come to our aid, we also ought freely to help our neighbor … that we may be Christs to one another." C. S. Lewis said the same thing in *Mere Christianity:* "The Church exists for nothing else but to draw men [and women] into Christ, to make them little Christs. If they are not doing that, all the cathedrals, clergy, missions, sermons, even the Bible itself, are simply a waste of time."

Most Christians recognize this basic *martyria* strategy. Most of us came into the Christian faith because we saw the reality of Jesus Christ alive in some other ordinary human such as a parent, coach, or teacher. A friend told me of his experience when he attended a Christian gathering of some thirty thousand persons (mostly men) in a large football stadium in the East. The gathering's leader asked the crowd to stand if they had come to their Christian faith while attending a mass rally, say, a Billy Graham revival. According to my friend, a few hundred persons stood and were applauded. Then the leader asked how many came to faith though the witness of other very ordinary persons or friends. Virtually the whole stadium rose to their feet.

Until mainline Protestant congregations grasp and endorse and equip their members for this foundational Christian strategy, programs of "outreach" or "evangelism" or "church growth" will probably founder.

Martyria in Biblical Perspective

The Word "Witness" in the Hebrew Bible: Courts, Claims, and Covenants When biblical scholars track the meaning of the word *martyria* (witness), they hear echoes from ancient Israel's courts and trials.

In most societies, as in ancient Israel, witnesses are indispensable for legal proceedings, justice allocation, and public treaties. The biblical scholar Allison Trites has carefully studied the role of witnesses in ancient Israel. She finds that "justice in the gate" was often carried out among the Israelites when village elders gathered to hear a dispute or an accusation.

In this setting, witnesses, who were mostly males, were summoned to clarify past events or verify disputed facts. When witnesses finished, the elders, acting as a court of justices, weighed the testimonies, announced their verdict, and then imposed a solution. According to Trites, the two essential ingredients of reliable witnesses were truthful testimony and personal integrity. She notes that such truth telling in public was simply another way of obeying the ninth commandment of the Decalogue, "You shall not bear false witness against your neighbor" (Trites, 222-30).

The obligation to "tell the truth" was, and is, foundational for justice and well-being in any community. Conversely, lying is fatal to the social fabric that binds community and neighbors.

The Old Testament (OT) also records a more expansive usage of the term "witness." Hebrew prophets, like Isaiah, created an imaginary courtroom where all the nations and their deities were assembled. Witnesses from other nations were summoned to testify to their gods. In such a "grand jury" God says to Israel, "You are my witnesses ... and my servant whom I have chosen, so that you [all] may know and believe me and understand that I am he. Before me no god was formed, nor shall there be any after me. I, I am the Lord and besides me there is no savior" (Isa. 43:10-11).

As to witnessing to the "nations of the world," the Old Testment parable-like story of a prophet named Jonah is without peer. After one of the Bible's most famous and harrowing detours, the unenthusiastic Jonah offered a one-sentence sermon and the entire city of Nineveh converted. Even the cattle got the message! But the sulking prophet scolded God for wasting God's grace on pagan Ninevites.

Disgusted with God's prodigal mercy, the depleted Jonah preferred to die. But God reminded Jonah that God's original covenantal intentions included more than the people of Israel. "Should I not pity Nineveh?" God asked Jonah. The Ninevites were persons "who do not know their right hand from their left," that is, they knew neither the Creator's redemptive grace nor the ways of living wisely.

Without Jonah's witness, the story concludes, the waiting people of Nineveh would continue in spiritual confusion. But Jonah continued to sulk, more distressed about a shriveled plant than a deprived and misguided community of people.

I once asked a friend who is a trial lawyer for a quick definition of a good witness. He replied that a good witness must (a) have had a firsthand experience, (b) be a person of credible and reliable character, and (c) be open to questioning. Those homespun criteria are not far from the insights of the well-known French philosopher and theologian Paul Ricoeur, who said there were four claims inherent in the biblical idea of "witness":

- The witness was not a volunteer but, rather, a disciple summoned by Jesus and then sent outward on a mission.
- The testimony of the disciple as witness centered around God's claim on human life.
- This testimony was directed to all peoples and is offered for all persons.

- This testimony was not merely one of words but also required appropriate action.[1]

With my lawyer friend's and Ricoeur's summaries in mind, I turn to the New Testament's record about witnessing.

Witness in the New Testament: Claims, Credibility, and Calling The word *martyria*, or witness, occurs over one hundred times in NT. Each of the four Gospels is busy with witnesses and advocates. Here is just a sampling of persons from very ordinary, though diverse, backgrounds: Mary, a peasant mother from Galilee; Simeon, a venerable devout Jew; Anna, an elderly prophetess of the tribe of Asher; John the Baptist, a wilderness prophet; Peter and Andrew, fishermen; an unnamed Samaritan woman; Nicodemus, an elite religious leader; an unnamed, healed demoniac from Gadara; devoted friends Lazarus, Mary, Martha, and Mary Magdalene; and a Roman army officer overseeing the crucifixion. Complementing these ordinary persons were extraordinary witnesses, such as angels and the transcendent voice of God.[2]

In his climactic trial before Pilate, Jesus himself summarized his ministry with the words, "You say that I am a king. For this I was born, and for this I came into the world, to testify [bear witness to] the truth" (John 18:37). And to ensure his followers would never forget his identity, Jesus, in an "upper room," broke bread and called it his body and poured out a cup of wine and called it his life blood. Both symbols would serve forever after as perpetual testimonies to his grace, presence, and mission.

Beyond the Gospels' narratives lie the memoirs of the earliest apostles, especially those of Peter and Paul. Their stories illumine their Holy Spirit-prompted witnessing. At trial before religious and civil authorities, Peter attested to the crucifixion and resurrection of Jesus and added, "And we are witnesses to these things" (Acts 5:32). Later, with some reluctance, Peter testified before an inquisitive Roman centurion named Cornelius, in the coastal town of Caesarea, about Peter's firsthand experience with the risen Lord (Acts 10).

1. For this summary, I am indebted to Thomas Long's book *The Witness of Preaching* (1989).

2. All three of the synoptic gospels record incidents where a voice from heaven says of Jesus, "This is my Son, the Beloved; listen to him" (Matt. 3:17; Mark 9:7; Luke 9:35).

Paul, the premier witness to Gentile societies, advocated for his Christian convictions in sophisticated Athens (Acts 17). On another occasion, Paul asserted, "I do not count my life of any value to myself, if only I may finish my course and the ministry that I received from the Lord Jesus, to witness to the good news of God's grace" (Acts 20:24). Later, in his dramatic trial before Roman ruler Herod Agrippa, Paul said, "I stand here, testifying to [all,] both great and small" (Acts 26:19-23).

Throughout all of the NT, witnesses from all walks of life testified to the gospel's foundations centered in the life, death, and resurrection of Jesus. Simultaneously, they demonstrated the significance of that gospel in their personal and public lives. Reviewing the New Testament record, witnessing for them was not an option; it was a mandate and privilege.

It ought not to be overlooked that the church's most valued and normative documents, the four Gospels, depended on source materials derived from "eyewitnesses."[3] Future readers of the Gospels were to be assured that the New Testament record was grounded in real people who possessed firsthand information and attested to transforming experiences. Luke reminded his readers that his sources "were handed on to us by those who from the beginning were eyewitness" (Luke 1:2).

Some scholars think that John's Gospel is organized around a succession of witnesses drawn from a broad spectrum of human society: John the Baptist (John 1); Nicodemus (John 3); a Samaritan woman and her neighbors (John 4); a blind man who received sight (John 9), along with others. John's culminating witness, Mary Magdalene, announced to the other disciples, "I have seen the Lord," and then told them what the resurrected Jesus had said to her (John 20:18). The author of this fourth Gospel (perhaps the apostle John) concludes his account unambiguously: "This is the disciple who is testifying to these things ... and we know that his testimony true" (John 21:24).[4]

---

3. The literature about the term "eyewitness" in the New Testament is extensive. See Richard Bauckham, *Jesus and the Eyewitnesses: The Gospels as Eyewitness Testimony* (2006).

4. In a later epistle, attributed to the apostle John, we read, "We declare to you what was from the beginning, what we have heard, what we have seen with our eyes, what we have looked at and touched with our hands, concerning the word of life ... we declare to you what we have seen and heard so that you also may have fellowship with us" (1 John 1).

In short, multiple and diverse persons testified to the uniqueness of Jesus the Christ and, simultaneously, affirmed publicly his transforming message in their lives.

Few biblical narratives about witnessing stir this author's imagination quite like that of the unnamed woman at a well in Samaria, north of Jerusalem. She is what theologians call the gospel's "living voice." The account in, John 4, begins with a jagged-edged encounter. When a tired and thirsty Jesus asks for a drink of water, she snips at him, " 'How is it that you, a Jew, ask a drink of me, a woman of Samaria?' (Jews do not share things in common with Samaritans)." Surfacing here are the tragic realities that divide the human family: class cleavage (she's poor), racial separation (she is part Gentile and part Jew), competing religious commitments (Samaritans claimed a truer allegiance to the writings of Moses than Jerusalem Jews), gender alienation (no rabbi dare speak to a woman in public), and a violation of countless other social protocols.

As this high-intensity encounter unfolds, the reader soon learns that this Samaritan woman is imaginative, inquisitive, quick-witted, spiritually thirsty, and gifted in the art of hospitality. Underway in this passage is an account of a very ordinary person becoming a learner and disciple. The more she inquired about Jesus, the more Jesus disclosed. And, simultaneously, the more she inquired about Jesus, the more she discovered herself and her God-endowed gifts.

With a startling turn, the narrator notes that the Samaritan woman returned to her village and invited others to "come and see" the one "who told me everything I have ever done" — that is, "come and see a man who told me who I am." The villagers honored her witness and invited this Jewish rabbi into their homes. Such hospitality scandalously transgressed countless social mores — mental models — of the day.

At the end of this Johannine narrative, there is a compliment that exceeds all other compliments for any Christian's witness: the villagers said to her, "It is no longer because of what you said that we believe, for we have heard for ourselves, and we know that this [Jesus] is truly the Savior of the world" (John 4:42). Again, mystery upon mystery unravels here. A plain and ordinary woman, introduced only as a "drawer of water" for others, emerges as an ambassador for the Savior of the world. Her unadorned "come and see" strategy for testifying, like that of so many others in the NT, must have radiated grace and confidence.

The Biblical Way of Witness: The Call to Any Disciple Within a Community In light of this brief account of biblical ideas about witnessing and advocating, it becomes clear that the gospel is entrusted to ordinary people who function in the ordinary environments of families, communities, and vocations. Clearly, pastors and other professionals are not the *sole* bearers of "tidings of great joy." The contemporary theologian Jürgen Moltmann puts it this way:

> The Christian church grew out of the apostolic proclamation of the gospel and is alive in the act of proclamation. But the expression "proclamation" ... [was not] limited to the public discourse of a preacher who is commissioned for that purpose.... This [proclamation] includes preaching, teaching, conversation with groups of individuals, storytelling, comforting, encouraging, and liberating ... [and] verbal witness in different relationships of life. (Moltmann, 2006, 206)

Neither is the formalized preaching event the *sole* occasion for Christian witnessing. Members of contemporary congregations are misguided and neglectful when they relegate *martyria* solely to professional clergy and their pulpit proclamations.

To the contrary, authentic and faithful witnessing occurs when a parent reminds a child at bedtime that she is the special friend of Jesus; or when a colleague or friend shares how the gospel gives meaning to his or her life journey; or when a Christian disciple refuses to follow directives of a superior that require deception or promote injustice; or when a disciple ushers a stranger into a Christian gathering.

Of course witnessing occurs from the pulpit, but the preaching event is not the only venue for the gospel's proclamation. Seen in this light, the embedded Protestant heritage of the "priesthood of all believers" frees congregational leaders to tutor and equip all parishioners to express their faith commitments with grace and confidence in public arenas.[5]

---

5. For an excellent treatment of the biblical understanding of "witness" and "witnessing," see Darrell L. Guder, *Be My Witnesses* (1985). Guder summarizes the biblical idea of *martyria* like this: *be* the witness; *do* the witness; and *say* the witness. This earlier work has been expanded in Guder's *The Continuing Conversion of the Church* (2000).

Before turning to develop two different but intertwined forms of contemporary Christian witnessing, I want to reiterate a prevailing thesis of this book: *all the faithful practices detailed in this book, including martyria, are symbiotically linked. Martyria rarely advances apart from koinonia and mathētēs.* Without communities (*koinonia*) to provide disciples (*mathētēs*) with instruction and encouragement, *martyria* usually stumbles and congregations turn inward. As noted elsewhere, Jesus spent three years teaching and empowering his disciples before sending them out to unfamiliar societies and diverse cultural environments.

In our day, congregational leaders are called to equip members for Christian witnessing in at least two ways: First, to teach them how to testify to the gospel they have experienced. *Second*, to help them envision their vocations as the venue where the gospel is acted out. Each of these witnessing initiatives depends on the empowerment of the Holy Spirit. Each requires sensitivity to social contexts and a "sense of place." Each requires graciousness, humility, and innovation. I turn to them now.

I. Martyria *as Testimony to the Gospel — Why Stories Matter*

If I were serving in a parish again, I would make Thomas G. Long's wise book *Testimony: Talking Ourselves into Being Christian* (2004) required reading. Long maintains that Christians talk about their faith because "it is a truly human act to want to tell the truth." We Christians cannot tell the whole truth about ourselves without talking about God. "Christians know that we cannot be fully human without speaking the truth about life and about ourselves, which is grounded in the truth about God.... When we talk about our faith ... we are coming more fully and clearly to believe. In short, we are talking ourselves into being Christian."

Christians' testimonies are "God's language in a world waiting for love," Long writes. But Christians will need to understand that the church is God's language school. When Christians are singing, praising, preaching, and passing the peace, they are not only praising God, they are also learning "how to talk in the world.... Worship is a dress rehearsal for speaking faithfully in the rest of life."

In worship, God is experienced as the one who speaks and who invites our human speech in return. This bond between worship and words, Long continues, is "built into the very essence of the gospel...." To participate in worship services is not only to hear and speak truthful and life-changing words inside the sanctuary, "but also to prepare ourselves for truthful and life-changing speech in other areas of life." The "new reality" experienced in worship requires a new way of speaking about the Christian faith in the world. That new way is the way of stories and narratives (Long, 2004, 6-7, 104, 53).

Witnesses Are Storytellers Effective Christian testimonies surface as narratives. "If pressed to say what the Christian faith and life are, we could hardly do better than 'hearing, telling and living a story,'" wrote Lutheran theologian Edmund Steimle. Countless other theologians remind mainline Protestants that the NT-based gospel itself is best understood within the framework of story or narrative.[6]

Stories explain *why* we believe, rather than simply *what* we believe. They are not, initially, doctrinal affirmations. Many contemporary persons are wary, if not put off, by abstract, didactic, creedal "proclamations from on high." Absolutists' claims sound hollow when disembodied from authentic persons and personalities.

By contrast, personal narratives relate how ordinary persons locate themselves *in* their witness, not just *behind* or *above* their testimony. Stories humanize a witness, especially when slippages and insecurities are acknowledged. At their authentic best, faith-forming stories interpret *how* the gospel gives meaning and hope to persons in their quite ordinary life journeys.

Stories Are Works of Art Testimonies are verbal creations. They weave together experience and imagination. Within the mystery of the Holy Spirit's presence, our faith is fashioned in synch with our personality, gifts, and "social location." Such a fashioning implies no one's faith story is automatically a template or normative for all others. As Brian McLaren recently wrote, our faith stories are created as "works in progress," interwoven with *The Story We Find Ourselves In* (2003). That is, we shape our faith narratives within the boundaries and grace of the essential gospel outlined in chapter 3. Our stories help vivify that gospel.

6. For these quotes and many other insights in this section, I am indebted to Thomas G. Long's *The Witness of Preaching* (1989), chapter 1.

Stories Can First Be Shared, Rehearsed, and Perfected Among Friends Many mainline Protestants can wax shy and even fear-stricken when asked to testify to their faith. But they need not remain forever paralyzed. Within a *koinonia*-based community, Christian friends can coach each other. Role-playing our testimonies among friends can generate confidence. It is not uncommon for lawyers to prepare their clients for presentations on the witness stand. In like manner, Christian friends can help each other to become more graceful, pointed, and context-appropriate when practicing how to tell their stories.

Stories Point Listeners Beyond the Storyteller Christian communities of our day are privileged to have access to an abundance of stories that testify to faith journeys of countless Christians. The stories mentioned in chapter 2 are examples of how Christians have narrated their faith to others. Allow me to recall one more.

In his unforgettable autobiography, *Surprised by Joy*, C. S. Lewis tells how his faith journey found traction:

> Remember, I had always wanted, above all things, not to be "interfered with." I had wanted (mad wish) "to call my soul my own." I had been far more anxious to avoid suffering than to achieve delight.... You must picture me alone that night in Magdalen [College], night after night, feeling ... the steady, unrelenting approach of Him whom I so earnestly desired not to meet. In the Trinity term, that which I so greatly feared had at last come upon me.... I gave in and admitted that God was God, and knelt and prayed: perhaps, that night, the most dejected convert in all England.... The Prodigal Son at least walked home on his own two feet. But who can duly adore that Love which will open the high gates to a prodigal who is brought in kicking, struggling, resentful, and darting his eyes in every direction for a chance to escape?" ... The hardness of God is kinder than the softness of men, and His compulsion is our liberation. (Lewis 1955, 228-29)

Equipping Disciples to Tell Their Faith Stories The challenge for leaders in twenty-first century mainline congregations remains clear: how will they encourage and equip sincere and faithful Christians to tell their own faith stories in a religiously pluralistic society that values highly the privatization of religious commitments?

Thankfully, we can find numerous models across America of thriving mainline congregations who coach their members how to witness to the gospel without embarrassment or arrogance.[7] Prominent among those leadership models is GraceNet initiatives, authored by Martha Grace Reese.[8] She embodies the experience of a researcher, corporate attorney, congregational pastor, middle judicatory minister, church consultant, author, and keen observer of contemporary mainline congregations.

Reese's widely used book, *Unbinding the Gospel*, grew out of two major research efforts. The *first* was a questionnaire sent to 262 congregations of the Christian Church (Disciples of Christ) that asked twenty-five thousand members about their witnessing and their churches' helpfulness. The two responses that ranked *lowest* were, "This church is effectively reaching unchurched persons" and "This congregation provides training in sharing Christ with others."

Reese's *second* research initiative, funded by the Lilly Endowment, was titled the "Mainline Evangelism Project." It was a four-year study of several hundred congregations. The goal of this research, she writes, "was to find churches that were doing effective evangelism and to discover their motivation.... How do they think? What are they doing? We found some exciting answers."

Reese repeatedly found three pivotal characteristics among members of growing congregations: *First*, members can articulate

---

7. Resources for how congregations can equip their members for faithful and gracious witnessing are plentiful. Every mainline denomination has an evangelism office with timely and appropriate resources. For the eager researcher, see Bryan Stone's *Evangelism After Christendom: The Theology and Practice of Christian Witness* (2007). The multiple publications of the Willow Creek Association in Barrington, Ill., can also be helpful, especially for the bashful. Begin with Mark Miller's *Experiential Storytelling: (Re) Discovering Narrative to Communicate God's Message* (2003) and move on to Lee Strobel and Mark Mittelberg's *The Unexpected Adventure: Taking Everyday Risks to Talk with People About Jesus* (2009). The chapter titled "Telling Your Story" in Kevin G. Harney's *Organic Outreach for Ordinary People* (2009) is another resource for shy mainliners. Throughout all of these resources, the New Testament strategy of "come and see" is writ large.

8. While the author of several books, Reese is the founder and president of GraceNet, Inc. Her continuing work in evangelism and church growth can be traced on the website www.GraceNet.info. Of particular importance is her essay "Best Practices to Start *Unbinding the Gospel* in Your Church," which is available online. Her annual reports to the Lilly Endowment, also available online, are memorable accounts of how she has pursued her GraceNet initiatives in ordinary congregations.

their love for God, their love for their church community, and their love for people who do not live with this faith. *Second,* persons in growing churches can tell you what difference their Christian faith makes in their lives. *Third,* growing congregations teach their members how to share their faith with others (Reese, 2008, 4, 6).

In part three of *Unbinding the Gospel,* Reese provides a helpful chart that identifies different groupings of persons *outside* mainline congregations (see below). The chart is useful for congregational leaders who desire to focus and refine their evangelistic endeavors. Below, I have adapted and expanded her original graphic illustration. Especially noteworthy is her identification of groups in contemporary American society where the gospel story has yet to be told effectively and, further, what challenges accompany a church's witness to the unchurched.

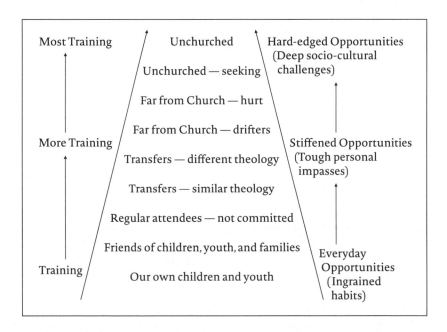

Reese's follow-up book, *Unbinding Your Church,* is a useful manual for pastors and leaders of mainline congregations. Through it she directs the *Unbinding the Gospel Project,* whose objectives are (a) to coach one thousand or more congregations in a two-year process of prayer, faith sharing, and evangelism, and (b) to study the dynamics of spiritual leadership and congregational transformation. This project can be followed by consulting the website cited in footnote 8.

2. Martyria *as Vocation —*
Why Our Everyday Responsibilities Matter

The concept of "vocation," as employed here, covers a wide swath of human practices. One's vocation is not less than the day job for which he or she derives financial compensation, but it is a more inclusive term. As maintained in the previous chapter, *a person's vocation is anywhere she or he has responsibilities.* Within this definition and perspective, a Christian's vocation can include a wide spectrum of activities, such as parenting, studying, and volunteer activities. As a pastor friend once put it, "Vocation has to do with defining relationships and purposeful living beyond the parameters of an individual life."

As we will explore in the following chapter on *diakonia,* or service, Christians whose daily vocations require them to work in the systems of modern society — family, medicine, law, education, government, manufacturing, farming, business (to name a few) — possess the greatest competence *and* opportunities to help transform those societal networks into more just, equitable, and life-affirming systems.

This expansive understanding of vocation reframes a long and embedded understanding of "the call" in the lives of men and women in the church's past. Prior to the Protestant Reformation, the term "vocation" was usually reserved for clergy and other religious persons, especially those in "holy orders." However, the Protestant Reformers, convicted by insights derived from the Scriptures, reconfigured that earlier heritage and insisted that all Christians, *by virtue of their baptisms,* are called into the service of the kingdom or reign of God.

Martin Luther and John Calvin maintained that any layperson's vocation that does not violate God's commandments and contributes to the welfare of one's neighbors should be understood as a "divine calling." Calvin insisted, for example, that a magistrate or a "civil authority is a calling, not only holy and lawful before God, but also the most sacred and by far the most honorable of all callings in the whole life of mortal men" (Calvin II, 1960). The same might be said for a business executive, union steward, social worker, lawyer, or high school coach. Since the Reformation, when Protestants are at their best theirs is a "world-formative" Christian faith, not a withdrawn, "world-adversive" faith.

Four centuries after the Reformers, American Presbyterians in their *Confession of 1967* re-affirmed the same vocational orientation for disciples: "The church calls every [person] to use his abilities, his possessions, and fruits of technology as gifts entrusted to him by God for the maintenance of his family and the advancement of the common welfare." Disciples, who are called to "strive first for the kingdom of God" (Matt. 6:33), do so in the ordinary places of daily work, home, school, and other arenas where they have responsibilities. Within this classical Protestant worldview, contemporary understandings of vocation become linked with the practices of *martyria* (witnessing).

The research of sociologist Robert Wuthnow, however, is again revealing. He found that, among churchgoing Americans, the relationship between faith and work is ambiguous.

In a nationwide survey, Wuthnow asked working people why they chose their line of work. They responded in ways that pointed to reasons other than religious commitments. Most (75 percent) said their decision was not influenced by religion, while only 10 percent said that religious values definitely influenced their choice of occupation. Wuthnow was surprised to find that the responses among persons who attended religious services every week were not significantly different from those of the larger public. He noted, "This is a striking finding" (Wuthnow, 1994c, 48-49).

Equally striking are testimonies of mainline parishioners who report little connection between their congregational life and their vocational life. On one occasion, while leading a workshop for church leaders outside of San Francisco, I urged them to pay attention to the interfacing of their faith and their daily work. To illustrate my concern, I mentioned the stressful and draining responsibilities of teachers of children with special physical and emotional needs. I intended to salute those gifted teachers as special ambassadors of the kingdom of God. Afterward, a woman who had waited around for an opportunity to speak broke into tears. I feared that I had offended her unintentionally, but she gathered herself and said, "I have been a special education teacher for fifteen years. It is hard. But I am doing what God has called me to do. This is the first time I have ever heard someone in my church affirm what I try to do for God every day."

Her small cluster of listeners, beginning with me, felt appropriately chastened.

This woman's lament is not unlike that of the prominent Lutheran layperson and steel-manufacturing executive William Diehl. Diehl has written that, in thirty years, his church (which he attended faithfully) failed to give him any guidance that connected his faith and his work. "I received no affirmation, no training, no support and no prayers.... There was absolutely no connection between Sunday and Monday" (Diehl, 12).

Yet congregational leaders need not become paralyzed. A growing cadre of scholars like Laura Nash (a Harvard University Business School professor) and Scotty McLennan (a Stanford University dean) find that women and men in contemporary business communities are experiencing an unfulfilled hunger to find ways to integrate their faith and their work. Nash and McLennon titled their findings *Church on Sunday, Work on Monday: The Challenge of Fusing Christian Values with Business Life* (2001). David W. Miller, director of Princeton University's Faith and Work Initiative, is a another prominent scholar exploring the ways spiritual identities "inform engagement with work issues such as ethics, values, vocation, meaning, purpose ... in a pluralistic world." The stated purpose of this initiative is to "equip students and leaders to integrate the resources of their faith with their work to transform their organizations and serve the greater good."[9] Congregational leaders will find these two studies informative and suggestive when planning for congregational workshops around vocational callings and challenges.

Recent Protestant theologians — sensitive to contemporary issues of secularization, modern economic systems, and the rise of religious pluralism — often speak of vocation as "partnering." Christians are summoned as partners in God's mission in the world. One theologian identifies vocation as partnering in arenas where there is "work to be done, a message to be proclaimed, service to be rendered, hostility to be overcome, injustice to be rectified" (Migliore, 247).

This more modern way of defining vocation as an expression of *martyria* was alive and well in the work of the late Fred Rogers, the creator and central character in the long-running television series

---

9. Miller, David, *God at Work: The History of the Faith at Work Movement* (2007). The initiative's website can be reach through www.princeton.edu/faithandwork.

"Mister Rogers' Neighborhood." Once, while addressing a group of seminarians, Rogers told about his long friendship and correspondence with one viewer named Tony, who lived in an impoverished city-center in New Jersey.

> I am very grateful to God for Tony. You see, I believe that God's Holy Spirit took whatever I was saying and doing years ago on that television set into Tony's miserable home and translated it into what Tony needed at the moment. Between that television screen and that little boy in need was a space of invisible holy ground used by God's spirit ultimately to bless us both. Is it any wonder that every time I walk into a studio to make a program, my prayer is always: "Dear God, in whatever we [I] do let some word that is heard be Yours."

Few definitions of a Christian disciple's vocation are the peer of Frederick Buechner's: "The place God calls you to is where your deep gladness and the world's deep hunger meet" (Buechner, 1973, 128).

What, then, is a doable agenda for current church leaders? How can we begin to structure congregation-based ministries to enable all members to embody the gospel by developing a maturing sense of vocation? How can at least some of our words in public arenas be "heard as Yours"?

At least four proposals are possible in every congregation. First, congregational leaders need to carve out time for the study of modern vocational challenges. One excellent place to begin is by consulting Douglas Schuurman's accessible yet comprehensive book *Vocations: Discerning Our Callings in Life* (2003). Christians "want to think about what vocation means and how it may be significant for their lives.... Christians, like so many modern people in our fragmented culture, are searching for ways to integrate their lives — public and private, religious and secular, home and office. The doctrine of vocation can provide invaluable help in contributing to such integration" (Schuurman, xiv). I have found Schuurman's work superbly grounded in biblical perspectives, theologically informed, and accompanied by practical and liturgical suggestions for congregations.

A *second* practice, inspired by William Diehl's book *The Monday Connection*, emerged among members of several Lutheran congregations who organized small groups that called themselves the "Monday Connection." They met on the first Monday morning of each month at a local restaurant. Participants rotated in presenting "case studies" derived from their work-worlds. Questions, Bible passages, and ethical issues were as common as coffee. One participant said, "Whenever possible, the group tries to find ways in which the worship service of the previous day is connected to the case study being presented. Was there something in the lessons, the sermon, the liturgy, or a hymn that related to the problem?"

The goal of every session, reports author Thomas Long, was the same: "to help people discover what Christ would have them do or say in a *specific situation in a workaday world*" (Long, 2004, 108).

A *third* initiative emerged from a Midwest congregation that sponsored weekend retreats centered around persons of similar vocations. It was envisioned that professionals such as middle-management executives, special-ed teachers, or social workers would gather for a two-day weekend to wrestle with the straightforward question "What does it mean to be Christian and ... ?"

The first retreat, led by a nationally prominent child oncologist who was a devout Christian, brought together a group of physicians. Early on, in well-led discussion groups, these doctors brought up complex ethical, professional, and relational issues that baffled them both as Christians and doctors. Frequently they appealed to the guest seminar leader for opinions and options, but as the weekend wore on they learned from each other. It soon became clear that disciple-like wisdom resided in many of the participants. One small group huddled around the retreat leader until the early morning hours, discussing how to handle their own feelings when their hi-tech medicine became insufficient to help heal patients they deeply cared about. Not surprisingly, attendees found ways to meet and confer after the retreat concluded.

Finally, a Lutheran congregation in Washington, D.C., mentioned in Schuurman's book, regularly uses a liturgy for church members seeking to fulfill faithfully their "world formative" vocations as Christian disciples.

Minister to Participant:
Your work and your worship are intimately interwoven.... Your work grows out of your worship and your worship grows out of your work. [Name] do you come today to acknowledge that the place where you work is as holy as the place where you worship?

Participant (kneeling):
I do.... Enabled by Christ's love for me, I shall endeavor to make each day's work a sacrament. I pray that my work will be cleansed of all spiritual and material selfishness, of all impatience or criticism, of all secret desire for recognition or reward. Turn, O God, my seeing into loving, that I may witness to the redeeming love of Jesus Christ for all [persons]. In his name I make my prayer. Amen. (Schuurman, 129)

This liturgical commissioning reminds this author of a passionate plea to all in mainline congregations by Anglican bishop and New Testament scholar N. T. Wright, in his book *For All God's Worth*. It is a rare hybrid of a prayer, challenge, and lament:

The church doesn't need people who know it all, or can do it all, or want to control it all.... We need Christian people to work as healers: as healing judges and prison staff, as healing teachers and administrators, as healing shopkeepers and bankers, as healing musicians and artists, as healing writers and scientists, as healing diplomats and politicians. We need people who will hold on to Christ firmly with one hand and reach out the other, with wit and skill and cheerfulness, with compassion and sorrow and tenderness, to the places where our world is in pain.... We pray that God will raise up a new generation of wounded healers; so that the healing love of Christ may flow out into the world, to confront violence and injustice with the rebuke of the cross, and to comfort the injured and wronged with the consolation of the cross. (Wright, 1997, 100-102)

Martyria in the Ordinary

I acknowledge that the faithful practice of witnessing, as outlined above, is not a comfortable discipline for many contemporary mainline Protestants. We circulate in a society sated with competitive ways of life; inclusive pluralistic faith claims; and self-selected, cocooned communities. However, gospel-driven witnessing — "giving a reason for the hope that lies within you" (1 Pet. 3:15) — remains a high calling for Jesus' disciples.[10] Most emphatically, twenty-first-century mainline congregations will be summoned to avoid the trap of relegating that witness exclusively to paid, professionalized clergy.

We mainliners have much to learn from our Christian brothers and sisters in independent churches who train their members well in the joys and courtesies of witnessing. In the end, "A saint is anyone who makes it easier to believe in God."

Once, after a lumbering lecture about Christians and *martyria*, a group of smiling students cornered me. "Yeah, we get it," they said:

"Talk the talk"

"Walk the walk,"

and "Live into your call!"

I wished I had dreamed up such a summary.

10. Eugene Peterson paraphrases this text from 1 Peter 3:15 like this: "Be ready to speak up and tell anyone who asks why you're living the way you are, and always with utmost courtesy" (*The Message*).

CHAPTER 8

Practicing the Arts of Serving: Compassion and Social Change
················
Diakonia

> ...They would sell their possessions and goods and distribute the proceeds to all, as any had need.
>
> — ACTS 2:45

Once, while I was moderating the annual meeting of our congregation in which we properly attended to budgets, reports, and elections, a young social worker waved her hand, wanting to speak.

I knew her well. She lived out her Christian faith on grimy inner-city streets, in decrepit apartments, and among the city's forgotten. With prophetic fire in her eye she asked, "Who really benefits from all these expenditures? It looks to me like most of what we spend here circles around for ourselves." Her well-aimed jab actually finds confirmation among sociologists who study American mainline congregations.

In his study of seven hundred Methodist congregations, Dan R. Dick found that 81 percent of the parishioners interviewed (3,794 of 4,684) stated that their primary involvement with their church was attending worship services, and the majority of those attendees were "mostly interested in what the congregation had to offer them personally" (Dick, 48).

Dick's research raises the probing question put forward to contemporary Protestant communities by Miroslav Volf, a Yale Divinity School theologian, in his book A Public Faith: How Followers of Christ Should Serve the Common Good. "What should be the main concern of Christ's followers when it comes to living well in the world today?"

His answer is that Christian communities are called to "*make plausible the claim that the love of God and of neighbor is the key to human flourishing.… [and] to actually believe that God is fundamental to human flourishing*" (Volf, 2011, 73-74).

In this chapter, I intend to revisit Jesus' mandate to love God and others by examining the faithful practice of Christian *diakonia*.

Diakonia, akin to the practice of *martyria* (witnessing) and sustained by *koinonia* (fellowship), is the gospel practiced in public arenas where Christians contribute to the flourishing of ordinary persons. *Diakonia* is a way of life that Jesus incarnated and, in turn, expects of his disciples.

Remembering that I seek to address lay leaders and pastors of the Baby Boomer and Gen X generations, I *first* will trace briefly the biblical mandates for *diakonia*; then explore that identifying affirmation of Jesus, who claimed, "I am among you as one who serves" (Luke 22:27).

Next, with biblical and theological affirmations in tow, I intend (a) to suggest sample illustrations of how congregations take on ministries of compassion in their communities; (b) to address how congregational-based disciples confront degrading social and cultural systems of our era; and, finally, (c) to outline the cross-cultural mission ventures that preoccupy many congregations in our day. Throughout this chapter we will hear echoes of Dietrich Bonhoeffer's ultimate maxim for Christian communities: "The Church is the Church only when it exists for others" (Bonhoeffer, 1972, 382).

Biblical Mandates for Diakonia

The Greek word *diakonia* in the New Testament (NT) is a fluid term.[1] Basically, *diakonia* means "service," or, in some specific contexts, "service at table" or "waiting at tables, serving food, pouring wine." In a more expansive sense, *diakonia* usually means caring for the physical needs of others. It implies a service that connects available resources to crippling human needs.

The New Testament records that the disciples in those earliest,

---

1. The word *diakonia* can be understood as "acts of mercy; service to neighbors, especially those who are the 'least'; service to creation; and service to the whole community." See G. Kittel's *Theological Dictionary*, vol. 2, 81-93.

post-Pentecost Christian congregations "would sell their possessions and goods and distribute the proceeds to all, as any had need" (Acts 2:45). According to Acts 6, seven persons, "full of the Holy Spirit and wisdom," were appointed to the tasks of serving (*diakonia*) others who were neglected and hungry. Thus, the office of deacon, whose title was derived from the term *diakonia*, was established in the earliest Christian communities.[2]

But modern readers of the New Testament, like those of the first century, cannot miss the startling, if not radical, implications of *diakonia*. The title of "servant" in the first century carried nuances of "inferior status."

Within the hierarchies of Greco-Roman society, no bona fide leader or religious person should ever be called "servant." "Busboys" or "water carriers" or "hewers of wood" carried no societal clout. It was counter-cultural, if not jarring, when Jesus said to his disciples:

> The kings of Gentiles lord it over them, and those in authority over them are called benefactors. But not so with you; rather the greatest among you must become like the youngest, and the leader like one who serves. For who is greater, the one who is at the table or the one who serves? Is it not the one at the table? But I am among you as one who serves. (Luke 22:25-27)

Few incidents in the Gospels reveal what Jesus meant by serving than when Jesus got up from the table, took off his robe, tied a towel around himself, poured water into a basin, and washed the disciples' feet (John 13). It was a dramatic inversion of social status. The one entitled to being served, serves. Not long afterward, Jesus elevated

---

2. One can trace the emerging office of deacon. *Diakonia* described (1) the collection and distribution of monies to needful communities in Corinth and Jerusalem (2 Cor. 8:1-6; Rom. 15:25, 30); (2) the help Timothy and Erastus gave to the apostle Paul (Acts 19:22); (3) unspecified acts of love that Christians showed to one another (1 Cor. 16:15; Heb. 6:10; Rev. 2:19). (4) In 1 Peter 4 the building up of the Christian community was deemed *diakonia*; and (5) in that pivotal New Testament letter on the nature of the church, the book of Ephesians, Paul urges congregational leaders to "equip the saints for the work of ministry (*diakonia*)." Summarizing the NT's message, one scholar and churchman, James McCord, writes: "The service [*diakonia*] which Christians, individually and corporately, offer to their neighbors springs from their relationship and obedience to Jesus Christ as Lord" (McCord, 99).

diakonia to another level when he said of himself, "For the Son of Man came not to be served but to serve, and to give his life a ransom for many" (Mark 10:45). Little wonder that the apostle Paul was awestruck when he wrote to the church in Philippi,

> Let the same mind be in you that was in Christ Jesus, who, though he was in the form of God, did not regard equality with God as something to be exploited, but emptied himself, taking the form of a slave [servant], being born in human likeness. (Phil. 2:5-7)

Not surprisingly, Christians down through the ages believe Jesus' crucifixion to be the ultimate expression of *diakonia*.

In light of this New Testament background, *diakonia* is a distinguishing marker of Christian discipleship. According Matthew 25, service to others, especially those are who are the "least" — the hungry, stranger, sick, prisoner — is equated with a disciple's devotion to Jesus himself. The Reformer John Calvin insisted, "It is impossible for us to wound, despise, reject, injure or in any way to offend one of our brethren but we, at the same time, wound, despise, reject, injure and offend Christ in him.... We cannot love Christ without loving him in our brethren."

Said in another way, the same gospel that ensures our union with Christ simultaneously incorporates a divine directive to shape a congregation's mission around serving and healing, justice seeking and generosity. The distinctive lifestyle of both individual Christians and Christian communities is demonstrated — witnessed to — when hope is restored to impoverished and powerless persons in their societies.

Thus, when congregations "go public" with their faith through the practices of *diakonia*, the biblical word for "ministry," they become participants in the kingdom of God "on earth as it is in heaven." Again, *diakonia* is the counterpart of *martyria*, and it is sustained through a congregation's practices of *koinonia*. Without *diakonia*, a congregation's *martyria* lacks integrity; without *koinonia*, it risks exhaustion. More serious, without *diakonia* Christian congregations opt out of their privilege to partner in the coming of the kingdom (or reign) of God.

Diakonia is not, then, some voluntary mission program that a Christian congregation freely chooses or neglects. As one theologian maintains, "The Church cannot withdraw from [human] affliction and suffering … without contracting out of its witness and betraying its Lord."

Leaders of congregations are deeply misinformed and misguided if they merely arrange for church members to ruminate about the Bible or fellowship with one another, while, at the same time, neglect to address their surrounding society's debilitating issues such as injurious poverty, homelessness, and demeaning racial/prejudicial structures.

In our own day, Martin Luther King Jr. put the *diakonia* challenge succinctly: "Life's most persistent and urgent question is, 'What have you done for others?'"

In the remainder of this chapter, I want explore how mainline congregations engage the human deprivations in their host communities and, thereby, participate as partners in the coming reign of God. Afterward, I will turn from abstract analyses to concrete illustrations in three arenas of congregational missional practices where gospel-prompted *diakonia* gains traction.

Diakonia among Mainline Protestants

Assessments of the practices of *diakonia* in mainline American Protestant congregations in the last half of the twentieth century are extensive.[3]

According to a massive survey taken in 2008 and 2009 (known as the U.S. Congregational Life Survey, with some 500,000 participants), many worshipers acted as "good neighbors." For example, 73 percent donated money to charitable organizations; 50 percent donated food to others; 28 percent loaned money to someone outside their own family; and 22 percent provided care for others who were very sick.

Participation in more corporative ways was different. Only 20 percent of the worshipers reported they worked with others to solve

---

3. Several sociologists seek to measure the dollar value of services offered by congregations. See especially Ram A. Cnaan, *The Invisible Caring Hand: American Congregations and the Provision of Welfare* (2002). This book discusses how American congregations became the hidden safety net of the American welfare system.

a community problem, and only 22 percent reported they participated in political and social justice activities (Woolever, 2010, 71-72).

Mark Chaves's earlier study of 1,200 American congregations came to another assessment: "[In] congregations with some social service programming, only ten individuals on average are involved as volunteers in those activities" (Chaves, 2004, 203). Chaves surveyed these same congregations later, in 2008, and did not find a meaningful change in members' civic involvement.[4]

In a collection of essays, *The Quiet Hand of God: Faith-Based Activism and the Public Role of Mainline Protestants* (2002), edited by Robert Wuthnow and John Evans, several sociologists tracked how mainline Protestants participated "quietly" in American public life. They tallied and summarized many of the current practices of *diakonia* in typical mainline congregations across the nation. Below are a few of their findings:

- While the vast majority of American congregations place a high priority on worship and fellowship along with the spiritual well-being of members, those same members also believe their congregation has public responsibilities in their communities. But they usually affirm that those responsibilities are best undertaken by inspiring members to take seriously their roles as citizens (p. 131).
- The emerging strategy for *diakonia* among mainline congregations is that of networking. "Increasingly the model of church life [among mainline congregations] becomes that of network, or referral system" (p. 19). In contrast to more independent congregations, mainline congregations tend to be more willing to build connections with nearby secular social agencies and nonprofit

4. Mark Chaves has also found that the "faith-based initiatives" begun in 1996 during the presidencies of Clinton and Bush made little impact on congregations and did not prompt congregations to get more involved in providing social services in their communities. The one exception to this generalization was in disaster relief. In 2006, Chaves found that 13 percent of congregations reported providing assistance following the 2005 Hurricane Katrina disaster in Louisiana and Mississippi. He concluded that congregations were most effective when collaborating with outside organizations such as Habitat for Humanity and were at their best when mobilizing "small groups of volunteers carrying out well-defined, limited tasks." See Chaves's summary article in *The Christian Century*, June 1, 2010, 22-24.

organizations. However, mainline churches tend to rely on their members who already hold influential positions in their "communities' civic hierarchies" (p. 124).

- As the gap between smaller and larger mainline congregations increases and as many smaller congregations struggle to survive, members in larger congregations are generally more willing to "mount a wider variety of social programs than smaller churches have sponsored in the past" (p. 19). Numerically smaller, maintenance-oriented congregations *appear* to be increasingly "self-contained." There are, of course, many and notable exceptions to these generalizations.
- There seems to be a correlation between the age of congregations and the *diakonia* services engaged. Strangely, more recently founded congregations are, apparently, *less* "civically engaged than older ones."
- While mainline congregations are more likely to promote social services, sponsor forums about public issues, open their buildings to community groups, and provide day-care centers for children, they are not, in general, more likely to engage directly in politics and legal entanglements. Accordingly, it is more acceptable for clergy to preach on broad social and moral issues that can be related to biblical themes than to speak directly about [particular] political issues (p. 387).

Wuthnow draws his own summary of the practices of *diakonia* in American congregational life. He concludes that most members of mainline congregations prefer to work more quietly, at the local level, especially by doing volunteer work in their communities, attending lectures about social issues, and supporting congregational activities like soup kitchens and day-care centers.

Mainliner Protestants, Wuthnow finds, do not draw high walls between themselves and the rest of society. However, because they often occupy relatively privileged places in their communities, mainline members usually believe they can be politically and socially influential in ways other than participating in religiously motivated movements in political arenas (p. 401).

Wuthnow adds a downside dimension to this "quiet" style of *diakonia* among mainline Protestants. He claims it often yields to a complacency toward broader social, economic, and political systems.

In the same summary he notes that evangelical Protestants are more willing to engage a "more activist political style" (p. 394).

With these sociologists' analyses lurking in the background, I turn to a gospel-derived, Spirit-empowered *diakonia* that can encourage a missional-based agenda for contemporary Protestant congregations. Three programmatic efforts can help fulfill that agenda: (1) creative acts of compassion in a congregation's surrounding community; (2) cooperative efforts to redress and change local social and cultural systems that perpetuate injustices; and (3) missional efforts across cultural boundaries.

The congregational *diakonia* practices outlined below are a very small sampling of the "quiet hand of God" at work. However limited and selective, they are illustrations of bona fide samples of compassion and justice-seeking ministries that I have investigated and, along with others, can vouch for their effectiveness.

1. Practicing Diakonia: *Creative Acts of Compassion*

Most congregations tailor their diaconal or service-oriented responses to the particulars of the socio-cultural realities of their host communities. Even the most thriving congregations concentrate on a few significant issues, or even a single one, in their host communities.

Obviously, the *diakonia* of rural congregations will evolve in different ways from those of inner-city congregations. However the practices of *diakonia* are conditioned by "local-option" preferences, the end result — helping persons to flourish — remains the common vision for many faithful congregations. Below are examples that illustrate how a few mainline congregations act out their faith in a diaconal way. They are ministries I have observed and respect.

(1) The building of the North Presbyterian Church in Kalamazoo, Michigan, is located near the neighborhood once dominated by the Western Michigan Psychiatric Hospital. During the 1980s, when the "chemical revolution" for treating mentally ill persons flourished, inmates of the hospital were flushed out. Some evacuees had no families to take them in, many were without the promise of employment, and most possessed only meager financial resources to make a new start in life. Under the extraordinary leadership of two compassion-

ate and Spirit-filled pastors and over a period of two decades, North Presbyterian church, with a membership of only 150 persons, refined and focused its ministry around the needs of those patients the hospital turned away. Many former patients became members, and several emerged as leaders in the congregation.[5]

(2) In November 1994, a small group of Midwest, mainline Christians launched a *diakonia*-based ministry now known as Kids Hope USA. The founding vision was to involve 500 churches across America who would embrace an opportunity to form "Jesus-with-skin-on relationships" with 100,000 at-risk public elementary school children. Out of that original vision, some 440 U.S. congregations became involved by 2010.

The Kids Hope program emphasizes the "power of one": one congregation, in one school, where one mentor meets once a week with one at-risk child for one hour. Each mentor has one prayer partner who prays for the child-mentor relationship. Required training seminars for local coordinators, mentors, and prayer partners are conducted by regional representatives of the Kids Hope organization. Following prescribed procedures, local leaders of this program annually assess the accomplishments of this diaconal ministry. Some of their evaluations can be followed on the Kids Hope USA website, KidsHopeUSA.org.

(3) For nearly two decades I lived in the quiet, bucolic university town of Princeton, New Jersey. Within ten miles of our home, a post–World War II and economic blight slowly descended on New Jersey's capital city, Trenton. By the last quarter of the twentieth century, it was estimated that nearly one-third of the citizens in the greater-Trenton area received 90 percent of their income from Social Security benefits and other state welfare agencies.

In the late 1980s a "dream team" from three area congregations gathered to combine their imaginations and energies in order to address the daunting issues of hunger and homelessness prevalent in their neighborhoods. Grounded in the historical practices of almsgiving and Jesus' mandate in the Gospels (especially Matthew 25), this small ecumenical group decided to focus on assisting low-income persons who had exhausted their financial resources.

5. I am indebted for this information to the Rev. Robert Rasmussen and the Rev. Dr. Fred Cunningham, pastors of this congregation.

According to one of the founding pastors, the new organization's goal was to "partner with others to secure food, housing, and employment for our neighbors in need." Eventually this "Crisis Ministry," as it came to be called, expanded organizationally and financially.

Eventually, by 2003, a Methodist pastor led a staff of volunteers and coordinated an ecumenical coalition of some thirty-five Jewish and Christian communities. Their current mission statement speaks of a determination to provide food for people in need; help with back rent for people facing eviction; provide security deposits for homeless people seeking to rent; assist with utility payments for people facing shut-off notices; and fund prescription medication for persons who have no other method of payment. The ministry's website links to dozens of local and national agencies engaged in similar ministries and advocacy. Members of congregations in the Princeton and greater-Trenton area have repeatedly testified that they learned best how and where to serve by first serving.[6]

(4) A Lutheran (ELCA) congregation of this author's acquaintance participates in a nationally prominent program called Interfaith Homeless Network (IHN). Three or four times a year this congregation provides safe, weeklong, hospitable shelter for homeless families. A small army of volunteers are coached and equipped with clear job descriptions to serve as local hosts in an efficient and gracious manner. Church classrooms are turned into bedrooms, a volunteer kitchen staff provides evening meals, and other members do laundry. The goal of this ministry is to provide temporary shelter for families until independent housing can be secured. IHN recruits other congregations in the city to ensure yearlong coverage for homeless families.

This particular ELCA congregation's housing program has been eminently successful. In 2010, 93 percent of the families served found permanent housing. The church's website claims this diaconal ministry is one way these church members "live out our faith by reaching hurting people.... It is about giving ourselves, gifting others with our time, helping by our physical presence."[7]

(5) The Kids' Food Basket (KFB) program in Grand Rapids,

6. See their website at www.thecrisisministry.org.
7. The home website of the IHN national program is www.familypromise.org. This particular Lutheran congregation's website is www.tlcgr.org.

Michigan, is an example of an organization that is not affiliated with a church or denomination but that involves many volunteers from local congregations.

KFB's expressed purpose is to address the acute and growing scandal of hunger among children of the city. On a per-capita basis, more Grand Rapids children are "food insecure" than children in Detroit or Chicago. By 2012, KFB's budget reached $1.4 million and the ministry now requires six paid staff persons.

Recognizing that children need some 3,000 calories a day to develop mentally and physically, KFB's evening meals provide one-third of a child's daily caloric needs. Funded by a variety of community sources, more than 6,000 sack suppers were prepared in a central location and then delivered to 32 city schools every day of the school year in 2012. This impressive social service organization is an example of Robert Wuthnow's "quiet hand" strategy mentioned above, where members of congregations connect with secular social agencies and nonprofit organizations to address local civic issues.[8]

(6) In a mid-sized city in northern Michigan, several congregations band together to address human needs with a "one-stop shopping" event on four Saturdays each year. Members of participating congregations shuttle visitors from various parts of the city. In addition to providing a food pantry and free clothing boutique, the churches recruit local physicians, dentists, chiropractors, optometrists, bankers, and lawyers to provide on-site advice as to where appropriate professional services are available in the city. Persons knowledgeable about local social service agencies sit at tables, dispensing helpful information.

When asked by a newspaper reporter where church leaders derived the idea for this event, the organizers said they learned how to do it by observing and copying the procedures of art festivals in and around their city and county.

Scholars who track *diakonia* practices do raise words of caution. A growing number of studies express some hesitancy, if not concern, about the styles and practices of some well-intentioned congregations that seek to share their largesse with surrounding impoverished communities. In her street-savvy book *Restorers of Hope*,

8. See the Kids' Food Basket website at www.kidsfoodbasket.org.

Amy Sherman details her understanding of New Testament *diako-nia*.[9] She envisions God's people as "Restorers," that is, as church members who

> treat needy people personally, flexibly, and creatively.... [They] build friendships with the disadvantaged while addressing people's personal, emotional, intellectual, and spiritual needs. [The challenge facing current church leaders] lies in redirecting their church's outreach to go beyond conventional commodity-based ministries to more relational development ones. (Sherman, 7, 136)

More cautious is Robert Lupton's *Toxic Charity: How Churches and Charities Hurt Those They Help (and How to Reverse It)* (2011). Lupton is the founder of FCS Urban Ministries (Focused Community Strategies) in inner-city Atlanta, Georgia, and author of the widely circulated monthly publication *Urban Perspectives*.[10]

Lupton finds that well-intentioned charity efforts administered by churches can become harmful to those they are striving to help. Out of forty years of experience and in-depth research in a single neighborhood, Lupton has assembled several guiding principles for congregations pursuing involvement with their impoverished neighbors. I have adapted and edited a few of his proverbs from his book and other publications:

- Discern if the need is a crisis or a chronic problem. If a crisis, then act; if the need is chronic, then help persons rebuild by planning a future with them.
- Exchange is better than giving. One-way charity often erodes human dignity.
- Lending is better than giving. Giving multiple times creates a humiliating dependency.
- Never do for others what they can do for themselves. "Compassionate intervention" can short-cut another's empowerment.
- Listen to what is not being said. Like good physicians, effective helpers listen, observe, question, and intuit.

9. See Sherman's website at www.centeronfic.org.
10. To learn more about this seasoned urban ministry, visit www.fcsministries.org.

In their research and grass-roots experience, both Sherman and Lupton insist that the vital signs of Christian *diakonia* point to initiating and maintaining relationships with impoverished and alienated neighbors. Both authors readily recognize that such relationships are "tall orders" for many mainline Protestants. Yet both affirm, with biblical wisdom, "the poor and the privileged need each other."

2. Practicing Diakonia: *Advocating for Community Change*

The "kingdom of God" is the gospel extended into every aspect of every realm of human life. When we pray "Thy kingdom come," we are praying that our world will open up to God's love and God's way. It is the petition that God will direct and give meaning to all human affairs and conditions.

As mentioned in chapter 3, some denominational manuals of operation designate congregations as "provisional expressions of the kingdom of God." Lofty as that label may sound, there are at least two distinctive features in those "provisional expressions" that will signal God's reign. First, Jesus repeatedly reminded his disciples that God's coming kingdom often arrives in unexpected ways. This kingdom, Jesus said, is like a tiny mustard seed that quietly grows and sprouts branches where birds can nest (Mark 5:30). When ordinary people do extraordinary services, take extraordinary risks, and thereby love their neighbors, they are, as Jesus once said of a devout inquirer, "not far from the kingdom of God" (Mark 12:34).

Justice seeking is the *second* dimension of a congregation's "provisional expression" of the kingdom of God. Justice is what love looks like in public arenas, and biblically understood justice has a distinctive agenda. Across the pages of Scripture, the people of God are repeatedly called to seek a fairer justice for those least cared about and excluded — most notably, the widow, the orphan, the alien, and the poor. As Nicholas Woltersdorff points out, love and justice converge when all persons' rights are honored because those rights are grounded in a loving God who created humans in God's own image.[11]

---

11. Wolterstorff has written extensively and passionately about the convergence of Christian love, justice, and human rights. One place to begin is his essay "Justice,

It is patently naïve for congregations to assume that the church can dismantle the complex, multiple political and social powers in American society that limit human flourishing. On the other hand, one notable sociologist finds, many congregations can respond to the kingdom's call through "*constructive subversion* [of those] frameworks of social life that are incompatible with the *shalom* for which we are made and to which we are called" (James D. Hunter, *To Change the World: the Irony, Tragedy, and Possibility of Christianity in the Late Modern Age*. Oxford University Press, 2010, p. 235. Emphasis his).

Below are three examples of contemporary congregations I know which engage in "constructive subversion." Please note that each of these *diakonia* initiatives required different "subversive" strategies and the mobilizing of multiple resources.

Housing for the Homeless Grand Rapids, Michigan, where I was a Presbyterian pastor, was increasingly plagued in the post–World War II decades by the collapse of affordable housing for a spreading urban population. In the late 1970s, three members of our congregation — a charismatic accountant, a laid-back bank mortgage officer, and a visionary associate pastor — partnered with a nearby Roman Catholic real estate agent and dared to take on the dehumanizing local issues of homelessness and substandard housing.

Together, with the help of other concerned friends, they walked dark streets, interviewed apartment dwellers, petitioned local zoning boards, solicited cooperation from other congregations, lobbied at city hall, and sought funds from denominations and local foundations. They focused their energies by concentrating on the spread of decrepit housing in a section of the city-center referred to as the "Heartside Neighborhood."

Walking as much by faith as by professional experience, they met weekly, early on Tuesday mornings, for prayer and divine guidance. They eventually called their dream project "Dwelling Place," a title derived from Psalm 90, incorporating in 1980.

After securing further denominational funding and gaining endorsement from governmental bureaucracies, they purchased and refurbished a 45-room defunct hotel and, later, acquired two

---

not Charity: Social Work Through the Eyes of Faith," found in *Hearing the Call: Liturgy, Justice, Church, and World*, ed. by Mark R. Gornik and G. Thompson (2011), 395-410.

nearby abandoned warehouses to create 300 safe and affordable apartments.

Nearly thirty years after that start-up, Dwelling Place owns more than 1,300 housing units. As an independent, nonprofit corporation, it is currently guided by a volunteer board of directors and managed day-to-day by a paid professional staff. Its talented executive director has been in place for two decades.

While the housing ministry for the homeless continues, Dwelling Place satellite ministries now include medical care, employment offices, and specialized housing for people who have mental illness.

As the initiatives of Dwelling Place evolved, persons from many center-city congregations working in concert with dozens of other leaders and agencies acted as "subversive advocates" within the political and economic networks of the city. Today hundreds of impoverished inner-city residents have a "dwelling place" of their own. Along the way, a threatened neighborhood was revitalized. Open spaces, affordable housing, restaurants, banks, and other vital urban services now populate the Heartside Neighborhood.[12]

Safety on Our Streets In 2007, a gathering of six local pastors from diverse religious communities banded together to address escalating street violence in the Michigan city of Flint. What emerged in that economically depressed community was an organization called FACT, or Flint Area Congregations Together.

FACTs earliest initiatives focused on the reduction of violence and the promotion of safety in public places, especially on the city's streets. To that end, pastors and parishioners explicitly urged — pressured — the mayor, the police department, schools, and other governmental agencies to address this crippling environment. Help with strategies came from representatives from the PICO National Network of faith-based community organizers. The Flint group's initial agenda has since expanded to address other civic issues affecting Flint's future, such as school improvement, neighborhood revitalization initiatives, and securing financial resources at the state's capital in Lansing.

12. For a history and current initiatives of this organization, see www.dwelling-placegr.org. The Flint Area Congregations Together website can be found at www.flintfact.org.

In 2013, twenty-seven Flint churches — including Baptists, Catholics, African Methodist Episcopal, Unitarians, and Presbyterians — participated in FACT's expanding initiatives, funding, and political lobbying.

Just Policies for Immigrants It is now a commonly accepted view that if substantive, nationwide changes are to address the injustices in American society, those changes will be accomplished mostly through lobbying government representatives and the imposition of new laws.

Only with the passage of the Civil Rights Act in 1964 was the blatant discrimination toward African Americans and other racial minorities curtailed and fuller access to this nation's political systems and leadership opened. While few would deny the strategic role that American churches played in that cultural revolution, it was governmental action, in the end, that reversed centuries of discriminatory practices.

With that heritage clearly in mind, many current mainline denominations are now seeking to mobilize and equip leaders in congregations to address current unjust laws and exclusionary practices that impede the flourishing of immigrant persons in American society.

In a quest for a "just immigration policy," several denominations, such as the Presbyterian Church (USA), now provide training workshops to suggest ways congregations and their leaders can address the unjust local and federal policies affecting thousands of immigrants, many of whom reside in the neighborhoods of mainline congregations. These workshops usually cover a theology of hospitality, community organizing skills, and procedures to identify immigration issues in a congregation's local context.[13]

Again, these very few examples of "constructive subversion" exemplify how congregations can become advocates for justice in public arenas. At the same time, they illustrate how mobilizing gifted

13. For further details see http://oga.pcusa.org/media/uploads/oga/pdf/network. The United Methodist Bishop Minerva Marano of California leads the United Methodist Interagency Task Force on Immigration and recently headed a direct appeal to President Obama in March 2013 to facilitate immigration policy reform for some 11 million undocumented immigrants in the United States.

and informed church members can initiate the implementation of *diakonia* in wider public arenas.

3. Practicing Diakonia in Cross-Cultural Contexts

From the church's earliest endeavors recorded in Acts, Jesus' disciples realized their mission to the wider Greco-Roman world would become, inevitably, cross-cultural. While the gospel is normative for all persons, in all ages and in all cultures, the expression and interpretation of that gospel is always conditioned by localized language and societal protocols. Within the past several decades, federal programs such as the Peace Corps and Americorps, as well as para-church organizations such as World Vision, Bread for the World, and Doctors Without Borders, have helped sensitize American churches to the realities and promises of globalization.

At the same time, scholars of world Christianity have now traced the transitions of the population centers of Christianity to South America, Sub-Saharan Africa, and nations of east Asia. In response, many globally sensitive congregations now design and implement "mission trips" labeled as "Short Term Mission" trips or STMs. Such STMs sponsored by congregations are now widespread and growing. To equip congregations, independent organizations and most denominational headquarters now produce abundant resources and sponsor training opportunities to assist congregations to facilitate such trips.

Among many other foci, church sponsored STM participants have cared for orphans, held Bible classes, evangelized, painted homes and church buildings, and cared for AIDs patients. Some American groups went as far away as China, Thailand, and Russia.[14]

Some church leaders and sociologists, however, have begun to wonder whether STMs are really transformative or whether they

14. The literature about STMs is also burgeoning. See the national association Alliance for Excellence in Short Term Missions for resources, conferences, and trends (www.aestm.org). Don C. Richter's *Mission Trips that Matter: Embodied Faith for the Sake of the World* (2008) can help congregational leaders to plan, guide, reflect, and evaluate their mission trips. Jann Treadwell, a seasoned Christian educator, offers practical ways to put together STMs and recounts the "transformative power" experienced in youth mission trips. See www.unboundmissiontrips.com.

sometimes simply operate as a sort of ecclesial tourism. In one instance, so reports a denominational magazine, a group traveling to the Sudan spent $37,000 on plane tickets and donated only $5,000 for construction costs. Another informed observer writing for *The Christian Century* regretted that "poorly conceived trips can distract hosts from their primary ministries, use up significant sums of money and energy on low-priority tasks, and create unreasonable expectations for visible results in a short period of time" (Radecke, 22).

In a review of thirteen in-depth studies of STMs, sociologist Kurt Ver Beek found "little or no positive [and enduring] impact from the STM trips in the lives of the participants" when that impact is measured by the criteria of (1) continued intercessory prayer, (2) further study about local social and political issues, and (3) sustained financial contributions sent abroad. On one occasion, Ver Beek noted, STM participants in Honduras spent $30,000 in order to construct one house that would cost $2,000 if built by local workers. Unless there were longer-ranged, accountable relationships between visitors and those visited, Ver Beek concluded, the impact of a STM quickly waned.[15]

Acknowledging the potential downside of STMs, there are numerous accounts of *positive* cross-cultural mission trips. Only two exemplary STMs will be cited here. Both of these, which I have personally witnessed, are excellent examples of cross-cultural *diakonia* put into practice.

(1) Every year during the past decade, a smaller Midwest congregation sponsors a ten-day house-building mission trip to an impoverished village in Michigan's sparsely populated Upper Peninsula. Each year, during the winter and spring, materials for one house are gathered and pre-prepped. Then, in early summer, some two dozen youth, college students, and carpenter-savvy adults travel north to "rough in" one house to the point where it is ready for occupancy. Earlier communications with social workers and housing authorities help identify the location and prospective occupants.

While on site, mission volunteers visit with the future homeowners, some of whom help with the construction chores. Intergen-

15. Calvin College sociology professor Kurt Ver Beek's research and surveys can be found in Robert Priest, ed. *Effective Engagement in Short-Term Missions: Doing It Right* (2012).

erational volunteers are commissioned in a worship service before they leave home, and they report to the congregation after they return. During the trip, daily devotions and evening reflections often reveal the Spirit's promptings and assurance. Bonds of friendship among co-workers naturally emerge and usually endure. Back home some have testified that they "experienced God and the meaning of being Christian for the first time." It is no surprise that recruiting both adults and teenagers for these work trips is rarely difficult.

(2) A mid-sized mainline congregation in New Jersey has maintained a ministry of compassion and justice in Haiti, the most impoverished republic in the Western Hemisphere. Some three decades ago, a few members of the congregation made contact with Pastor Luc Deratus and his "Harmony Ministries," near Port-au-Prince. An enduring relationship began when the New Jersey congregation sponsored a modest fund drive to purchase goats for the village near Pastor Luc's school.

In subsequent years, as cross-cultural friendships deepened, groups of parishioners have traveled annually to Haiti and, in the past decade, have established a medical clinic, refurbished church buildings, started a food pantry, and distributed medicines, clothing, and school supplies. In 1999, when Pastor Luc lacked funds to hire additional teachers, the congregation responded with a successful "Sponsor-a-Student" campaign. The following year, some 200 students attended the Haitian school.

This cross-cultural ministry remains committed to reciprocity and collegiality. Every other year, Pastor Luc preaches and teaches in the New Jersey congregation. Since the tragic earthquake in Haiti in January 2010, six other congregations have teamed up with the founding congregation and expanded this diaconal mission. This enlarged group of congregations, in accord with the leaders of Harmony Ministries, has recently launched plans and funding to design and build a new educational facility.

Several common characteristics at work in these two missional endeavors make them noteworthy. Each of them started with manageable, attainable goals; avoided sponsoring annual mission trips to multiple locations; cultivated friendships with residents who were, in varying degrees, culturally different from themselves; maintained reciprocal involvements; and experienced the joys and meaningfulness of serving in God's coming kingdom.

A Summary Theological Perspective:
Diakonia as *Missio Dei* (the Mission of God)

During the closing decades of the twentieth century, countless numbers of Protestant theologians and denominational leaders pressed mainline congregations to expand the theological horizons implicit in *diakonia*. At issue is whether leaders of congregations understand the practices of *diakonia* as a few local programmatic service-oriented ventures *or* as their mission as servants in the coming kingdom of God, where justice and *shalom* flourish.

Jürgen Moltmann is one prominent voice urging churches to identify their mission "as participation in the history of God's dealings the world" (Moltmann, 1977, 65). The biblical scholar C. J. H. Wright offers another but similar perspective: "Mission (if biblically informed and validated) means our committed participation as God's people, at God's invitation and command, in God's own mission within the history of God's world for the redemption of God's creation" (Quoted in Van Gelder, 101).

Illuminating every congregation's missional efforts is Jesus' own summation of his *and* his disciples' mission: "'As the Father has sent me, so I send you.' ... He breathed on them and said to them, 'Receive the Holy Spirit'" (John 20:21-22).

A prayer from the Church in Wales gives that understanding of *diakonia* a final blessing. It is called the *Missio Dei* Prayer:

> God the Sender, send us,
> God the Sent, come with us,
> God the Strengthener of those who go, empower us,
> that we may go with you
> and find those who will call you
> Father, Son, and Holy Spirit
> (from *Prayers Encircling the World*, 1998).

CHAPTER 9

Practicing the Arts of Worship —
Word, Sacraments, Prayer
....
Leitourgia, PART ONE

They devoted themselves to ... the prayers. ... [And] as they spent much time together in the temple, they broke bread at home.

— ACTS 2:42, 46

"Worship is the point of concentration," wrote the distinguished authority Geoffrey Wainwright, "at which the whole of the Christian life comes into ritual focus" (Wainwright, 1980, 8). Thus, with *leitourgia*, or worship, we arrive at the last of the five gospel-driven faithful practices of Christian congregations.[1]

It comes last, but not because it is least. On the contrary, worship is the ultimate faithful practice. As an intentional response to the gospel, worship enfolds, enables, and critiques all the other practices addressed in this book. Many call worship the parent of every other faithful practice.

In worship, Christians learn what we are to believe, say, and do in God's world. With the gospel as its heart, Christian worship simultaneously expresses and forms our faith. Little wonder that in her sem-

---

1. In this chapter I employ *leitourgia* as a synonym for public or corporate Christian worship. *Leitourgia* derives from two Greek words, *leitos* ("concerning the people") and *ergon* ("work or service"). The word later developed into the equivalent of "the public service or work for another." Christian *leitourgia* is the "work of the people," offered as service to God. Further, since the first century CE, Christian communities have used the word "liturgy" (derived from *leitourgia*) as a generalized term for patterns of communal worship services as well as for specific rites and structures employed in many Christian traditions.

inal study *Congregations and Community,* Nancy Ammerman concluded that "worship is an event that is meant to express the unifying vision of a congregation" (Ammerman, 1997, 55).

During the past several decades, however, mainline Protestant worship practices in America have come under relentless vetting. Prompted in part by encounters with other churches in which casual atmospheres, minimalist symbols, and electronic media prevail, some mainline church leaders have lost confidence in traditional practices. Others believe that new worship practices will attract new faces into the life of their congregations. Not infrequently, murmurings circulate. Tensions escalate into "worship wars." Tracing these controversies is outside the boundaries of this chapter, though detailed chronicling can be found elsewhere.[2]

In this chapter, however, I offer several theological affirmations for the shaping of Christian worship in a congregation. I believe they can help leaders understand and assess their current worship practices. In the following chapter, I will emphasize leaders' responsibility to oversee congregational worship in three venues: worship of the gathered community; worship across the congregation in family settings; and the personal or private worship of each member.

Before launching into the daunting issues surrounding Christian worship, leaders can profit by listening to a few social scientists who, over the past two decades, have held stethoscopes to the spiritual heartbeats of American society.

Revisiting Worship Across the American Landscape

In the mid-1990s, the distinguished American historian of religions and television commentator the late Houston Smith once asked a group of pastors and professors, "What is it that the church has that cannot be gotten elsewhere?"

Smith, the son of Methodist missionary parents in China and a frequent visitor in American congregations, observed,

2. To trace these skirmishes, see Thomas G. Long's wise and witty work *Beyond the Worship Wars: Building Vital and Faithful Worship* (2001).

If people do not hear from mainline churches the news of a world that is vastly more real than the one we normally experience, they will go where they do hear that news.... Mainline churches are good at good works and social action, and pretty good at community formation, but parishioners can fill these needs in other ways. And many do (quoted in Marty 1995, 5).

Wave after wave of sociological evidence supports Smith's barbed comment. While Americans, both inside and outside churches, long for "an encounter with the Transcendent," many are not, apparently, experiencing that encounter in traditional, mainline congregations' worship services.

A poll conducted in 2005 by Princeton Survey Research Associates (and published in *Newsweek*) found that only 21 percent of persons over 18 years of age said they felt a "strong connection to God" while in a house of worship, and only 2 percent did so while reading a sacred text. Robert Wuthnow's analysis of modern American-styled spirituality has helped clarify the reasons for this drought.

In *After Heaven: Spirituality in America Since the 1950s*, Wuthnow charted an irreversible trend. During the last half of the twentieth century, Americans drifted *from* confidence in sacred institutions and their worship traditions *to* fluid and individualized quests. "Faith is no longer something people inherit but something for which they strive" (Wuthnow 1998, 8).

In a later study, in 2003, Wuthnow found that *private* or *personal* experiences, rather than institutional ones, are now central to many Americans' understanding of what it means to grow spiritually. Nearly 61 percent of Americans believe that "personal experience is the best way to understand God," while only 33 percent say that "church doctrines and teachings are the best way to understand God." Further, 56 percent of the public think "God can be known as people empty their minds and look inside themselves."

Not surprisingly, Wuthnow also found that most contemporary seekers in pursuit of a personal spiritual experience rarely "find enough strength to serve others" or "actually experience the presence of God in their [daily] lives" (Wuthnow 2003, 48).

Identifying Christian Worship

The word "worship" derives from an older English form of "worth-ship." Only an ultimately worthy person, social reality, or natural phenomenon qualifies for one's ultimate allegiance. In worship, we acknowledge the absolute worthiness of the "Other" and, when compared, the relative worthiness of everything else.

At the same time, in worship experiences, humans are drawn to something or someone of immense magnetism. We are fascinated with irresistible beauty and drawn into a mystery beyond ourselves. In Christian worship a confluence of human capacities comes into play. Few have explained that convergence more eloquently or more comprehensively than William Temple, a twentieth-century Archbishop of Canterbury, in England.

> To worship is
>> to quicken the conscience by the holiness of God,
>> to feed the mind with the truth of God,
>> to purge the imagination by the beauty of God,
>> to open the heart to the love of God,
>> to devote the will to the purpose of God.
> All this is gathered up in that emotion which cleanses us from selfishness because it is the most selfless of all emotions — adoration. (Temple, 1942, 30)

This often-quoted, multilayered view of Christian worship may feel out of sync in current American congregations, but I find it an antidote to the frenzied search to identify authentic Christian worship in our day.

Clearly, many mainline Protestant churches are adrift with changing liturgical styles, competing musical aesthetics, and continual experimentation. How, then, are their leaders to choose among the multiple worship options surfacing in contemporary Protestantism?

Fortunately, there is an abundance, perhaps an overload, of resources now available. Every mainline denomination underwrites offices and publications to assist congregational leaders through the maze of options. In addition, a small library of scholars augment the helpful denominational worship resources. Worship leaders can easily consult them to avoid further frustration and indecision.[3]

Founders of Protestantism wrote extensively about worship. In the broadest of terms, worship for them involved a twofold rhythm. Martin Luther said that in Christian worship, "nothing else be done in it than that our dear Lord himself talks to us through His holy word and that we, in turn, talk to him in prayer and songs of praise."

"We are lifted up even to God," wrote John Calvin, "by the exercises [practices] of religion. What is the design of preaching of the word, the sacraments, the holy assemblies and the whole external government of the church, but that we may be united to God?" (Quoted in Dearborn and Coil, 21-22).

The contemporary Christian philosopher, Nicholas Wolterstorff, summarizes worship this way: "Worship is a meeting between God and his people, a meeting in which both parties act — God the initiator and we as the responders" (Wolterstorff 1986, 10).

No responsibility of leaders of congregations is more satisfying or more perplexing than overseeing worship practices for the people

---

3. The literature about Christian worship is so voluminous that it defies easy classification, let alone simplified summations. But congregational leaders need not be paralyzed, since many "entry-level" texts are readily available. Begin with James F. White, *Introduction to Christian Worship* (2001); and Robert E. Webber, *Worship Old and New* (1994). Then move to *Worship at the Next Level*, ed. by Tim A. Dearborn and Scott Coil (2004). This text outlines the issues facing mainline Protestants. See especially the essays by Miroslav Volf ("Worship as Adoration and Action"), Robert Webber ("The Crisis of Evangelical Worship: Authentic Worship in a Changing World"), and John D. Witvliet ("Beyond Style: Rethinking the Role of Music in Worship.") If pressed to make a choice, Webber's book would top my list of nominations.

Of high import is the document prepared for leaders of congregations by the Evangelical Lutheran Church in America, titled *Principles for Worship* (2002). Encyclopedic in scope and style is *The Oxford History of Christian Worship*, ed. by G. Wainwright and K. B. Westerfield Tucker (2006). For the growing interest in cataloging the worship practices around the world, see *Christian Worship Worldwide: Expanding Horizons, Deepening Practices*, ed. by C. E. Farhadian (2007). And worship websites abound. One can begin with www.experiencingworship.com.

Finally, leaders can visit the website of the Calvin Institute of Christian Worship (www.worship.calvin.edu) for a treasure trove of resources. Inquisitive church leaders can enroll in an annual conference each January, at which more than 200 contributors address a variety of worship issues and strategies in North America. See www.worship.calvin.edu/symposium.

of God. The remainder of this chapter will address, however abbreviated, what I understand as the essentials of Christian worship. I call them waypoints. In chapter 10, I will address the responsibilities of leaders to oversee the celebration of worship in three venues in congregations: community gatherings, family circles, and private settings.

Waypoints for Charting Christian Worship in Congregations

Contemporary travelers chart their journeys via Global Positioning Systems (GPS). Integral to GPS planning are waypoints — "ports of call" — that mark favored destinations and define routes. The several worship waypoints marked below are intended to help leaders navigate their way through the currents and crosscurrents of twenty-first-century Christian worship practices. In keeping faith with one of the purposes of this book, I will note several resources and accessible studies for each waypoint.

Waypoint 1: Christian Worship as a Response to the Gospel The biblical scholar Walter Brueggemann once said we Christians are "story-formed creatures." The story that forms our identity and calling is the gospel. As outlined in chapter 3, this gospel — with its essential, expansive, expressed, and experiential dimensions — also gives Christian worship and liturgy their distinctiveness. The striking feature of Christian worship, writes Nicholas Wolterstorff, is that it "focus[es] not just on God's nature but on God's actions which took place in historical time ... [and] in liturgy we imitate the central acts of the biblical narrative" (Wolterstorff, 1990, pp. 128-29). Another theologian, William Dyrness, puts the same affirmation this way:

> One of the boundaries that Christians of all kinds have placed on worship practices reflects the particular narrative to which [Christians are] connected. Christians believe that the practices of worship are to shape the believer *in and through the story of Jesus Christ*. Of course, all Christians also believe that the narrative of this life is vitally connected to God's creation of the world, the call of Israel, and the emerging of the young church in the New Testament. All Christians believe this is more than a morality tale; it is a series of

events that structures all of history, accomplishes salvation, and thus forms a believer's spiritual life. (Dyrness, 48)

When we Christians are at our best in designing worship services, we will seek to make the gospel clear and persuasive.[4]

Authentic Christian worship is jeopardized when congregational leaders neglect the biblically and historically attested gospel and give way to stale and lesser narratives like "themes for today." A savvy observer of American congregations once panned the growing use of the "Hallmark Card Lectionary," where congregations celebrate the likes of Labor Day, Grandparents' Day, National Dairy Week, Mother's Day, Father's Day, Memorial Day, and Independence Day; while others insist on gathering in a church parking lot to "Bless the Bikes" (motorcycles) or on concluding a service with an anointing of a local professional football team.

Little wonder that church leaders of any era can feel uneasy by the sober warning given to the Christian community in Ephesus for abandoning their "first love," namely, the message of the gospel (Rev. 2).

Waypoint 2: Christian Worship Prioritizes the "Means of Grace" — the Word of God, Sacraments, and Prayer For a very long time theologians employed the expression "means of grace" as a shorthand term to summarize the provisions by which God initiates, nurtures, and deepens humans' faith, especially in worship experiences. Each of the means of grace directs our attention to God's action. Most Protestant traditions and confessional statements place three practices as indispensable "means" for worship: the hearing of the Word of God, the receiving of the sacraments, and the offering of prayers. An influential nineteenth-century spokesperson for American Presbyterians, the devout Charles Hodge, put it this way:

> By means of grace are not meant every instrumentality which God may please to make the means of spiritual edification [avail-

---

4. The New Testament scholar Ralph P. Martin finds these primary elements in the worship of Christians in the NT: (1) the centrality of Christ, who embodied the revelation of God as Father and in whose name the worship of God occurred; (2) the awareness of the Holy Spirit; and (3) a responsibility to care for others. See "Patterns of Worship in New Testament Churches," *Journal for the Study of the New Testament* (1989).

able] to his children. The phrase is intended to indicate those institutions which God has ordained to be the *ordinary* channels of
grace, i.e. of the supernatural influences of the Holy Spirit, to the
souls of men. The means of grace, according to the standards of
our Church, are the *Word, sacraments, and prayer.* (Hodge, 466, Emphasis mine)

This revered tradition underscores why these non-negotiable
means of grace are the foundational patterns around which Christian worship in a congregation is centered. When the people of God
gather in response to the gospel, their worship practices and liturgies
are to be ordered in such a way that

- all may listen for the Word of God when the Scriptures are read
  and preached, because the Word of God in Jesus Christ is the
  definitive source of our knowledge of God and God's will for
  humanity;
- all are invited to recall the waters of their baptism when they
  were anointed with the Holy Spirit and incorporated into Christ's
  community, and thereafter, all are invited to sit at the Messiah's
  table, where the "sign and seal" of the gospel of nurturing grace
  is clarified and tasted; and
- all are invited to pray, corporately and individually, alongside of
  our "elder brother," Jesus, who taught that the proper practice of
  prayer begins with the words, "Our Father, who art in heaven...."

These prescribed means of grace, notes Nicholas Wolterstorff, signal
how God is acting here and now. Within the Holy Spirit's intervention and through the liturgy of corporate worship services, we

do not *just* enter the sphere of *God's presence* ... nor *just* enter the
sphere of the *God who acts.* [Through the liturgy we] enter the sphere
of God *here-and-now acting.* In participation of the Lord's Supper ...
[and] in the reading of Scriptures and the preaching of the sermon,
nor do we only hear what God said millennia ago, but God speaking *to us here and now....* And in the greeting, in the benediction,
in the law, in the declaration of pardon, God gives us *here and now*
God's word of grace and God's light for our path. (Wolterstorff,
1985, 67)

Chapter 3 addressed the first two of these means of grace — the Word of God and the sacraments — but a brief comment about prayer as a third "means of grace" is necessary.

In a recently published autobiography, the Methodist theologian Stanley Hauerwas put it this way: "All along, I discovered that the work of theology is the work of prayer.... I hold no conviction more determinatively than the belief that prayer names how God becomes present to us and how we can participate in that presence by praying for others" (Hauerwas, 281).

One of Hauerwas's mentors, Karl Barth, affirmed similarly: "The [Christian] community is constituted as it prays" (Barth 1962, 705). In fact, a recent reappraisal of Barth's entire body of writing concluded that Barth believed "there can be no human knowledge of God and no theological knowledge of our humanity apart from the sustained act of prayer.... His theology and his life manifested what it means to 'begin and end in prayer'" (Barth 2002, ix).

Praying in worship services, as a means of grace, is as varied and vivifying as the worldwide human family. Once, when I served as a guest preacher in a large Christian community in Kathmandu, Nepal, the presiding elder called the people of God to prayer. Immediately, the congregation stood and each congregant began to pray out loud! Rather than a raucous dissonance, a lovely symphony of prayers filled the plainly decorated auditorium. I felt moved and encouraged and joined in this novel (at least for me) practice.

After a while, when the rhythms softened, the elder drew us to a conclusion by inviting us to offer our Lord's Prayer. If I were ever in a pastorate again, I would experiment with this liturgical practice even among reserved, taciturn Presbyterians.

These non-negotiable means of grace for Christian worship properly remind leaders, whether clergy or laity, that they are not totally free to proffer ad hoc worship topics and designer liturgies. In this regard, an insight from the martyred German theologian Dietrich Bonhoeffer is worth pondering. In a letter to an inquisitive but skeptical friend, Bonhoeffer wrote that Christians must be careful of where and when they can presume to encounter God.

> Either I determine the place in which I will find God or I will allow
> God to determine the place where He will be found. If I say where
> God will be, I will always find there a God who in some way corre-

sponds to me, is agreeable to me. But if it is God who says where He will be, then that will truly be a place which, at first, is not agreeable to me at all, which does not fit well with me. That place is the Cross of Christ. And whoever will find God there must draw near to the cross in the manner which the Sermon on the Mount requires. That does not correspond to our nature at all." (Bonhoeffer 1986, 44-45)

Bonhoeffer's observation reminds contemporary congregations what Christians have affirmed from their beginnings. To the Christian community in Corinth the apostle Paul wrote, "For I have decided to know nothing among you except Jesus Christ, and him crucified ... so that your faith might rest not on human wisdom but on the power of God" (1 Cor. 2:2-5).

Waypoint 3: Worship Honors a Wide Range of Human Feelings and Experiences Worship is a passionate affair. In worship, says C. S. Lewis, "we must suppose ourselves to be in perfect love with God — drunk with, drowned in, dissolved by that delight which ... flows from us incessantly in effortless and perfect expression."

Humans praise spontaneously, Lewis noted. "We delight to praise what we enjoy because that praise not merely expresses but completes the enjoyment.... This is so even when our expressions are inadequate, as of course they usually are" (Lewis 1958, 95-96).

While praising God in worship entails multiple human faculties — body movement, intellect, imagination, memory — wholesome worship engages our affectional centers. It invades our emotional reserves. The common biblical word that embraces those centers and reservoirs is "heart."[5] And "the heart has reasons the mind knows not of," opined the French mathematician and philosopher Blaise Pascal.

The language and grammar for heartfelt worship usually begins with the Hebrew Psalms.[6] They have provided vocabulary and mel-

---

5. In the Bible, the word "heart" carries a wide range of meanings. Sometimes "heart" means the seat of human personality and capacities. At other times it refers to humans' center of rationality and decision-making as well as the engine of human emotion and passion. For example, "I will put my law within them, and I will write it on their hearts" (Jer. 31:33). Thus the people of God are called to love God with all their "heart, soul, mind, and strength" (Deut. 6:5; Luke 10:27).

6. For an accessible and insightful introduction, see John D. Witvliet, *The Biblical Psalms in Christian Worship: A Brief Introduction and Guide to Resources* (2007).

ody for Jewish and Christian worship for 2,500 years. What gives the Psalms particular energy and utility is the wide range of human passions expressed in them. They are "stained with the glad sweat of life itself." On the one hand are the psalms of lament. One scholar compares these "Psalms of Disorientation" to American blues music. Here is a small sampling: *forsakenness* ("My God, my God, why have you forsaken me?" Ps. 22); *brokenness* ("Has God forgotten to be gracious?" Ps. 77); *alienation* ("You have caused my companions to shun me ..." Ps. 88); *lament* ("By the rivers of Babylon — there we sat down and ... wept." Ps. 137).

On the other hand, the Psalms are testimonies of exuberance and delight: *pleasure* ("In your presence is fullness of joy; in your right hand are pleasures forevermore." Ps. 16); *gratitude* ("O give thanks to the Lord, for he is good, for his steadfast love endures forever," Ps. 136); *awesomeness* ("Bless the Lord, O my soul. O Lord my God, you are very great. You are clothed with honor and majesty, wrapped in light as with a garment.... [You look] on the earth and it trembles. [You touch] the mountains and they smoke." Ps. 104).

And between the poles of lament and praise are the passions of personal faith: *intimacy* ("The Lord is my shepherd ..." Ps. 23); *guilt* ("Against you, and you alone have I sinned ..." Ps. 51); *self-worth* ("The Lord is my light and my salvation; whom shall I fear?" Ps. 27). Psalm 145 is an unparalleled expression of *hopefulness* and *trust*. In this psalm, attributed to King David, the sovereign God's "kingdom is an everlasting kingdom" and his "dominion endures throughout all generations." At the same time, this sovereign God's "compassion is over all that he has made." Israel's God is "faithful in all his words," "upholds all who are falling," and "satisfies the desire of every living thing."

I list these few Psalm passages in light of the high probability that many parishioners enter corporate worship services with entangled feelings surging beneath cool exteriors. Corporate worship that is coldly cerebral (read: a pacified congregation) or merely informative (read: sermons as lectures) or routinely perfunctory (read: misunderstood rituals) leaves the heart parched, as if were "in a dry and weary land where there is no water" (Ps. 63).

At a deep psychic level, gospel-driven worship generates an irrepressible delight in God. "How lovely is your dwelling place, O LORD of hosts," proclaimed the psalmist, "My soul longs, indeed it faints for the courts of the LORD; my heart and my flesh sing for joy to the living God" (Ps. 84). That Psalm reminded Don E. Saliers of the "delight-taking" in worship. He thought the traditional hymn "Simple Gifts" got it right (Saliers 1998, 33):

> 'Tis the gift to be simple, 'tis the gift to be free,
> 'tis the gift to come down where we ought to be,
> and when we find ourselves in the place just right,
> 'twill be in the valley of love and delight.

Ideally, there can be times in mainline congregations' worship services when God's beauty is so irresistible that we worship God solely for who God is and not bother about what God might or might not do for us. Few have expressed this delight more winsomely than Jonathan Edwards (1703-1758). The young and brilliant Edwards, one of America's premier theologians, once tried to explain to his father this inexpressible sense of beauty when encountering the gracious God:

> I walked abroad alone, in a solitary place in my father's pasture, for contemplation. And as I was walking there, and looking up on the sky and clouds, there came into my mind so sweet a sense of the glorious majesty and grace of God, that I do not know how to express. I seemed to see them both in sweet conjunction; majesty and meekness joined together; it was a sweet and gentle and holy majesty; and also a majestic meekness; an awful sweetness; a high and great and holy gentleness. (Quoted in Faust and Johnson, 60)

Because faith and feelings are so intimately related, the people of God have usually appealed to the arts and sought the assistance of artisans. The employment of the arts in Christian worship is another waypoint.

Waypoint 4: Christian Worship Is Interwoven with — and Enhanced by — the Arts If worship is a passionate affair, then expressions of human feelings in worship belong to the arts and artists. As long as Jews and Christians can remember, poets, musicians, dancers, liturgists, novelists, storytellers, dramatists, iconographers, sculptors, clothiers, filmmakers, and architects were invited into their communities as cherished companions.[7] When Robert Wuthnow's research team asked a cross section of Americans over a four-year period about their faith journeys, they found that

> music, poetry, paintings, sculpture, and dance played meaningful and inspiring roles. [These arts] draw people closer to God, often expressing what cannot be put into words. They spark the religious imagination and enrich personal experiences of the sacred.... Many [contemporary] people are experimenting with the arts in their devotional lives, at their houses of worship and their efforts to serve others.... For many churches, it has also been a dynamic source of vitality." (Wuthnow 2003, xiv)

Tracing the import of the arts in worship is an intimidating but worthy topic. Any leader who wants to explore the role of the arts in worship will find shelves upon shelves of helpful resources.[8]

Many have found the work of historian and theologian Robin Jensen especially insightful. In worship, she writes, "We make use of the poetic, the visual, the sensory, the aesthetic and the kinesthetic ... [to stretch] beyond simple prose to find a variety of ways to discover and relay the message of the gospel, to speak the unspeakable." The arts protect "the divine mystery while at the same time revealing it.... Art gives only external form to what we shape in our imaginations. Once it is objectified, we may share it with others, as well as revise, polish or even repudiate it." But she adds a note of caution: the arts in worship events can easily become ends in themselves and thus "become essentially idolatrous" (Jensen 363, 365).

In every era of the church's past and present, multiple art genres have enhanced services of worship. The visual arts — painting, stained-glass, tapestry, sculpture, metal work, to name a few — of-

---

7. Mark Chaves's important study of American congregations found that, with the exception of worship services, no other programs in congregations surpassed the finances and commitments to art performances, from children's Christmas pageants to adult choir concerts and film festivals. See Mark Chaves, *Congregations in America* (2004) chapter 6.

8. For an extraordinary rich collection of visual art, see www.eyekons.com. Most of their paintings are available for bulletins, PowerPoint presentations, and background projections in sanctuaries.

fered worshipers unforgettable means of entering into a larger experience of the gospel.

"The world is charged with the grandeur of God," as poet Gerard Manley Hopkins once phrased it.[9] In this chapter, however, I will confine my abbreviated observations to only two artistic genre, architecture and music.

Architecture. Historian and theologian Donald Bruggink, in his copiously illustrated book *Christ and Architecture*, begins with this premise: "Architecture for churches is a matter of gospel. A church that is interested in proclaiming the gospel must also be interested in architecture, for year after year the architecture of the church proclaims a message that augments the preached word or conflicts with it" (Bruggink and Doopers, 1).

The quest for theologically-informed structures is not new. God's instructions for the building of the tabernacle and temple in ancient Israel signaled the interplay of structures and God's salvific message. Since then, architectural designs have preoccupied the imaginations — and finances — of leaders of countless worshiping communities. Some even suggest that architectural design is the premier ecclesial art form — and with good reason. Church buildings, which can become sacred places, stir human imaginations when light, color, and contours unite with the multiple human trades and materials employed in their construction.

At the same time, the parameters of cultural tastes and economic resources shape church buildings. The dark Gothic-inspired churches on the East Coast, the glass cathedrals on the West Coast, and the concrete block buildings with one lonely cross-topped steeple ("prayers in stone") in the Heartlands witness to each congregation's understanding and needs for the practices of worship.

Complementing these more traditional structures are the twentieth-century American church buildings patterned after public auditoriums. Minimal Christian symbols and a prominent lectern at center stage testify to what leaders believe worshiping communities want and need.

9. For a brief yet comprehensive survey of the role of the visual arts in Christian worship, see Marchita Mauch's essay in *The Oxford History of Christian Worship*, ed. by G. Wainwright and K. Westerfield Tucker (2006) pp. 817-837. Special attention is given to the Christian visual arts in Africa, East Asia, and the Pacific.

Finally, all architectural forms employed by worshiping communities need continual interpretation. Congregants are entitled to understand why various architectural expressions such as building shapes; traditional symbols like the cross, pulpit, and table; and stained-glass windows and utilization of light become *active* instruments to facilitate participants' worship of their gracious God.

Music. No artistic expression of faith outdoes or replaces music. Music works its own magic on the human heart. Music infiltrates the sealed crevices in the soul, liberates imprisoned passions, and expresses our deepest human longings.[10] As Eugene Peterson observes, "Song is heightened speech.... Song does not explain, it expresses; it gives meaning to the trans-literal. Song is more than words and there are no words to convey what that 'more' is precisely" (Peterson 2005, 176).

Few musical experiences can compete with singing. As one worshiper said to Robert Wuthnow, the sociologist, "Sometimes when we're singing and the Spirit is moving, it is almost like the roof goes away and you can see the heavens. When we are all in sync, you can feel the spirit moving" (Wuthnow 2003, Preface). Every lover longs to sing to the other. Singing immerses insolated selves into a community. It is a basic practice of *koinonia*. Once, on a "Prairie Home Companion" broadcast, Garrison Keillor explained what happens when people sing together. "[At Christmas] we sing all the songs we know [with] all the people we love.... We stand shoulder to shoulder and sing songs together.... [It is a] sensuous, democratic experience."

Utilizing music in worship services, however, requires careful

10. A quote from the movie "Shawshank Redemption" is too insightful to pass over. In this film, the mild mannered Andy Dufresne (played by Tim Robbins) commandeered the prison's public address system and then broadcast for all to hear a piece from a Mozart opera. Later, his friend "Red" Redding (played by Morgan Freeman), reflected:

I have no idea to this day what those two Italian ladies were singing about. Truth is, I don't want to know. Some things are better left unsaid. I'd like to think they were singing about something so beautiful, it can't be expressed in words, and it makes your heart ache because of it. I tell you, those voices soared higher and farther than anybody in this grey place dares to dream. It was as if some beautiful bird had flapped into our drab little cage and made these walls dissolve away, and for the briefest of moments, every last man in Shawshank felt free.

consideration. Thomas Long has argued persuasively in *Beyond the Worship Wars: Building Vital and Faithful Worship* (2001) that worship leaders need to focus on participation rather than performance. If the sole intent of church music performances is to excite and heighten listeners' aesthetic experience, then the concert hall is a more appropriate setting (Long 2001, 109).

Rather, all music is in service of worshipers participating in the liturgy. John D. Witvliet's essay "Beyond Style: Rethinking the Role of Music in Worship" is especially insightful and comprehensive. Witvliet proposes six criteria for helping congregations' worship committees to discern "what is best" for corporate Christian worship. One of the six criteria can be summarized like this: an important test for worship leaders "is to see how effectively, honestly, and knowingly a worship band or organist can get a congregation to sing well together. Music in worship is not primarily about individual choice, participation or preference but about the entire congregation" (Dearborn and Coil, 163-79).

Again, even though I have briefly mentioned only two examples of art forms, Holy Spirit-inspired Christian worship welcomes art and artists of all kinds. "Faith resides in the soul-deep level of human experience. To reach that depth in human or divine communication, or to unleash the secrets of the heart in prayer, we need symbols. Mere words will not suffice" (Dearborn and Coil, 161).

Waypoint 5: *Christian Worship and Diakonia Are Symbiotically Related* C. S. Lewis once observed, "We only learn to behave ourselves in the presence of God." Perhaps he had in mind an oft-quoted fifth-century phrase in the Christian church, "The rule of prayer is the rule of belief and of action." This historic proverb is in sync with a very long line of biblical prophets who leaned hard on the people of God who presumed to worship God while neglecting or oppressing others.

The uncompromising Amos, putting his own security at risk, spoke for God: "I hate, I despise your festivals, and I take no delight in your solemn assemblies.... Take away from me the noise of your songs; I will not listen to the melody of your harps. But let justice roll down like waters, and righteousness like an ever-flowing stream.... Alas for those who are at ease in Zion" (Amos 5:21, 23-24).

Jesus participates in that same prophetic heritage: "Why do you call me 'Lord, Lord,' and do not do what I tell you?" (Luke 6:46). His instructions to his disciples to feed the hungry, heal the sick, welcome the stranger, clothe the naked, and visit the prisoner were necessary obligations for honoring him (Matt. 25).

In short, worshipers in any era who assume that their cultic exercises excuse them from the practices of *koinonia, martyria,* and *diakonia* are deeply misinformed. As Richard Foster once observed, "Worship begins in holy expectancy, it ends in holy obedience. Holy obedience saves worship from becoming an opiate, an escape from the pressing needs of modern life" (Foster, 173). Worship without *diakonia* is what Bonhoeffer called "cheap grace."

Countless Christian theologians track the reciprocal relationship of worship and seeking justice. A section from Jürgen Moltmann's *The Church in the Power of the Spirit* is typical:

> No one who prays in Christ's name and cries out for redemption can put up with oppression. No one who fights against injustice can dispense with prayer for redemption. The more Christians intervene for the life of the hungry, the human rights of the oppressed and the fellowship of the forsaken, the deeper they will be led into continual prayer.... Prayer therefore leads to political watchfulness, and political watchfulness leads to prayer. (Moltmann, 287)

Congregational leaders can find a thoughtful discussion of this waypoint of Christian worship in *Worship at the Next Level*, especially the Miroslav Volf's essay "Worship as Adoration and Action: Reflections on a Christian Way of Being in the World." He warns, "The more God is pushed out of our world — out of the spheres of nature, of society, and individual human beings — the more difficult it will be to address this loving God in prayer and thanksgiving and to stand before this holy God in awe and reverence" (Dearborn and Coil, 33).

Waypoint 6: Christian Worship Involves Mystery Unfathomable mysteries infiltrate authentic Christian worship. On the one hand Christian worship dares to engage, however minimally and delicately, the "beyond-all-knowing God," as the poet Gerard Manley Hopkins once put it. The renowned twentieth-century Roman Catholic theologian Karl Rahner, meditating on the phrase "hallowed be thy name" in the Lord's Prayer, once asked what he was to call God:

What can I say to you, my God? Shall I collect together all the words that praise your holy Name? Shall I give you all the names of this world, you, the Unnameable? ... Shall I say: Creator, Sustainer, Pardoner, Near One, Distant One, Incomprehensible One, God both of flowers and stars, God of the gentle wind and of terrible battles, Wisdom, Power, Loyalty and Truthfulness, Eternity and Infinity, you are All-merciful, you are the Just One, you Love itself? (Quoted in Appleton, 361)

Far at the other end of a theological and cultural idiom, Anne Lamott in our day claims, "The words 'wow' and 'awe' are the same height and width.... They could dance together. Even when, maybe especially when, we don't cooperate, this energy — the breadth, the glory, the goodness of God — is *given*" (Lamott 2012, 84). No matter where one might look in the Christian theological spectrum of believers, mystery and worship belong together.

Sociologists and social surveys continually assess what American worshipers experience in worship services. Some of their findings are less than complimentary. According to one 2009 survey, while eight out of ten worshipers reported they experienced joy and inspiration, only about one in four worshipers reported a sense of "awe" or "mystery" during worship services.[11]

Waypoint 7: Christian Worship Follows Time-honored Rhythms The practices of Christian worship gravitate around timing and seasons, rather than place or space. Deep in the DNA of all worship rituals of the people of God is the rhythmic precedent of "Sabbath keeping." Observing Sabbaths, as one scholar put it, creates "an island in time," when the people of God become "attuned to holiness in time."[12]

From the earliest narratives in Genesis when God rested (Gen. 2)

11. Several researchers are tracking worship experiences in American congregations. See especially the works of Cynthia Woolever at Hartford Seminary's Institute for Religious Research, especially her *Field Guide to U.S. Congregations: Who's Going Where and Why* (2010).

12. In her book *Sabbath in the Suburbs: A Family's Experiment with Holy Time* (2012) MaryAnn McKibben Dana observes, "There are some things that spontaneity simply cannot offer.... [Sabbath] provides a steadiness and stability which ... at best, creates the possibility of investing time with special meaning, experience with special value, and life with a moment of transcendence" (Dana, 39).

to the Fourth Commandment (Exod. 20), the Sabbath was a required time-out when God's people were to rest from their time-consuming activities and realign themselves with what is holy.

Biblically speaking, the word "holy" carries overtones of "separateness" or "differentness." "Keeping Sabbath" acts out the declaration that God's people are not ultimately captive to the secular world and its values. It is an intentional, weekly affirmation that the people of God belong not to their work or their rulers or their society's priorities, but their ultimate allegiance is centered in God alone.

"Sabbath keeping" reflects worship's rhythms: work and rest, giving and receiving, being and doing, activism and surrender.

Mentored by the time-honored practices of "keeping Sabbath," Christians and their congregations configure Christian worship in other rhythmic patterns: practicing daily devotions; following liturgical seasons such as Advent, Lent, and Pentecost; and participating in retreats. For a very long time in the history of the church, the practice known as the "liturgy of the hours" followed a prescribed structure of scriptural reflection and prayers for various times of the day. Each of these "hours" came to be designated by a special name: *Lauds* at daybreak, *Sext* at midday, *Vespers* at eventide, and *Compline* at night before retiring.

One, though not the only, discernible outgrowth of disciples honoring the rhythms of worship appears when their lifestyles change. Diana Butler Bass, a keen observer of contemporary mainline congregations, tells about Nora Gallagher's spiritual journey while attending an Episcopal congregation in Santa Barbara, California. Gallagher visited the congregation in the mid-1990s as a postmodern tourist but stayed long enough to become a persuaded pilgrim.

Gallagher "ceased moving through space in which others dwelt," Bass notes, and inhabited the community's routines by "adopting its time, its seasons, its ethics and its patterns."[13] These rhythms of worship practices not only transformed a seeker's faith journey, but they also enabled that mainline congregation to reinvent itself into

---

13. One can read about Nora Gallagher's faith journey in her book *Things Seen and Unseen* (1998). Her journey's account is organized around traditional seasons of the Christian year: Advent, Christmas, Epiphany, Lent, Eastertide, Pentecost, and Ordinary Time. "[I live] by a calendar that runs parallel to my Day Timer, a counterweight, one time set against another. The church calendar calls into consciousness the existence of a world uninhabited by efficiency" (Gallagher, 3).

an "*open* monastic community — a place of spiritual practices, hospitality, worship and justice" (Bass, 60-61).

The evidence continues to accumulate. When mainline congregations, under the promptings of the Holy Spirit, advocate, teach, and implement the rhythmic practices of personal and community worship, their members usually discover new meaning and direction in their lives. Along the way, they might even be "surprised by joy."

Navigating the Shoals of Worship Services as Entertainment

I was once asked by a seminary student, "How will we know when we are leading worship or merely entertaining?" Her question sticks around like a stone in my shoe. Delineating the difference is not easy. Authentic worship is engaging and fascinating. Yet having to choose between tired, traditional liturgies and television-oriented formats can leave any mainline congregational leader paralyzed.

But this much is clear: it is a mistake to assume that "contemporary worship" with its amplified guitars, drums, and folksy preaching is inherently entertaining, while traditional gatherings with organs, trained choirs, and accommodating preachers are the more genuine product. Any worship service can descend into little more than weekly titillations where parishioners report they got "a little something out of it."

Recall those Athenians who told the apostle Paul to come back again with his strange proclamations about God and Jesus' resurrection. His listeners, it was reported, rather enjoyed "hearing something new" (Acts 17).

A few, though not exhaustive, markers to distinguish authentic Christian worship from mere entertainment can be drawn:

- It tends toward entertainment when audiences are sung to and offered tidbits of religious advice. In contrast, Christian worshipers seek to engage and listen for a Word from God, mediated through the Bible and clarified by the Holy Spirit.
- Entertainment events idolize celebrities. In Christian worship, however, a restrained and subdued admiration of worship leaders is more appropriate. John the Baptist's attitude still sets the standard: "He [Jesus] must increase, but I must decrease" (John

3:30). As a counter-move to idolization, several persons, prefera-
bly both male and female, can lead public worship services.

- Most corporate worship services require music, but the best liturgical music is to be performed *with* the congregation rather
than *to* it. It tends toward entertainment when soloists, choirs,
and instrumental performances become substitutes for a congregation's participation. Further, any instrument (such as organs!)
can be played so loudly that one cannot hear one's worship partners sing. The genre of music matters less than the goal of assisting all worshipers to lift their voices in praise in a way that
excludes no one.

- Christian worship often calls for change. Having heard God's
Word, we can be summoned to redeem a toxic attitude, to rec-
oncile a fractured relationship, to support financially a worthy
cause, to take up a hard responsibility, and to engage with others in a justice-seeking mission in our host society. Mere entertainment offers "cheap grace" and, often, idolizes self-defined
satisfactions.

- In the end, vital Christian worship posits God as its sole focus. As
Eugene Peterson has written, worship is not about me, "not my
potential, not how I can leverage some supernatural assistance
into getting ahead or a better job ... or peace of mind. Rather
[worship is about] a God in whose love I practice love, God in
whose holiness I become more human, God by whose forgiveness and grace I become the person I am created and saved to
be" (Peterson 2011, 19).

The distinguished Lutheran theologian George Lindbeck once
wrote that "worship is both the summit and the source of the church's
life." Few leaders in gospel-affirming mainline congregations would
disagree. These same leaders are called, as I see it, to organize worship
opportunities in three settings or venues in their congregations. Addressing these different worship settings will require consultation
and employment of a wide variety of resources. On the way to the
summit that Lindbeck envisions, leaders will be invited to reimagine and, perhaps, revamp entrenched ways of worship gatherings.
Such a leadership opportunity will, however, require another and
final chapter.

CHAPTER 10

Practicing the Arts of Worship — Community, Family, Personal

....

Leitourgia, PART TWO

> *All your works shall give thanks to you, O Lord, and all your faithful shall bless you.*
>
> — PSALM 145:10

Relying on the previous chapter's explanations of the ingredients of Christian worship, I maintain in this chapter that leaders of mainline Protestant congregations are privileged to inspire and facilitate worship in three venues:

- the corporate worship of their community,
- family worship throughout the congregation; and
- personal or private worship by each member, young or old.

Each of these venues is grounded in the gospel, but overseeing each requires different envisioning, different planning, and different resourcing.

As noted in the previous chapter, Christian worship, in whatever the setting, gathers *as well as* sends. It both *expresses* and *forms* faith. In this chapter, I envision these worship venues as the primary places and ways that disciples continually reform their lives, lifestyles, and vocations, and thereby further the reign of God "on earth as it is in heaven."

I turn to these three worship settings with no little hesitancy. As noted previously, the historical and prescriptive literature about Christian worship is so immense that easygoing summaries are not readily assembled. Nevertheless, I do maintain that the few and highly selective references cited in this chapter can be helpful and instructive to leaders and worship committees in mainline congregations. Once again, as a reminder to my readers, the mainline church leaders I seek to address are those of the Baby Boomer and Gen X generations.

Venue I: Corporate Worship in Christian Community

Most leaders of congregations acknowledge their responsibility to provide for corporate worship when the people of God gather. Study after study reveals that most congregation-based energies and resources are funneled into weekly worship services. And for good reason. After interviewing some 1,236 American congregations, sociologist Mark Chaves concluded, "Congregations' central purpose is, of course, the expression and transmission of religious meaning, and corporate worship is the primary way in which that purpose is pursued.... If that event fails to occur, a congregation ... would no longer be a congregation" (Chaves 2004, 127-28).

Another sociologist added this dimension: "The majority [of members] experience the congregation only by attending worship services. Thus, what they get from their religious community must happen during worship" (Woolever 2010, 47).

However, while worship events are the most staple and repeated ministry for congregations, contemporary Protestant worship services vary greatly. Consequently, shaping worship services becomes an enormous challenge when lay leaders, pastors, worship committees, and influential members observe the wide range of worship options in their local communities and on television.

As a shortcut way to address this challenge, I will use the historic and composite word "liturgy" (derived from *leitourgia*), to describe the public worship patterns, rituals, and orderings of Protestant corporate worship.[1] Every worship gathering of Christians incorporates

---

1. As mentioned previously, I employ the word "liturgy" as a generalized term to describe the patterns and rituals in public worship when Christian communities gather. For an encyclopedic survey of Christian liturgical options and developments, see G. Wainwright and K. B. Westerfield Tucker, eds., *The Oxford History of Christian Worship* (2006).

some kind of liturgical order. As soon as a leader calls to the gathered people, "The Lord be with you" or "Good morning, welcome!" or a hymn is nominated to be sung or a person reads a passage of Scripture or an offering is taken for a common cause, then *some* variety of liturgical ordering (*ordo*) is *already* under way.

Risking oversimplification, I suggest there are three clusters of liturgical orientations influencing current mainline denominations' patterns of worship: *traditional, Americanist,* and *eclectic.* Since each of these liturgical orders, or their variations, can be found throughout twenty-first-century mainline congregations, each deserves some explanation, however abbreviated. Such explanations will, I hope, help congregational leaders to identify where they are located in the spectrum of liturgical options in America.

Traditional Liturgical Patterns The first liturgical genre, *traditional,* has deep historical roots in ancient synagogue services, the early church's traditions, the medieval Mass, the Protestant Reformers' orders of service, the influential Anglican *Common Book of Prayer,* the Vatican II (1962) liturgical reforms of the Roman Catholic Church, and various Protestant Ecumenical gatherings since the 1950s. More recent examples can be found in the worship directories of mainline denominations such as the *United Methodist Book of Worship* or the *Book of Common Worship* (Reformed and/or Presbyterian), *the Lutheran Book of Worship* (ELCA), and *The Worship Sourcebook* (2nd ed.) of Faith Alive Christian Resources of the Christian Reformed Church and the Calvin Institute of Christian Worship.

Generally, these history-sensitive worship services are ordered around four basic acts or movements: (1) an appropriate word for the assembling of the people; (2) listening for the Word of God in Scripture readings and preaching and a response to that Word through praying; (3) the celebration of the gospel through the breaking of bread and the pouring of wine, with prayers of thanksgiving; and, finally, (4) the sending of the people into the world to witness and serve.

In this liturgical tradition, the gospel finds particular expression through the proclamation of the Word of God in Scripture lessons, sermon, and the celebration of the sacraments of baptism and the Lord's Supper. Under the Holy Spirit's influence, the Word keeps the sacraments from degenerating into magic and superstition. The sacraments keep the Word from degenerating into rationalistic propositions and numbing literalism. The two, emphasized in this tradition, are intended to be interwoven. When both are celebrated, the people of God are drawn into the joy and "Paschal mysteries" of the gospel's promises and life-affirming hope.

Many liturgy scholars find the template for these four movements implicit in Isaiah 6. There a holy God and a forgiven people reciprocally address each other before the people are sent to outward on God's mission in the world. The length, variations, and intensity of each of these four acts or movements may differ. Each can be enlivened by congregational singing. Historically, prayers of the people came *after* the Word in the sermon. That is, as noted in Isaiah 6, one listens for a word *from* God before one dares to speak *to* God in response.

Acknowledging denominational differences and local church variations, this four-act liturgical service usually follows a common pattern. Here is how one contemporary congregation in the Reformed tradition engages this traditional liturgical format:

I. Gathering
    Greeting
    Hymn(s) of Praise
    Prayer for the Presence of the Triune God
    Prayers of Confession
    Assurance of Pardon
    Renewal of Baptismal promises
    Hymn or Psalm of Thanksgiving

II. Listening and Responding to the Word of God
    Old Testament Reading
    Psalm Reading
    New Testament Reading
    Homily or Sermon
    Affirmation of Faith
        (Usually the Apostles' Creed or Nicene Creed)
    Prayers of Response to the Word and Intercession
    Hymn of Affirmation

III. The Holy Communion (Lord's Supper)
    Passing of the Peace to One Another

        Preparation of the Table
        The Peoples' Offering
        The Great Prayer of Thanksgiving
        The Lord's Prayer
        Breaking of Bread, Pouring of Wine
        Celebration of the Lord's Supper
        Hymn of Celebration

IV. Commissioning for Service in God's World
        Reminder of Disciples' Missional Responsibilities
        Charge to Act in Faithful Living
        Hymn of Commissioning
        Benediction
        Dismissal.

To make sure the "whole counsel" of God's Word is presented to the people of God, a lectionary (prescribed Old and New Testament readings) is usually followed.[2] In a three-year cycle, biblical texts and suggested liturgies provide a frame of reference to honor the life, death, resurrection, and ascension of Jesus and the empowering presence of the Holy Spirit at Pentecost and beyond. The liturgical calendar, emphasizing Advent, Epiphany, Lent, Eastertide, and Pentecost narratives, ensures that the total Word of God is proclaimed and its missional call interpreted and affirmed. In short, this liturgical ordering seeks to vivify the narrative of God's covenant inititatives, convenant fulfillments and covenant communities.

Obviously, this classical liturgical format does not easily submit to parishioners' individualized tastes. Neither does it accommodate preachers' self-selected sermon topics or the celebration of secular holidays. Further, artistic expressions of any kind — music, banners, projected images — serve this liturgical ordering and are not ends in themselves.[3]

In summary, this traditionalist liturgy incorporates both clergy and parishioners as vital participants; the Word of God is central;

2. For an overview of the role and use of the traditional lectionary, see William Willimon, "The Lectionary." *Theology Today* 58 (2001): 333-341. This article is available online.

3. For a thorough interpretation of the role of the arts in Christian worship, see especially Nicholas Wolterstorff, *Art in Action* (1980).

the sacraments are essential rather than occasional; and missional responsibilities as expected rather than optional.

Americanist Liturgical Models A second liturgical stream in twenty-first-century North American Protestantism I shall call *Americanist*. This liturgical stream has its headwaters in colonial America and then broadens and deepens in the mid-nineteenth century. One large tributary to this New World style appeared on the national scene in the 1830s and 1840s through the revivalist Charles G. Finney.[4]

Finney called for "new measures" in liturgical patterns. Robust singing of hymns and extemporary prayers "filled by the Spirit" served as preludes to the much anticipated sermon. When properly implemented, this liturgical strategy generated an "emotional curve" in which swelling emotions urged a "decision for Christ." It was designed to inspire, as historian Mark Noll remarked, "a true religion of the heart."

Finney's liturgy placed the preacher in a dominating, or even charismatic, role. Preaching was *"the appointed means of promoting religion,"* Finney insisted, "and it was left to the discretion of the Church to determine, from time to time, what *measures* should be adopted, and what [liturgical] forms pursued, in giving the gospel its power."

Finney's services, attuned to the pragmatic predispositions of American culture, prescribed practical ways for living the faith. "Anything brought forward as doctrine, which cannot be made use of as practical, is not the preaching of the gospel," wrote Finney in his *Lectures on Revival* (1835). In addition to his practical manuals about running revivals, he was an ardent abolitionist, a supporter of women's voting rights, and an advocate of a life of holiness. His "new measures" included the use of advertisements, the incorporation of multidenominational sponsorship of revivals, and the expansive use of musical instruments to augment his extemporaneous sermons (Wainwright and Tucker 2006, 607-608).

4. Charles Grandison Finney (1792-1875) was born in Connecticut, raised in the "burned-over" lands of western New York, studied for the practice of law, and joined and pastored in the Presbyterian circles whose theological standards he later rejected. He founded the Broadway Tabernacle in New York City and taught at Oberlin College in Ohio until his death. Many historians refer to him as the "Father of Modern Revivalism."

Many nineteenth-century Christian communities, however, re-fused to adopt Finney's "new measures." One notable critic of Fin-ney's worship strategies was Horace Bushnell, an influential Con-gregationalist preacher and scholar in Hartford, Connecticut. His famous book *Christian Nurture* (1847) was a counterweight to Finney's revivalist liturgical formats. In contrast to Finney's "crisis manage-ment" services, Bushnell opted for home and church schooling so that a "child would grow up as a Christian and never know himself [or herself] as being otherwise."

By the end of the nineteenth century and well into the twenti-eth, these two American liturgical streams, Finney's and Bushnell's, merged and generated a distinctive American way of worship among many mainstream Protestants. In place of the "emotional curve" tactic, these congregations, rural and urban, promoted "home-like" environments. Early twentieth-century Protestant architecture in America's urban centers provides clues to this amalgamated way of worshiping. Sanctuaries were shaped in an auditorium style with a prominent stage, an elevated pulpit, and sloping floors. At the same time, churches were outfitted with kitchens, parlors, and dining rooms, to simulate a "home away from home."[5]

The newly formed Federal Council of Churches (1908) published the "Seven Principles of Public Worship," which emphasized "social gospel" issues and recommended worship liturgies that honored La-bor Day, World Peace, and later, Race Relations Sunday.

In such a mixed liturgical milieu, several mainline denomina-tions appointed committees to "consider liturgical revision" and to untangle "the web that was liturgical identity." Typical was the northern Presbyterians' *Book of Common Worship*, distributed in 1906. According to its preface, worship leaders were instructed to seek a "golden mean between a too great laxity and a tyrannical uniformity." The long custom of congregational self-rule, however, was clearly evident on the cover page, which read, "For Voluntary Use."

Eventually the twentieth-century liturgical patterns in many mainline congregations blended selected aspects of traditional lit-

---

5. For a fuller development of this early-twentieth-century trend, see Jeanne Hal-gren Kilde, *When the Church Became Theatre* (2005). This historian traced how changes in the design of church buildings reflected changes in liturgical patterns.

urgies, congregational autonomy, and American socio-cultural agendas. For these reasons, I call the resulting liturgical adaptations *Americanist*. One way to identify these Americanized liturgical adaptations is to consult the "orders of worship" now recommended in several mainline Protestant worship manuals. With many variations, most prescribe the following:

Prelude Music
Call to Worship
Singing with people standing
Prayer of Confession and Assurance of Pardon
Hymn or Choral Presentation
Pastoral Prayer by minister
Lord's Prayer by all
Old Testament lesson (may be read responsively)
New Testament lesson (may be read responsively)
Collection of people's offerings
Singing of a hymn
Sermon, often "topical," rather than a scriptural exposition
Short Prayer for the blessing of the Word
Concluding hymn
Apostolic Benediction
Postlude Music

The telltale signs of this *Americanist* liturgical tradition are clear: the minister as preacher remains the central actor; the offering or "collection" occurs in the middle of the service; choirs (sometimes more than one) usually perform in various places; the Lord's Supper is celebrated, but only occasionally; prayers are offered as "pastoral prayers" followed by the Lord's Prayer in unison; and the sermon, based on a biblical text or a topic usually chosen by the pastor, is positioned near the service's conclusion. Finally, parishioners are sometimes urged to respond and, perhaps, "change their ways" in the presence of the entire community before departing.

The long shadows of this American-styled liturgical tradition remain well into the twentieth-first century: the pastor remains the primary liturgical performer; a well-rehearsed, robed choir is positioned up front in the chancel; and the sermon-event functions as the apex of this liturgical order. With the exception of Episcopal and

Lutheran churches, this Americanized liturgical pattern often dominates in smaller congregations in mainline denominations.[6]

Eclectic Liturgical Options A third liturgical genre — one notoriously difficult to define precisely — is *eclectic*. This broader category is to meant include terms like "contemporary worship" or "blended worship," as well as multiple varieties of "seeker services."[7]

Some scholars trace the origins of these liturgical realignments to the Reformed Church in America's Rev. Robert Schuller. In the early 1960s his "drive in" ministry in Southern California, his weekly "Hour of Power" television broadcasts, and his popular clergy seminars gained national attention.

During the first decade of the twentieth-first century, sociologist Cynthia Woolever found that 22 percent of some 3,000 Protestant congregations experimented with new styles of worship services, and an additional 18 percent altered their existing worship patterns. The need to "meet the needs of current and prospective members" drove many leaders to initiate liturgical changes in corporate worship services (Woolever 2010, 26).

Another survey, conducted in 2009 by the Hartford Institute for Religion Research, found that 64 percent of the congregations that switched to "contemporary worship" in the past five years increased their worship attendance by 2 percent. Increasingly, mainline congregations have arranged for two Sunday services, one more "traditional" and the other more "contemporary." Often, these two services take place in two different locations in a church's building, with two different types of musical instruments to accompanying the congregation's singing, different worship leaders, and, sometimes, two different sermons.

Usually, eclectic liturgies follow the format of praise songs with upbeat music *and* prescriptions to initiate intimate encounters with the gracious God. "Seeker services" are a variation of this genre. The

6. See especially Peter Bush and Christine O'Reilly, *Where 20 or 30 Are Gathered: Leading Worship in the Small Church* (2006).

7. The literature about "contemporary worship" is extensive. Three excellent resources can help leaders clarify trends and options in Protestant worship. One is Cornelius Plantinga and Sue A. Rozeboom's *Discerning the Spirits: A Guide to Thinking About Worship Today* (2003). Another is Robert Webber's classic treatment in *Planning Blended Worship: The Creative Mixture of Old and New* (1998). Third, personnel in denominational offices provide practical and thoughtful resources for pastors and committees of worship.

goal of this liturgical style, notes one authority, is to lead Christian worship without the impediments of outdated language, classical symbols, and conventional music. One advocate characterizes them as "proto-evangelism" worship; others insist it is not, properly speaking, a Christian worship service at all but only an occasion for non-committed seekers to "check out" the gospel, and, at the same time, visit the congregation's life-coping seminars.

Recognizing that contemporary Americans receive much of their information in a visual way, modern media techniques, such as multiple television screens and PowerPoint presentations, are usually employed. Sermons are designed to teach the founding elements of Christian faith or counsel parishioners on "life's challenging issues." Usually, sermons are oriented to the uninitiated and biblically ill-informed.

Most important, witnesses are invited "up front" to explain why faith is essential for a meaning-filled life. Leaders plan these services very carefully and often design them to fit some particular purpose, a particular religious season, a secular holiday, or moral challenges. Generally, the sacraments of baptism and the Lord's Supper are not observed in large assemblies, but are reserved for small group gatherings. Both the *Americanist* and *eclectic* styles are intentionally post-traditionalist and often bypass mainline denominational publications and patterns of establishment liturgies and rituals.

A way to illustrate *one* strand of this *eclectic* style is to consider the order of worship at the large Willow Creek Community Church in South Barrington, Illinois. Beginning in the 1970s, Willow Creek leaders shaped their popular worship styles, and by 2012 the church's format had changed very little:

Music (usually by a contemporary musical group)
Soloist
Chorus (with congregation singing along)
Dramatic skit or visual presentation
Testimony by prominent person
Song (by singers and band)
Message
Music
Dismissal and/or benediction
(See Wainwright and Tucker 2006, 629)

Again, this liturgical style seeks to connect with persons who are utterly out of touch with biblical narratives, traditional worship liturgies, and the doctrinal/creedal language of classical Protestantism. Avoiding prayers of confession and a collection of funds, this *eclectic* format oscillates between familiar songs and minimal liturgical repetition. Some proponents maintain that music alone, usually of a contemporary variety, provides all worshipers with sufficient liturgical expression.

Corporate Worship in Review Corporate worship in any liturgical style commands more attention, financial investment, and planning than any other weekly activity in a congregation. However, in a 2008 national study of American congregations, sociologist Cynthia Woolever found that "half of all [Protestant] worshipers say they are not growing in their faith" (Woolever 2010, 47).

Don Saliers of Emory University offers an explanation as to why mainline worship services can remain ineffective:

> Many persons whom I have interviewed about their worship experience consistently name three factors that prevent their deeper participation: (1) when worship is "done for us"; (2) when worship is "done to us"; and (3) when "we don't understand what is going on." Each of these factors bears directly upon the style and substance of Christian liturgy.

By the first, Saliers means that clergy, preachers, and singers do everything, while parishioners "don't want to do anything but listen and sing." By the second, he means the liturgy is usually oriented toward worshipers. By the third, he underscores a widespread lack of education about the basic elements of Christian worship (Saliers 1998, 73-75).

Among the most daunting questions leaders dare to ask about any phase of their congregations' ministries is this: "How do we know what we are doing is what we claim we are doing?" I contend that one primary role of leaders in any organization is to "clarify the realities" operative in their organization.

However limited and even intimidating, there are ways for church leaders to probe what "realities" happen in the hearts and minds of parishioners during worship services. Sociologists and contemporary practical theologians now regularly employ research tools to record faith stories, circulate questionnaires, conduct interviews, sponsor focus groups, and examine case studies. Such tactful inquiries eliminate conjectures or reliance on inadequate sampling of experiences when planning future worship services. They provide an *informed* look at worship experiences before leaders and worship programmers leap into feasible alternatives.[8]

Venue 2: Christian Worship in Families

"Every Christian family ought to be as it were a little church consecrated to Christ." So counseled American theologian Jonathan Edwards, in his famous "Farewell Sermon" to a congregation that had just dismissed him. Countless other theologians, educators, and practitioners of most religious traditions would endorse Edwards's insight about families.

As one contemporary scholar put it, "The incubators of faith are not church staff but parents and guardians." And for good reasons. As I noted in chapter 6 (*Mathētēs*), most of the essential practices of discipleship of the Christian faith are initiated, nourished, interpreted, and cultivated within the "sacred shelters" of families. In families, children *and* parents acquire a vocabulary for faith expression when memorizing Scripture verses and catechisms. Family-based rituals of worship, such retelling biblical stories, annual celebrations of baptisms, and prayers before and after meals reinforce the joys of belonging (*Koinonia*).

When the "means of grace" central to Christian worship — Scripture, sacraments, and prayer — are intentionally celebrated and interpreted in family circles, it is not coincidental that "little churches" emerge at home.

At the same time, however, families may be the hardest place to sustain consistent worship practices.

Most Americans are acutely aware of the fragility of families and fragmentation of contemporary family life. In a humorous but poi-

8. For an excellent example of how one mainline congregation circulated a questionnaire to discern how its worship services were received, see Martha L. Moore-Keish's *Do This in Remembrance of Me* (2008).

gnant account, MaryAnn McKibben Dana, records the stress of trying to balance her family's frenetic suburban existence while caught in a relentless list of work, errands, car pool, dishes, email, bills, and yard work responsibilities. "Life," she confessed, "felt like a 500-piece jigsaw puzzle with 600 pieces" (Dana 2012).

It is not surprising that sociologists find widespread disregard of regularized family worship experiences. Beginning with the research mentioned in chapter 6, the *Effective Christian Education: A National Study of Protestant Congregations* revealed that two-thirds of the Protestant members surveyed reported they never gave time to help children or youth to grow in the Christian faith at home. Of the adults between thirty and fifty years of age, only 11 percent recalled having conversations about faith issues with their fathers.

Sociologist Robert Wuthnow once directed a study that compared two hundred adult persons (Christians and Jews) who grew up with religious training with those who had not. Those interviewed were women and men of diverse racial, educational, and class backgrounds. In *Growing Up Religious* (2000), he concluded that their spirituality had been most affected "when it [had] been practiced at home as well as in formal organizations.... Spirituality is likely to survive — *if parents and grandparents are committed to its importance*" (Wuthnow 2000, 236).

Rather than supply further documentation of the demise of family worship, we need to turn our attention toward more hopeful directions.

As a friend and seasoned Christian educator recently reminded a group of pastors, "It is not nearly enough to insist or even convince parents *what* they should do, but, rather, a congregation must provide them with resources and models for *how* to do those things in family worship." She then pointed to an abundance of resources and models available to equip church leaders with their responsibilities to provide worship experiences for contemporary families. For starters, there are three places where mainline church leaders can turn for help. These are (1) denominationally generated resources, (2) a few well-known textbooks, and (3) a comprehensive website that specializes in faith formation and worship ministries in families. Happily, most of these references are now available online.

Practical Denominational Resources Protestant denominational leaders have not remained mesmerized and silent. Virtually every mainline denomination produces an abundance of updated and creative curricula for family worship. The Presbyterian Church (USA) issued in 2005 a study document for congregations, titled "Transforming Families."[9] After lamenting that contemporary families are disconnected from their nurturing responsibilities and noting that most Presbyterians now expect church professionals to provide for the faith development experiences of children and youth, the denomination continually produces "Creative Ideas for Family Worship" series (with CDs). In the Lutheran tradition, the ELCA produces guides for family life and worship in the *Living Lutheran* series. Through its *Faith Alive* series, the Christian Reformed Church in North America publishes the WE curriculum, designed for cross-generational worship gatherings.[10]

Helpful Texts About Family Worship Supplementing these denominational resources are monographs on family worship. I mention only two but reliable and accessible references. Marjorie J. Thompson's *Family the Forming Center*, a work mentioned in chapter 6, outlines multiple ways for families to celebrate the presence of God. Creating a "sacred space" such as an altar with candle or homemade cross; practicing daily rituals such as mealtime graces; bedtime Bible stories; and conversations about the various seasons of the church year embody means for "practicing the presence of God" in the midst of home life.

Thompson is particularly helpful in her chapter titled "Prayer in the Family." She believes that prayer, as a means of grace, lies at the center of family spirituality. She cites an example of one family who sets aside time at the breakfast table for sharing what the day holds for each and then praying briefly for each other. On such occasions "both children and adults realize that no special words or particular phrases are necessary" while praying. Single words or short phrases, Thompson notes, can express one's joy in God: "Thank you," "Bless the Lord," or, "Alleluia."

Thompson further develops why the "study of Scripture and

9. This wide-ranging document is available online. See http://www.pcusa.org/media/uploads/_resolutions/transformingfamilies.pdf.

10. These denominations' materials are available online. See www.thethoughful christian.com for PC(USA); www.elca.org/Living-Lutheran; and www.WeCurriculum .org for the Reformed curricula.

the practice of prayer are inseparable." Families, she continues, are in a unique position to integrate biblical stories and personal stories. With such practices, families become transporters of God's Word.

As in the past, the Psalms, memorized and discussed, hold a pivotal place in the life of faith in family circles. In the end, Thompson urges church leaders "to develop hands-on workshops and classes to enable parents to integrate their daily practical care of children with spiritual development." To facilitate such occasions, she lists illustrations, periodicals, videos, and more books (Thompson 1996, 141).

If Thompson's book is more foundational and wide-ranging, Delia Halverson's *Side-by-Side: Families Learning and Living in Faith Together* (2002) is a basic resource for planning family worship events around the seasons of the church year and interpreting the Christian sacraments in family circles. According to one experienced Christian educator of my acquaintance, Halverson's work is especially useful for families who are seeking how to begin worshiping at home.

A Research Center for Family Worship Finally, there is an extraordinary website sponsored by the LifelongFaith Associates and led by John Roberto. This New England-based association publishes online the *Lifelong Faith Journal*, which is both a repository of contemporary research about American families as well as a provider of practical strategies for faith formation in children. In a recent essay (2007), Roberto and others listed ten "best practices" for children's faith formation. One of those practices provides ways for children to experience and imagine how their own personal stories are intertwined with the Bible stories.

A more recent issue of this journal (Summer 2013) charts a growing network that connects congregations across denominational lines who share articles, videos, and digital tools for promoting faith formation in children and families. Coursing through these scholars' ministry, and quoted on their website's home page, is a hypothesis lifted from the notable sociologist Christian Smith: "If formation in faith does not happen there [in families] it will — with rare exception — not happen anywhere."[11]

11. See www.lifelongfaith.com and www.21stCenturyFaithFormation/com.

Venue 3: Private Christian Worship

Christian disciples of every age and every culture testify that the quiet, private routines of prayer, scriptural meditation, and discernment focus their worship of God. The precedent for such personal worship experiences has a very long pedigree. For more than three thousand years, the people of God "prayed the Psalms," whose words, raw and uninhibited, are offered to the Holy One for "all sorts and conditions of men [and women]," as the *Book of Common Prayer* puts it.

During the era when Jewish synagogues emerged in Babylonia and across the Middle East (as early as 600 BCE), the times for prayers became regularized according to the hours of the day, usually morning, midday, and night. These scheduled, set-aside hours continued and expanded into the New Testament era. The Gospels record numerous occasions where Jesus departed before daylight "to a deserted place, and there he prayed" (Mark 1:35). After crowds gathered to hear him and pressed him to cure their diseases, "he would withdraw to deserted places and pray" (Luke 5:16). And on another occasion, Jesus, prior to selecting his disciples, "spent the night in prayer to God" (Luke 6:12). He admonished his disciples to go into their closets to pray (Matt. 6:6).

Acts of the Apostles makes numerous references to when the disciples prayed, say, at the "ninth hour" (mid-afternoon) (Acts 3:1) or the "sixth hour" (noon) (Acts 10:9). The apostle Paul urged the Christians at Thessalonica to "rejoice always, pray without ceasing" (1 Thess. 5:16-17). The earliest known manual used by early Christian congregations, called the *Didache* (circa 50-70 CE), instructs disciples to pray the Lord's Prayer three times a day, usually morning, noon, and night.[12]

Beginning in the second and third centuries and continuing to the Reformations of the sixteenth century, treasuries of private devotions and prayers multiplied. Monastic communities such as the Desert Fathers in Egypt, Benedictines in Italy, and the Jesuits in Spain, France, and Asia developed "Rules" or protocols for private devotions.

---

12. For contemporary leaders who might want to know how their earliest counterparts led congregations, see Aaron Milavec, *The Didache: Text, Translation, Analysis, and Commentary* (2003).

Both Martin Luther and John Calvin in the sixteenth century wrote extensively and passionately about a disciple's devotional life. Luther taught that the Lord's Prayer was a framework that shaped one's prayers, meditations, and praise. In an often-repeated story, Luther's barber once asked him how to pray, and Luther told him to start and end with the Lord's Prayer.

In his *Institutes of the Christian Religion*, Calvin wrote similarly about the Lord's Prayer as a primary means of grace. "For he [Jesus] prescribed a form for us in which he sets forth as in a table all that he allows us to seek of him, all that is of benefit to us, all that we need to ask" (Calvin 897).

In the English language, the influential Anglican *Book of Common Prayer* (first published in 1549) is currently used in more than fifty nations and has been translated into more than a 150 languages. In one of its prayers during the Advent season, the worshiper asks that he or she may properly "hear . . . read, mark, learn, and inwardly digest . . . thy holy Word."

"All theological reflection," wrote theologian Karl Barth in his 1962 lectures to American audiences, "begins and ends in prayer."

With this legacy and wisdom in mind, where might contemporary leaders of congregations find resources to encourage their friends and parishioners to "Be still, and know that I am God!" as Psalm 46 counsels?

Presently, there is an overabundance of accessible resources to help parishioners slake their spiritual thirst. Mainline denominational central offices employ talented and informed personnel to enable congregational leaders to provide for worship in private venues. The Upper Room, affiliated with the United Methodist Church, has published daily devotional guidance for private worship for nearly seventy-five years.[13] Upper Room materials now circulate to 2.5 million Christians around the world and are translated into more than forty languages. Their meditations about Scripture passages are usually written by their regular readers and usually grow out of real-life faith experiences originating in diverse places and circumstances.

This same Upper Room has comforted countless Christians who are homebound or ill. More recently, a new publication, *Alive Now*, also published by the Upper Room organization, seeks "to nourish

---

13. See www.alivenow.upperroom.org.

people who are hungry for a sacred way of living." This journal employs Scripture verses, prayers by church leaders, poems, spiritual direction, and readings from resource books.

Finally, the Upper Room also publishes a first-rate journal called *Weavings*, which incorporates meditations, poetry, and biblical reflections. These resources are usually published online, as well as in standard printed booklets.

Other denominations regularly produce personal devotional curricula. One example is the Evangelical Lutheran Church in America's *Daily Faith Programs*, which provide daily studies of the Bible based on current lectionary readings. Another is the Presbyterian Church (USA)'s monthly devotional publication *These Days*, written by clergy and laity. Scripture passages, space for prayer lists, questions to stir reflection, and life experiences are regular features of most denominational devotional publications. Most are available online.

Among the surplus of textbooks designed to promote personal religious practices, two volumes merit particular consideration by church leaders. The first is *Soul Feast: An Invitation to the Christian Spiritual Life* (2005), a premier introduction to the "devout life" or "spiritual formation" by Marjorie J. Thompson.

Thompson, whose helpful book on family devotional practices was mentioned above, was a student and friend of Henri J. M. Nouwen at Yale University. Of Thompson's work, Nouwen, the renowned authority on contemporary spirituality, once said, "When you have read and lived this book, you have been in touch with the best that Christian spirituality has to offer."

With grace and clarity, Thompson outlines the basic ingredients of private or personal worship: meditative reading of Scripture, prayer, fasting, confession, and openness to others' direction. Such disciplines practiced over time become daily habits, she believes. Her survey of the "Spiritual Yearnings of Our Time" and her chapter on "Approaches to Prayer" remain luminous guides for twenty-first-century Christians.

The other recommended textbook is *Spiritual Disciplines Handbook* (2005) by Adele Ahlberg Calhoun. Different in style and format from Thompson's work, Calhoun approaches multiple disciplines of faith formation as if they were a series of workshops, complete with introductory essays, Scripture texts, reflective questions, spiritual exercises, and bibliographies. Church leaders could lift any of disciplines she addresses and generate workshops on their own turf. Possible topics range from Sabbath keeping to spiritual direction.

Two other pivotal resources for private worship need mentioning, no matter how abbreviated and severely selected. I refer to the dependence on the biblical Psalms and the testimonies of other Christians.

If Christian worship in any venue is intended to drench the whole of life with an awareness of the empowering presence of God, then no resource of devotional literature and language exceeds the Psalms.

"The most valuable thing the Psalms do for me," C. S. Lewis once wrote, "is to express the same delight in God which made David dance." They have an uncanny way of putting appropriate words to the wide spectrum of deep human feelings of love, trust, doubt, lament, anger, despair, and hope. The psalmists' figures of speech are universally understood and, when combined with music for the human voice, provide fitting expressions for the praise of God.

At the same time, as Walter Brueggemann observed in his book *Praying the Psalms,* many "Psalms offer speech when life goes beyond our faint efforts to control," especially when men and women are faced with the "rawness of human reality" (Brueggemann, 19).

In addition, many of the Psalms instruct all persons with political and economic authority to attend to the oppressed and impoverished. "Give the king your justice, O God.... May he defend the cause of the poor of the people, give deliverance to needy, and crush the oppressor" (Ps. 72).

For centuries, individuals and families have memorized the Psalms, such as the Psalm 1 and 23. To that list I again recommend Psalm 145. Some biblical scholars describe it as an "anthology," because it draws together insights, expressions, and the hope of many other Psalms. Few psalms, in my opinion, conjoin so eloquently the majesty, providence, and grace of God. Inclusivity abounds in this psalm. "The Lord is good to all, and his compassion is over all that he has made." At the same time, while the "Lord is near to all who call upon him in truth," the psalmist warns those deviating from that truth.

Apparently, this psalm was repeated in private and public three times a day in some Jewish communities of Jesus' day. John Calvin saluted this psalm as the most beautiful composition of the "sweet singer of Israel," David.

In addition to Scripture, the church's legacy of devotional resources overflows with modern testimonies of Christians who attest to the faith-forming experiences through their practices of private worship. Two authors, Elizabeth O'Connor and John Baillie, will have to suffice. I readily confess they rank very high among my mentors. During the last third of the twentieth century, O'Connor chronicled the extraordinary ministries and missional orientation of the Church of the Saviour in Washington, D.C. In *Journey Inward, Journey Outward*, she writes of "engagements on the journey inward."

> This God with whom we will be engaged for the rest of our days come to us across a great distance, and at the same time He is the divine force at the core of our own lives. He is a God whom we will know in many ways, but one of the primary ways is *prayer grounded in Scriptures*. As people on an inward-outward journey ... we will take time to be with God in the quiet places of our spirit, so that we can come to know a different quality of life.... What will make us open to being addressed by God in the events of life, to hearing his Word in newspaper headlines and committee meetings ...? Is it not precisely because God does address us in the arena of life that we must prepare ourselves [in private] to hear Him there? (O'Connor, 17-18)

My other tutor has been John Baillie, a twentieth-century Scottish pastor and Edinburgh University theology professor and the author of the sterling prayers found in his *Diary of Private Prayer*.

I am aware that many contemporary Christians find Baillie's formal, King James-like phrasing, as well as his biased gender language, off-putting. However, in three mainline congregations of my acquaintance, ordinary members adapted Baillie's language, offered his thirty morning and evening prayers as their own, and then met monthly to share their prayer experiences. Some reported this discipline of twice-a-day praying to be transforming. Virtually every element of private worship is engaged in the very first morning prayer Baillie lifted to God:

> Eternal Father of my soul, let my first thought today be of Thee, let my first impulse be to worship Thee, let my first speech be Thy name, let my first action be to kneel before Thee in prayer.

> For Thy perfect wisdom and perfect goodness;
> For the love wherewith Thou lovest mankind;
> For the love wherewith Thou lovest me;
> For the great and mysterious opportunity of my life;
> For the indwelling of Thy Spirit in my heart;
> For the sevenfold gifts of Thy Spirit:
>> I praise and worship Thee, O Lord.

Yet let me not, when this morning prayer is said, think my worship ended and spend the day in forgetfulness of Thee. Rather from these moments of quietness let light go forth, and joy, and power, that will remain with me through all the hours of the day;

> Keeping me chaste in thought;
> Keeping me temperate and diligent in my work;
> Keeping me humble in my estimation of myself;
> Keeping me honourable and generous in my dealings with others;
> Keeping me loyal to every hallowed memory of the past;
> Keeping me mindful of my destiny as a child of Thine.

O God, who hast been the Refuge of my fathers [and mothers] through many generations, be my Refuge today in every time and circumstance of need. Be my Guide through all that is dark and doubtful. Be my Guard against all that threatens my spiritual welfare. Be my Strength in time of testing. Gladden my heart with Thy peace; through Jesus Christ my Lord. Amen. (Baillie, 9)

John Baillie's daily prayers, admittedly, may not serve as a suitable model for every twenty-first century-disciple but they remain fresh and meaningful for many. More recently, other authors have adopted Baillie's morning and evening routine for praying and meditating.[14]

Whatever resources are consulted and employed, I submit that leaders remain privileged to help shape the totality of a congregation's faithful practices of *leitourgia* (worship). That privilege, I maintain, extends not only to corporate worship services, but also to family venues and to the practices of personal devotions. Jesus' definitive

14. A student of John Baillie, J. Barrie Shepherd, has written a supplement to Baillie's famed book of prayers. Titled *Diary of Daily Prayer* (2002), it, too, has thirty morning and evening prayers. Shepherd, a prolific author of devotional literature was, until 2000, pastor of the First Presbyterian Church in New York City.

announcement to a woman near a Samaritan well still inspires that privilege and suffuses every faithful practice of Christian worship: "God is spirit, and those who worship him must worship in spirit and truth" (John 4:24).

Afterword

According to that master of practical wisdom, Yogi Berra, "If you don't know where you are going, you could wind up someplace else." It has my primary purpose of this book to help current mainline Protestant congregations to discern where they are headed. More specifically, I have urged leaders of these congregations to envision how the gospel, focused essentially in Jesus Christ and illuminated by the Holy Spirit, calls them to endorse particular faithful practices. These five biblically informed, Spirit-infused faithful practices, I contend, are prescribed for all the people of God, young and old, to keep them from "winding up someplace else."

From its outset, I have thought of this book as both a textbook and a testimony. As a primer for lay leaders, the five faithful practices, explained here are foundational for any congregation's ministry and witness. They are interdependent, and no one practice can thrive in isolation from the others.

While admitting they are no small assignments for all church leaders, all five of these faithful practices need to be operative if congregations are to flourish as "provisional expressions of the kingdom of God." Along the way, this textbook has sought to provide resources to equip current leaders in their calling. Those resources are plentiful and accessible. Most of them are referenced in "Works Cited."

At the same time, this book serves as a testimony to countless numbers of congregations who have enacted these faithful practices. There is an old and exaggerated adage among sociologists and historians that says, "Nothing is real unless it is local." Memorable examples of these faithful practices can be found in many mainline congregations. The few I have recorded here are offered as means of encouragement and illustration for all congregational leaders.

In 1962 the distinguished Protestant theologian Karl Barth visited the United States. During his whirlwind tour of American sights (especially Civil War battlegrounds) and visits with notable persons (including Martin Luther King Jr. and Billy Graham), the then seventy-seven-year-old Swiss citizen delivered a series of lectures in Chicago, Princeton, Richmond, and San Francisco. Barth said that the lectures were a "brief account" of what he "learned and represented ... during my five years as a student, twelve years as a preacher, and subsequent forty years as a professor." He called these lectures *Evangelical Theology: An Introduction*.

Among the multiple insights in these lectures, two stand out for this author. *First*, the church community, Barth insisted, "is confronted and created by the Word of God.... [But this] community does not speak with words alone ... [but] by its attitude to world problems ... by its silent service to all handicapped, weak and needy in the world" (Barth 1964, 38).

Second, the "theological work" of Christian communities "must have the character of an offering in which everything is placed before a living God." That means, Barth would add, every must congregation begin "once again at the beginning." And all new beginnings "are disclosed and set in proper light by prayer" (Barth 1964, 165).

Works Cited

Adams, Joanna. 2001. "Atlanta as Church Context" in *Hope for the World Mission in a Global Context*, edited by W. Brueggemann. Louisville: Westminster John Knox.

Ammerman, Nancy. 1997. *Congregations and Community*. New Brunswick: Rutgers University Press.

———and Carl Dudley. 2003. *Congregations in Transition: A Guide for Analyzing, Assessing, and Adapting in Changing Congregations*. San Francisco: Jossey-Bass.

Anderson, Ray S. 2001. *The Shape of Practical Theology: Empowering Ministry with Theological Praxis*. Downers Grove, IL: InterVarsity.

Appleton, George, ed. 1985. *The Oxford Book of Prayer*. New York: Oxford University Press.

Arnold, Jeffery. 1997. *Staring Small Groups: Building Communities That Matter*. Nashville: Abington.

Baab, Lynne E. 2008. *Reaching Out in a Networked World: Expressing Your Congregation's Heart and Soul*. Herndon, VA: Alban Institute.

Banks, Robert and Benice M. Ledbetter. *Reviewing Leadership: A Christian Evaluation of Current Approaches*. Grand Rapids: Baker Academic.

Baillie, John. 1958. *A Diary of Private Prayer*. London: Oxford University Press.

Barth, Karl. 1962. *Church Dogmatics*. IV.67.4. Edinburgh: T&T Clark.

———. 1964. *Evangelical Theology: An Introduction*. Trans. Grover Foley. New York: Doubleday.

———. 2002. *Prayer: Karl Barth (50th Anniversary Edition)*. Ed. by Donald E. Sailers. Louisville: Westminster John Knox.

Bass, Diana Butler. 2004. *The Practicing Congregation: Imagining a New Old Church*. Herndon, VA: Alban Institute.

Bass, Dorothy C. 1997. *Practicing Our Faith*. San Francisco: Jossey-Bass.

Bass, Richard, ed. 2007. *Leadership in Congregations*. Herndon, VA: Alban Institute.

Bauckham, Richard. 2006. *Jesus and the Eyewitnesses: The Gospels as Eyewitness Testimony*. Grand Rapids: Eerdmans.

Becker, Penny Edgell. 1999. *Congregations in Conflict: Cultural Models of Local Religious Life*. New York: Cambridge University Press.

Benson, Peter and Carolyn H. Eklin. 1990. *Effective Christian Education: A National Study of Protestant Congregations*. Minneapolis: Search Institute.

Bishop, Bill. 2008. *The Big Sort: Why the Clustering of Like-Minded Americans Is Tearing Us Apart*. New York: Houghton Mifflin.

Bonhoeffer, Dietrich. 1972 (1970). *Letters and Papers from Prison*. Ed. Eberhard Bethage. New York: Macmillan.

———. 1986. *Meditating on the Word*. Boston: Cowley Publications.

———. 1995 (1937). *The Cost of Discipleship*. Austin, TX: Touchstone Publishing.

———. 2005 (1939). *Life Together* and *Prayerbook of the Bible*. Minneapolis: Fortress.

Bosch, David. 1985. *The Lord's Prayer: Paradigm for a Christian Lifestyle*. Pretoria, South Africa: Christian Medical Fellowship.

Branson, Mark Lau. 2007. "Forming God's People" in *Leadership in Congregations*. Ed. Richard Bass. Herndon, VA: Alban Institute.

Bruce, A. B. 1904 (1871). *The Training of the Twelve*, 5th ed. New York: G. H. Doran Company.

Brueggemann, Walter. 2007. *Praying the Psalms*. Winona, MN: St. Mary's Press.

Bruggink, Donald J. and Carl H. Doppers. 1965. *Christ and Architecture: Building Presbyterian/Reformed Churches*. Grand Rapids: Eerdmans.

Buechner, Frederick. 1973. *Wishful Thinking: A Theological ABC*. New York: Harper & Row.

———. 1984. *Love Feast*. New York: Harper & Row.

———. 1991. *Telling Secrets*. New York: HarperOne.

———. 1997. "Doubt and Faith" in *Fiction and Faith: Twelve American Writers Talk about Their Vision and Word*. Ed. W. Dale Brown. Grand Rapids: Eerdmans.

———. 2006. *Secrets in the Dark: A Life in Sermons*. New York: HarperOne.

Burge, G. M. 1999. "The Greatest Story Never Read: Recovering Biblical Literacy in the Church." *Christianity Today*. Aug. 9, 1999: 45-49.

Burns, Kenneth. 2008. "The Americanist." *The Christian Century*. July 15, 2008: 32-33.

Bush, Peter and Christine O'Reilly. 2006. *Where 20 or 30 Are Gathered: Leading Worship in the Small Church*. Herndon, VA: Alban Institute.

Caird, G. B. 1980. *Language and Imagery of the Bible*. London: Duckworth.

Calhoun, Adele Ahlberg. 2005. *Spiritual Disciplines Handbook: Practices That Transform Us*. Downers Grove IL: InterVarsity.

Calvin, John. 1960. *Institutes of the Christian Religion*. 2 vols. trans. by F. L. Lewis. Philadelphia: Westminster.

Campbell, Heidi. 2005. *Exploring Religious Community Online: We Are One in the Network*. New York: Peter Lang.

———. 2012. "Understanding the Relationship between Religion Online and Offline in a Networked Society." *Journal of American Academy of Religion* 80 (2012): 64-93.

Carroll, Jackson. 2000. *Mainline to the Future: Congregations for the 21st Century*. Louisville: Westminster John Knox.

———. 2006. *God's Potters: Pastoral Leadership and the Shaping of Congregations*. Grand Rapids: Eerdmans.

Chaves, Mark. 2004. *Congregations in America*. Cambridge: Harvard University Press.

———. 2008. "Continuity and Change in American Congregations: Introducing the Second Wave of the National Congregations Study." *Sociology of Religion* 69: 415-440.

Works Cited

———. 2010. "Thanks, But No Thanks: Congregations Say No to Faith-Based Initiatives." *The Christian Century*, June 1, 2010: 22-24.

———. 2011. *American Religion: Contemporary Trends*. Princeton: Princeton University Press.

Christopher, J. Cliff. 2008. *Not Your Parent's Offering Plate: New Vision for Financial Stewardship*. Nashville: Abington.

Cnaan, Ram A. 2002. *The Invisible Caring Hand: American Congregations and the Provision of Welfare*. New York: New York University Press.

Coggins, R. G. and J. L. Houlden, eds. 1990. "Gospel" in *A Dictionary of Biblical Interpretation*. London: SCM Press.

Cole, A. H., ed. 2011. *A Spiritual Life*. Louisville: Westminster John Knox.

Cross, Gary. 2002. *An All Consuming Society*. New York: Columbia University Press.

Dana, MaryAnn McKibben. 2012. *Sabbath in the Suburbs: A Family's Experiment with Holy Time*. St. Louis: Chalice.

Dean, Kenda Creasy. 2010. *Almost Christian: What the Faith of Our Teenagers Is Telling the American Church*. New York: Oxford University Press.

Dearborn, Tim A. and Scott Coil, eds. 2004. *Worship at the Next Level: Insights from Contemporary Voices*. Grand Rapids: Baker Books.

Devries, Mark. 2008. *Sustainable Youth Ministry: Why Most Youth Ministry Doesn't Last and What your Church Can Do About It*. Downers Grove, IL: InterVarsity.

Dick, Dan R. 2007. *Vital Signs: A Pathway to Congregational Wholeness*. Nashville: Disciple Resources.

Diehl, William. 1991. *The Monday Connection: A Spirituality of Competence, Affirmation, and Support in the Workplace*. San Francisco: Harper.

Dolan, Tom. 2011. "So You Think You Are Friendly." *Congregations Magazine*: 14-18.

Donahue, Bill. 1996. *The Willow Creek Guide to Leading Life Changing Small Groups*. Grand Rapids: Zondervan.

———. 2006. *Leading Life Changing Small Group Leaders*. Grand Rapids: Zondervan.

Donne, John. 1991. *The Complete English Poems*. New York: Alfred A. Knopf.

Dunn, James D. 1992. *Jesus' Call to Discipleship*. New York: Cambridge University Press.

——— and John Rogerson, eds. 2003. *Eerdmans Commentary on the Bible*. Grand Rapids: Eerdmans.

Duvall, Michael. 1999. *Creating Congregations of Generous People*. Herndon, VA: Alban Institute.

Dykstra, Craig. 2002. "Theological Understanding of Christian Practices" in *Practicing Theology: Beliefs and Practices in Christian Life*. Ed. Miroslav Volf and Dorothy C. Bass. Grand Rapids: Eerdmans.

Dyrness, William A. 2009. *A Primer on Worship: Where We've Been, Where We Are, Where We Can Go*. Grand Rapids: Eerdmans.

Eason, Steven P. 2004. *Making Disciples, Making Leaders*. Louisville: Geneva Press.

Eck, Diana L. 2001. *The New Religious America: How a "Christian Country" Has Now Become the World's Most Religiously Diverse Nation*. San Francisco: HarperCollins.

Edison, Margaret. 1999. *W;t* (sic). New York: Faber and Faber.

Emerson, Michael and Christian Smith. 2000. *Divided by Faith: American Religion and the Problem of Race in America*. New York: Oxford University Press.

Farhadian, C. E., ed. 2007. *Christian Worship Worldwide: Expanding Horizons.* Grand Rapids: Eerdmans.

Faust, C. H. and T. H. Johnson. 1962. *Jonathan Edwards: Representative Selections*, rev. ed. New York: Hill and Wang.

Fee, Gordon. 1994. *God's Empowering Presence: The Holy Spirit in the Letters of Paul.* Peabody, MA: Hendrickson Publishers.

————. 1996. *Paul, the Spirit, and the People of God.* Peabody, MA: Hendrickson Publishers.

———— and Douglas Stuart. 2003. *How to Read the Bible for All Its Worth.* Grand Rapids: Zondervan.

Ferguson, Everett. 1996. *The Church of Christ: A Biblical Ecclesiology for Today.* Grand Rapids: Eerdmans.

Fitzmyer, Joseph. 1979. "The Gospel in the Theology of Paul" in *Interpretation: A Journal of Bible and Theology*, XXXII : 339-50.

Ford, David F. 2004. *The Shape of Living: Spiritual Directions for Everyday Life.* Grand Rapids: Baker.

Foster, Richard J. 1988. *Celebration of Discipline: The Path to Spiritual Growth.* New York: HarperCollins.

Fuller, Robert C. 2001. *Spiritual, But Not Religious: Understanding Unchurched America.* New York: Oxford University Press.

Gallagher, Nora. 1998. *Things Seen and Unseen.* New York: Random House.

Garcia, Alfredo. 2010. "Methodist Study Finds Four Marks of Church Vitality." *Christian Century.* August 24, 2010: 15.

Guder, Darrell L. 1985. *Be My Witnesses: The Church's Mission, Message, and Messengers.* Grand Rapids: Eerdmans.

————. 2000. *The Continuing Conversion of the Church.* Grand Rapid: Eerdmans.

Hall, Douglas J. 1990. *The Steward: A Biblical Symbol Come of Age*, rev. ed. Grand Rapids: Eerdmans.

Halverson, Delia. 2002. *Side-by-Side: Families Learning and Living in Faith Together.* Nashville: Abington.

Harney, Devin G. 2009. *Organic Outreach for Ordinary People.* Grand Rapids: Zondervan.

Harris, Maria. 1989. *Fashion Me a People: Curriculum for the Church.* Louisville: Westminster John Knox.

Hauerwas, Stanley. 2010. *Hannah's Child: A Theologian's Memoir.* Grand Rapids: Eerdmans.

Hays, J. D. and J. Scott Duvall, eds. 2011. *Baker Illustrated Bible Handbook.* Grand Rapids: Baker.

Hays, Richard. 1996. *The Moral Vision of the New Testament.* San Francisco: HarperCollins.

Herrington, Jim, Mike Bonhem, and James H. Furr. 2000. *Leading Congregational Change: A Practical Guide for the Transformational Journey.* San Francisco: Josey-Bass.

Hershel, Abraham. 1983. *I Asked for Wonder: A Spiritual Anthology.* Ed. S. H. Dresner. New York: Crossroad.

Hodge, Charles. 1952 (1872). *Systematic Theology*, Vol. III. Grand Rapids: Eerdmans.

Hoge, Dean R., Benton Johnson, and Donald Luidens. 1994. *Vanishing Boundaries: The Religious Mainline Protestant Baby Boomers.* Louisville: Westminster John Knox.

Hollinger, David and Charles Capper. 2006. *The American Intellectual Tradition*, 5th ed. Vol. 1. New York: Oxford University Press.

Works Cited

Hudson, Jill M. 2004. *When Better Is Not Enough: Evaluation Tolls for the 21st Century Church.* Herndon, VA: Alban Institute.

Hunter, James D. 2010. *To Change the World: The Irony, Tragedy, and Possibility of Christianity in the Late Modern Age.* New York: Oxford University Press.

Jacobsen, Eric O., ed. 2009. *The Three Tasks of Leadership: Worldly Wisdom for Pastoral Leaders.* Grand Rapids: Eerdmans.

Jensen, Robin M. 2001. "The Arts in Protestant Worship." *Theology Today,* 58 (2001): 359-368.

Johnson, Luke T. 1996. *Scripture and Discernment: Decision Making.* Nashville: Abington.

Kilde, Jeanne H. 2005. *When the Church Became Theater: The Transformation of Evangelical Architecture and Worship in the Nineteenth Century.* New York: Oxford University Press.

Kirkpatrick, Thomas. 2005. *Small Groups in the Church: A Handbook for Creating Community.* Herndon, VA: Alban Institute.

Kittel, G. 1964-1976. *Theological Dictionary of the New Testament.* 10 Vols. Trans. and ed. G. W. Bromiley. Grand Rapids: Eerdmans.

Koenig, John. 1985. *New Testament Hospitality: Partnership with Strangers as Promise and Mission.* Minneapolis: Fortress.

Lakoff, George. 2003. *Metaphors We Live By.* Chicago: University of Chicago Press.

———. 2004. *Don't Think of an Elephant! Know Your Values and Frame the Debate.* White River Junction, VT: Chelsea Green Publishing.

Lamott, Anne. 1999. *Traveling Mercies.* New York: Pantheon.

———. 2012. *Help, Thanks, Wow: The Three Essentials of Prayer.* New York: Riverhead Books.

Latini, Theresa F. 2011. *The Church and the Crisis of Ministry: A Practical Theology of Small Group Ministry.* Grand Rapids: Eerdmans.

Lee, Sang Hyun. 1988. *The Philosophical Theology of Jonathan Edwards.* Princeton: Princeton University Press.

Lewis, C. S. 1952. *Mere Christianity.* New York: MacMillan.

———. 1955. *Surprised by Joy.* New York: Harcourt, Brace and Company.

———. 1956 (1942). *Screwtape Letters.* New York: MacMillan.

———. 1958. *Reflections on the Psalms.* New York: Harcourt Brace Jovanovich.

Linn, Susan. 2004. *Consuming Kids: The Hostile Takeover of Childhood.* New York: The New Press.

Long, Thomas G. 1989. *The Witness of Preaching.* Louisville: Westminster John Knox.

———. 2001. *Beyond the Worship Wars: Building Vital and Faithful Worship.* Herndon, VA: Alban Institute.

———. 2004. *Testimony: Talking Ourselves into Being Christian.* San Francisco: Jossey-Bass.

Lupton, Robert. 2011. *Toxic Charity: How Churches and Charities Hurt Those They Help (and How To Reverse It).* New York: HarperOne.

Mallory, Sue. 2001. *The Equipping Church: Serving Together to Transform Lives.* Grand Rapids: Zondervan.

Martin, Ralph P. 1989. "Patterns of Worship in the New Testament." *Journal for the Study of the New Testament* 12 (1989): 59-85+.

Marty, Martin, ed. 1995. *Context: Martin Marty on Religion and Culture.* 27: 5. Chicago: Claretians.

———. 2000. *Context: Martin Marty on Religion and Culture.* 32: 18 Chicago: Claretians.

————. 2009. *Context: Martin Marty on Religion and Culture*. 41: 4 Chicago: Claretians.

Mayer, David, et. al. 1995. *Starting Small Groups and Keeping Them Going*. Minneapolis: Augsburg.

McCord, James and T. L. Parker. 1966. *Service in Christ: Essays Presented to Karl Barth on His 80th Birthday*. Grand Rapid: Eerdmans.

McEntyre, Marilyn Chandler. 2009. *Caring for Words in a Culture of Lies*. Grand Rapids: Eerdmans.

McLaren, Brian. 2003. *The Story We Find Ourselves In*. San Francisco: Jossey-Bass.

————. 2008. *Finding Our Way: The Return of the Ancient Practice*. Nashville: Thomas Nelson.

Meacham, Jon. 2006. *The American Gospel: God, the Founding Fathers, and the Making of a Nation*. New York: Random House.

Melchert, Charles F. 1998. *Wise Teaching: Biblical Wisdom and Educational Ministry*. Harrisburg, PA: Trinity Press International.

Migliore, Daniel L. 2004. *Faith Seeking Understanding: An Introduction to Christian Theology*, 2nd ed. Grand Rapids: Eerdmans.

Milavec, Aaron, ed. 2003. *The Didache: Text, Translation, Analysis, and Commentary*. Collegeville, MN: Liturgical Press.

Miller, D. R. and C. M Olsen. 2012. *Discerning God's Will Together: A Spiritual Practice for the Church*. Lanham, MD: Rowman and Littlefield.

Miller, Herb. 2007. *New Consecration Stewardship Sunday Program*. Nashville: Abington.

Miller, Mark. 2003. *Experiential Story Telling: (Re)Discovering Narrative to Communicate God's Message*. Grand Rapids: Zondervan.

Miller, Vincent J. 2005. *Consuming Religion: Christian Faith and Practice in a Consumer Culture*. New York: Continuum.

Minear, Paul S. 2004 (1960). *Images of the Church in the New Testament*. Louisville: Westminster John Knox.

————. 2004 (1950). *The Kingdom and The Power: An Exposition of the New Testament Gospel*. Louisville: Westminster John Knox.

Moltmann, Jürgen. 1974. *The Crucified God: The Cross of Christ as the Foundation and Criticism of Christian Theology*. New York: Harper & Row.

————. 1977. *The Church in the Power of the Holy Spirit*. New York: Harper & Row.

————. 1992. *The Spirit of Life: A Universal Affirmation*. Minneapolis: Fortress.

————. 1993. *The Way of Jesus Christ*. Minneapolis: Fortress.

————. 1994. *Jesus Christ for Today's World*. Minneapolis: Fortress.

————. 2010. *Sun of Righteousness, Arise!: God's Future for Humanity and the Earth*. Minneapolis: Fortress.

Monroe, Kelly, ed. 1996. *Finding God at Harvard: Spiritual Journeys of Thinking Christians*. Grand Rapids: Zondervan.

Moore-Keish, Martha L. 2008. *Do This in Remembrance of Me*. Grand Rapids: Eerdmans.

Mulder, John M. and H. T. Kerr, eds. 2012. *Finding God : A Treasury of Conversion Stories*. Grand Rapids: Eerdmans.

Myers, David G. 2001. *The American Paradox: Spiritual Hunger in an Age of Plenty*. New Haven: Yale University Press.

Nash, Laura and S. McLennon. 2001. *Church on Sunday, Work on Monday: The Challenge of Fusing Christian Values with Business Life*. San Francisco: Jossey-Bass.

Works Cited

Neumark, Heidi B. 2003. *Breathing Space: A Spiritual Journey in the South Bronx*. Boston: Beacon.

Nouwen, Henri. 1975. *Reaching Out: The Three Movements of the Spiritual Life*. New York: Doubleday.

———. 1981. *A Cry for Mercy: Prayers from the Genesee*. New York: Doubleday.

O'Conner, Elizabeth. 1968. *Journey Inward, Journey Outward*. New York: Harper and Row.

O'Connor, Flannery. 1988. *Habit of Being*. New York: Farrar, Straus, Giroux.

Ogden, Greg. 1990. *The New Reformation: Returning the Ministry to the People of God*. Grand Rapids: Zondervan.

———. 2007. *Discipleship Essentials: A Guide to Building Your Life in Christ*. Downers Grove, IL: InterVarsity.

O'Reilley, Mary Rose. 1994. "Deep Listening: And Experimental Friendship." *Weavings* IX (1994): 22-24.

Osmer, Richard. 2005. *The Teaching Ministry of Congregations*. Louisville: Westminster John Knox.

Ott, E. Stanley. 1989. *The Joy of Discipling: Friend with Friend, Heart with Heart*. Grand Rapids: Zondervan.

Outler, Albert. 1971. *Evangelism in the Wesleyan Spirit*. Nashville: Tidings Publishers.

Owens, L. Roger. 2010. *The Shape of Participation: A Theology of Church Practices*. Eugene, OR: Cascade Books.

Parish, Bobbi. 1991. *Creating Your Own Sacred Text: Develop and Celebrate Your Spiritual Life*. New York: Broadway Press.

Peterson, Eugene H. 1993. *The Message: The New Testament in Contemporary English*. Colorado Springs: NavPress.

———. 1995 *The Message*. Colorado Springs: Alive Communications, Inc.

———. 1999. *The Unnecessary Pastor*. Grand Rapids: Eerdmans.

———. 2005. *Christ Plays in Ten Thousand Places: A Conversation in Spiritual Theology*. Grand Rapids: Eerdmans.

———. 2011. "Living with the Triune God." *Books and Culture* 17 (2011): 19.

Placher, William ed. 2005. *Callings: Twenty Centuries of Christian Wisdom on Vocation*. Grand Rapids: Eerdmans.

Plantinga, Cornelius and Sue A. Rozeboom. 2003. *Discerning the Spirit: A Guide to Thinking About Worship Today*. Grand Rapids: Eerdmans.

Potter, David. 1954. *People of Plenty: Abundance and the American Character*. Chicago: University of Chicago Press.

Prothero, Stephen. 2007. *Religious Illiteracy: What Every American Should Know — and Doesn't*. New York: Harper Collins.

———. 2010. *God Is Not One: The Eight Rival Religious That Run the World*. San Francisco: HarperOne.

Putnam, Robert D. 2000. *Bowling Alone: The Collapse and Revival of American Community*. New York: Simon & Schuster.

Radecke, Mark N. 2010. "Misguided Missions: Ten Worst Practices." *The Christian Century*, June 18, 2010: 22.

Redman, Robert. 2001. "Welcome to the Worship Awakening," *Theology Today* 58 (2001): 369-83.

Reese, Martha Grace. 2008. *Unbinding the Gospel: Real Life Evangelism.* 2nd ed. St. Louis: Chalice.

———. 2008. *Unbinding Your Church.* (Pastor's and Leaders' Guide). St. Louis: Chalice.

Rice, Jesse. 2009. *The Church of Facebook: How the Hyperconnected Are Redefining Community.* Peabody, MA: David C. Cook.

Richter, Don C. 2008. *Trips That Matter: Embodied Faith for the Sake of the World.* Nashville: Upper Room.

Robinson, Anthony. 2007. "'Follow Me': The Renewed Focus on Discipleship." *The Christian Century,* September 4, 2007: 23-25.

———. 2011. "What Do the Bylaws Say? Order and Disorder in the Church." *The Christian Century,* May 17, 2011: 10-11.

Rogerson, J. W. 1999. *An Introduction to the Bible.* London: Penguin Books.

Roof, Wade Clark. 1999. *Spiritual Marketplace: Baby Boomers and the Remaking of American Religion.* Princeton: Princeton University Press.

Roozen, D. A. and C. K. Hardaway. 1993. *Church and Denominational Growth.* Nashville, TN: Abingdon.

Ronsvalle, John and Sylvia. 1996. "The End of Benevolence? Alarming Trends in Church Giving." *The Christian Century.* October 23, 1996: 1010-1014.

Sailers, Don E. 1998. *Worship Come to Its Senses.* Nashville, TN: Abingdon.

———, ed. 2002. *Prayer: Karl Barth (50th Anniversary Edition).* Essays by I. John Hesselink, Daniel L. Migliore, and Donald K. McKim. Louisville: Westminster John Knox.

Sample, Tex. 1990. *U.S. Lifestyles and Mainline Churches.* Louisville: Westminster John Knox.

———. 1994. *Ministry in an Oral Culture.* Louisville: Westminster John Knox.

Schnase, Robert. 2008. *Five Practices of Faithful Congregations.* Nashville: Abingdon.

Schor, Judith, ed. 2000. *Consumer Society Reader.* New York: Free Press.

———. 2005. *Born to Buy: Commercialized Children and New Consumer Culture.* New York: Scribner.

Schuller, David S., ed. 1993. *Rethinking Christian Education.* St. Louis: Chalice.

Schuurman, Douglas. 2004. *Vocations: Discerning Our Callings in Life.* Grand Rapids: Eerdmans.

Senge, Peter, et. al. 1990. *The Fifth Discipline: The Art and Practices of the Learning Organization.* New York: Doubleday/Currency.

———. 2004. *Presence: Exploring Profound change in People, Organizations, and Society.* New York: Doubleday/Currency.

Shepherd, J. Barrie. 2002. *Diary of Daily Prayer,* 2nd ed. Louisville: Westminster John Knox.

Sherman, Amy L. 1997. *Restorers of Hope: Reaching the Poor in Your Community with Church-based Ministries That Work.* Wheaton, IL: Crossway Books.

Smart, James D. 1970. *The Strange Silence of the Bible in the Church.* Philadelphia: Westminster.

Smith, Christian. 2000. *Christian America? What Evangelicals Really Want.* Berkley: University of California Press.

———. 2005. *Soul Searching: The Religious and Spiritual Lives of American Teenagers.* New York: Oxford University Press.

Works Cited

———and Michael Emerson. 2008. *Passing the Plate: Why American Christians Don't Give Away More Money.* New York: Oxford University Press.

Smith, James K. A. 2009. *Desiring the Kingdom: Worship, Worldview, and Cultural Formation.* Grand Rapids: Baker.

Stark, Rodney, et. al. 2008. *What Americans Really Believe.* Waco, TX: Baylor University Press.

Stewart, John W. "The Emergence of Congregational Studies in Oldline American Protestantism." *International Journal of Practical Theology,* 6 (2002): 253-287.

Stewart, S. M. and J. W. Berryman. 2000. *Young Children and Worship.* Louisville: Westminster John Knox.

Stobel, Lee and Mark Mittelberg. 2009. *The Unexpected Adventure: Taking Everyday Risks to Talk With People about Jesus.* Grand Rapids: Zondervan.

Stone, Bryan. 2007. *Evangelism after Christendom. The Theology and Practice of Christian Witness.* Grand Rapids: Brazos.

Swenson, Kristin. 2009. "Biblically Challenged: Overcoming Scriptural Illiteracy." *The Christian Century.* Nov. 2, 2009: 22-25.

Sweet, Leonard. 1994. *Faithquakes.* Nashville: Abingdon.

———. 2000. *Postmodern Pilgrims: First Century Passion for the 21st Century World.* Nashville: Broadman and Holman.

———. 2011. *Real Church in a Social Network World: From Facebook to Face-to-Face Faith.* Colorado Springs: WaterBrook Press.

———. 2012. *I Am a Follower: The Way, Truth, and Life of Following Jesus.* New York: Thomas Nelson.

Swinton, John and Harriet Mowat. 2006. *Practical Theology and Quantitative Methods.* London: SCM Press.

Taylor, Charles. 2007. *A Secular Age.* Cambridge: Belknap Press of Harvard University Press.

Temple, William. 1942. *Hope for the World.* London: MacMillan.

———. 1955. *Readings in St. John's Gospel.* London: MacMillan.

Thompson, Marjorie J. 1996. *Family, the Forming Center: A Vision of the Role of Family in Spiritual Formation.* Nashville: Upper Room.

———. 2005. *Soul Feast: An Invitation to the Christian Spiritual Life.* Louisville: Westminster John Knox.

Torrance, Thomas F. 1980. *Christian Theology and Scientific Culture.* Belfast: Christian Journals Limited.

Trites, Allison. 1977. *The New Testament Concept of Witness.* New York: Cambridge University Press.

Updike, John. 1982. *Beck Is Back.* New York: Alfred A. Knopf.

Van Gelder, Craig. 2009. *The Missional Church and Leadership Formation.* Grand Rapids: Eerdmans.

Ver Beek, Kurt. 2012. "Lessons from the Sapling: Review of Quantitative Research on Short-term Missions." In *Effective Engagement in Short-Term Missions: Doing It Right.* Ed. Robert Priest. Pasadena, CA: William Carey Library Publishers, 476-501.

Vest, Norvene. 1997. *Friend of the Soul: A Benedictine Spirituality of Work.* Cambridge, MA: Crowley.

Volf, Miroslav. 1996. *Exclusion and Embrace: A Theological Exploration of Identity, Otherness, and Reconciliation*. Nashville: Abington.

———. 2011. *A Public Faith: How Followers of Christ Should Serve the Common Good*. Grand Rapids: Brazos.

——— and Dorothy C. Bass, eds. 2002. *Practicing Theology: Beliefs and Practices in Christian Life*. Grand Rapids: Eerdmans.

Wainwright, Geoffrey. 1980. *Doxology: The Praise of God in Worship, Doctrine, and Life: A Systematic Theology*. New York: Oxford University Press.

——— and K. B. W. Tucker, eds. 2006. *The Oxford History of Christian Worship*. New York: Oxford University Press.

Warner, Stephen. 1994. "The Place of Congregations in the Contemporary American Religious Configuration" in *American Congregations*. Vol. 2. Ed. James P. Wind and James W. Lewis. Chicago: University of Chicago Press.

———. 2005. *A Church of Our Own: Disestablishment and Diversity in American Religion*. New Brunswick, NJ: Rutgers University Press.

Webber, Robert W. 1994. *Worship Old and New*. Grand Rapids: Zondervan.

———. 1998. *Planning Blended Worship: The Creative Mixture of Old and New*. Nashville: Abington.

Wentz, Richard. 1997. *The Culture of Religious Pluralism*. Boulder, CO: Westview Press.

White, James F. and John D. Witvliet. 1986. "Looking Back, Looking Ahead in Worship." *Reformed Worship* 38 (1986): 4-52.

———. 2001. *Introduction to Christian Worship*. 3rd ed. Nashville: Abington.

Willard, Dallas. 2006. *The Great Omission: Reclaiming Jesus' Essential Teachings on Discipleship*. San Francisco: HarperCollins.

Willimon, William H. 1998. *Acts: Interpretation: A Bible Commentary for Teaching and Preaching*. Louisville: Westminster John Knox.

———. 2001. "The Lectionary." *Theology Today*. 58 (2001): 333-41.

———. 2011. "Impractical Christianity" in *A Spiritual Life*. Ed. A. H. Cole. Louisville: Westminster John Knox.

Witvliet, John D. 2007. *The Biblical Psalms in Christian Worship: A Brief Introduction and Guide to Resources*. Grand Rapids: Eerdmans.

Wolfe, Alan. 2003. *The Transformation of American Religion: How We Actually Live our Faith*. Chicago: University of Chicago Press.

Wolterstorff, Nicholas. 1985. "Worship and Justice." *Reformed Liturgy and Music* 2 (1985): 67-71.

———. 1986. "Genius of Reformed Worship," *Reformed Worship* 2: 8-11.

———. 1987. *Lament for a Son*. Grand Rapids: Eerdmans.

———. 1990. "The Remembrance of Things (Not) Past: Philosophical Reflections on Christian Liturgy" in *Christian Philosophy*. Ed. Thomas Flint. Notre Dame, IN: Notre Dame University Press.

———. 1991. "Justice as a Condition of Authentic Liturgy." *Theology Today* 48 (1991): 24-39.

———. 1996. "The Grace That Shaped My Life" in *Finding God at Harvard*. Ed. Kelly Monroe. Grand Rapids: Zondervan.

———. 2003. "Imitating God: Doing Justice as a Condition of Authentic Worship," *Reformed Worship* 68: 4-5.

Works Cited

―――. 2011. *Hearing the Call: Liturgy, Justice, Church, and World*. Grand Rapids: Eerdmans.

―――. 2011. *Justice in Love*. Grand Rapid: Eerdmans.

Woolever, Cynthia and Deborah Bruce. 2002. *A Field Guide to U.S. Congregations: Who's Going Where and Why*. Louisville: Westminster John Knox.

―――. 2010. *A Field Guide to U.S. Congregations: Who's Going Where and Why*, 2nd ed. Louisville: Westminster John Knox.

Wright, N. T. 1994. *Following Jesus: Biblical Reflections on Discipleship*. Grand Rapids: Eerdmans.

―――. 1997. *For All God's Worth: True Worship and the Calling of the Church*. Grand Rapids: Eerdmans.

―――. 2006. *Simply Christian: Why Christianity Makes Sense*. New York: HarperCollins.

―――. 2013. *The Case for the Psalms: Why They Are Essential*. New York: HarperOne.

Wuthnow, Robert. 1988. *The Restructuring of American Religion: Society and Faith Since World War II*. Princeton: Princeton University Press.

―――. 1993a. *Christianity in the Twenty-first Century: Reflections on Challenges Ahead*. New York: Oxford University Press.

―――. 1993b. "Small Groups for New Notions of Community and the Sacred," *Christian Century*. December 8, 1993: 1,236-40.

―――. 1994a. *Sharing the Journey: Support Groups and America's New Quest for Community*. New York: Free Press.

―――. 1994b. "I Come Away Stronger": *How Small Groups Are Shaping American Religion*. Grand Rapids: Eerdmans.

―――. 1994c *God and Mammon in America*. New York: Free Press.

―――. 1996. *Poor Richard's Principles: Recovering the American Dream through the Moral Dimension of Work, Business, and Money*. Princeton: Princeton University Press.

―――. 1997. *The Crises in the Churches: Spiritual Malaise, Financial Woe*. New York: Oxford University Press.

―――. 1998. *After Heaven: Spirituality in America Since the 1950s*. Berkley: University of California Press.

―――. 2000. *Growing Up Religious: Christians and Jews and Their Journeys of Faith*. Boston: Beacon.

―――. 2003. *All in Sync: How Music and Art Are Revitalizing American Religion*. Berkley: University of California Press.

―――. 2005. *America and the Challenges of Religious Diversity*. Princeton: Princeton University Press.

―――. and John H. Evans. 2002. *The Quiet Hand of God: Faith-Based Activism and the Public Role of Mainline Protestantism*. Berkley: University of California Press.

Index

Index

Index

Lupton, Robert, 148; guiding principles of for dealing with impoverished people, 148

Luther, Martin, 118; on the devotional life, 194; on the parable of the "Prodigal Son," 36; on vocation, 130; on worship, 161

Lutheran World Federation, 92

Mainline congregations, 2, 2n1; changes in membership affiliation in, 10; membership cultures in, 96; membership decline in, 9; and the trend toward larger, multifaceted congregations, 9-10

"Mainline Evangelism Project," 128-129

Making Disciples, Making Leaders: A Manual for Developing Church Officers (Eason), 113n15

Mallory, Sue, 112n14

Marano, Minerva, 152n13

Marble Collegiate Church (New York City), 8

Martin, Ralph P., 163n4

Martyria (witnessing), 6, 22, 29, 56, 60, 116-118; the etymological root of *martyria*, 116; as God's coming to people through God's people, 108, 118-119, 124, 135-136; *martyria* as "martyr," 116; *martyria* as "witness" or "advocate," 60, 116; qualities of a good witness, 120; as vocation, 130-135; witnesses in the New Testament, 121-123, 122n4; the word "witness" in the Hebrew Bible, 119-121; the word "witness" in the New Testament, 121. See also *Martyria* (witnessing), as testimony to the gospel

Martyria (witnessing), as testimony to the gospel, 125-126; equipping disciples to tell their faith stories, 127-130; groupings of persons outside mainline congregations on which evangelistic endeavors are focused, 129 (chart); stories are works of art, 126; stories can first be shared,

rehearsed, and perfected among friends, 127; stories point listeners beyond the storyteller, 127; witnesses are storytellers, 126

Mathētēs (discipling), 6, 29, 56, 60, 91-93; dearth of *mathētēs* practices in contemporary mainline congregations, 94-97; essential practices of discipleship, 97-99 (*see also* Discernment; Faith formation; Learning); *mathētēs* as "apprentice," 60, 91, 93; *mathētēs* as "disciple," 91, 93; and the name "Matthew," 60, 91; the New Testament's focus on discipleship, 93-94. See also *Mathētēs* (discipling), strategic actions for growing mature disciples

Mathētēs (discipling), strategic actions for growing mature disciples, 107-108; assess progress, 113-115; listen to youth to reconfigure youth ministries, 110; prayerfully select leaders, 111-112; sponsor friendships, 108; teach adults, 109; train every leader, 112-113; visit other congregations, 110-111

Mauch, Marchita, 170n9

Mayer, David, 77-78, 79

McCord, James, 139n2

McLaren, Brian, 58n1, 126

McLennan, Scotty, 132

Meacham, Jon, 26

"Means of grace," 163-166, 189. *See also specific means of grace:* Prayer; Sacraments; Scripture

Mega-churches, 9-10, 15

Melchert, Charles, 93n1

Mental models, 13-14; as active, 13; revelation of through metaphors, 13. *See also specific mental models:* Consumerism; Deism; Homogeneity; Individualism; Religious pluralism; Spirituality

Mere Christianity (Lewis), 27-28, 28n14, 118

Migliore, Daniel, 42n6, 46, 68; on the sacraments, 44; on vocation, 132

Milavec, Aaron, 193n12